# THE FIRST IMMORTALS

Raising the Dead

## KAHLEDE

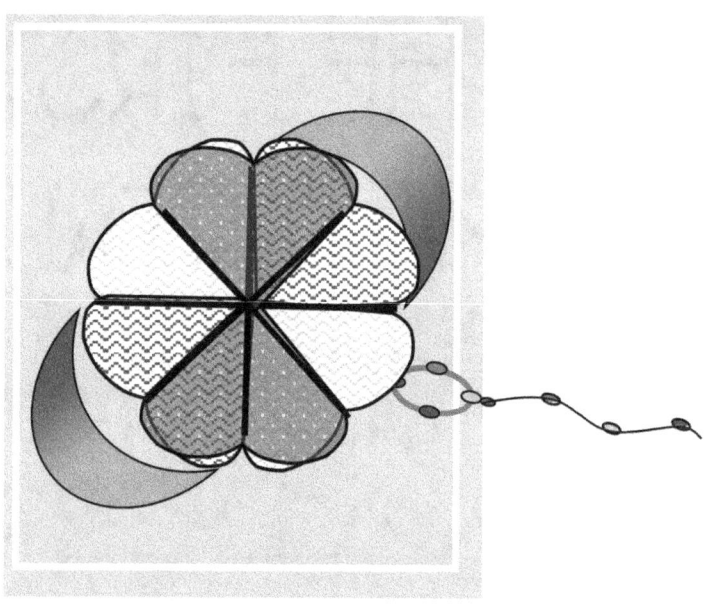

The Geometry of Life (see page 216)

# THERE ARE NO MIRRORS IN HEAVEN

Book 2

# THE FIRST IMMORTALS

Raising the Dead

## KAHLEDE

This edition published in 2022

by Kahlede

ISBN 978-1-64871-707-9 (print)

ISBN 978-1-64871-743-7 (ebook)

Copyright © Kahlede 2022

The right of Kahlede to be identified as the author of this work has been asserted by him in accordance with the *Copyright, Designs and Patents Act 1988*.

All rights reserved.

No part of this publication may be reproduced, stored in or introduced into a retrieval system, or transmitted, in any form, or by any means (electronic, mechanical, photocopying, recording, or otherwise) without the prior written permission of the publisher. Any person who does any unauthorised act in relation to this publication may be liable to criminal prosecution and civil claims for damages.

Printed in Australia.

# CONTENTS

| | |
|---|---|
| PREFACE | 12 |

## PART ONE
## THE MYSTERY OF IT ALL

| | |
|---|---|
| **BACK TO BASICS** | **16** |
| Cyclic, Palingenetic Time, Versus Linear Chronological Time | 16 |
| Free Will Versus Predestination | 23 |
| The Fractal Nature of Reality | 24 |
| Time Out | 27 |
| Competing Number Systems | 29 |
| Computer Code in the Mind | 40 |
| **PATTERNED FAMILY RELATIONSHIPS** | **43** |
| Islam, Judaism, Christianity, Combined | 48 |
| Rita's Story | 49 |
| Inherited Family Temperaments and Patterned Predispositions | 52 |
| Familiar Chaos | 57 |
| Learning by Proxy | 59 |
| Shedding Some Light | 68 |

## Contents

| | |
|---|---|
| Man Know Thyself | 72 |
| Enlightenment | 82 |
| Fractal Universal Gender Patterning | 87 |
| Matrix Protocols of Engagement | 94 |
| The End Meets its Beginning | 95 |

## FOUNDATIONS — 102

| | |
|---|---|
| Righteousness Equals Happiness | 105 |
| Imagination versus Mindfulness | 107 |
| Manifesting | 111 |
| Numbers Have Natures if not Feelings | 112 |
| The Voluptuous Number Seven | 116 |
| Waking | 121 |
| Fractal Eve | 125 |
| YHWH's Face | 127 |

## SOME POINTS TO PONDER — 131

## SABBATH MILLENNIUM OF PEACE — 155

| | |
|---|---|
| Yahshua's Timing | 159 |
| Raising the Ego | 162 |
| Sins Forgiven – Karma and the Power of Mindfulness | 164 |
| Coming Clean | 167 |
| Death and Memory – Reincarnation Verses Resurrection | 174 |
| Samsara | 179 |
| One Law: Love Truth | 191 |

# PART TWO
# THE OLD AND THE NEW

## MOSES IN NOAH'S ARK — 196

Intertextuality — 197
Patterned Spirit World — 203
Let Three-Dimensional Solidness Evolve — 209
Noah's Two Arks — 214
Stella and Fella — 216
Three Dimensions Plus Time (Cronos) Again — 226
Evil and the Grave — 232

## TIME TO CALL IT A DAY — 235

Anunnaki: Mesopotamian Reptilian Gods of the Earth and Underworld — 239
Evolutionary Epochs Verse Moses' Creation Days — 245
Linear Versus Cyclic — 253
Two Contrary Points, Plus Two Alternating Twilights — 259
Creation's Three Marriage Patterns — 263
YHWH and Time — 271

## LEAPING FORWARD INTO THE PAST — 277

Getting Personal — 282
Sacred Geometry — 285
Finding the Centre — 289

CONTENTS

| | |
|---|---|
| Walkabout – Making the Magic Work for You | 296 |
| From Marriage to Incest | 302 |
| Colour Patterns | 306 |
| Cyan Genesis | 309 |
| Going Home | 313 |
| Back to the Stars | 315 |
| Final Revision | 321 |
| Mirror, Mirror | 324 |

## APPENDIX – BITS AND PIECES     333

## LIST OF FIGURES

| | |
|---|---|
| Figure 1. The flower of life. Phi inside Pi | 115 |
| Figure 2. The Pattern of a Week | 119 |
| Figure 3. Yin and yang. Two inside one. | 147 |
| Figure 4. Inserting baptism as a surrogate cardinal point | 175 |
| Figure 5. Fractal phenomena inside phenomena | 190 |
| Figure 6. Comingling constellations at the Great Pyramid of Giza | 217 |
| Figure 7. The contention between XY Adam and the classical XX figure-8 Eve as represented by circumcision's pattern | 221 |
| Figure 8. Eve inside Adam with a common centre | 223 |
| Figure 9. Seeing eye to eye with our ancestors | 235 |

Figure 10. The Sumerian God, Ningishzida. 239
Figure 11. The Great Serpent of Norse mythology
Figure 12. The oldest symbol: Cross inside a revolving circle 256
Figure 13. Family circle or COG 259
Figure 14. First set of twilight marriages 263
Figure 15. Format of the second set of marriages 264
Figure 16. The third marriage format as described by Moses, which resembles a doughnut torus 266
Figure 17. The Pattern as a Network Science model 267
Figure 18. A single Creation Day as a COG 277
Figure 19. The versatility of the four cardinal points 286
Figure 20. The patterned geometry of a typical journey 289
Figure 21. The flag of the United Kingdom. 290
Figure 22. The maths of joined gender symbols 291
Figure 23. Four-leaf clover representation of a COG 300

# LIST OF TABLES

| | |
|---|---|
| Table 1. Different ways of looking at the numbers | 120 |
| Table 2. The first two Creation Days joined – Sunday to Monday | 262 |
| Table 3. Ways of seeing a day | 287 |

## LIST OF BOXES

| | |
|---|---|
| Box 1. Palingenesis, the Eternal Return or Wheel of Life | 17 |
| Box 2. Fractals | 20 |
| Box 3. Trivalent Logic (3VL) | 30 |
| Box 4. Extending Dualities to Trialities Deepens the Foundations of Dynamics | 36 |
| Box 5. Knights Templar | 46 |
| Box 6. Dog Breeds | 56 |
| Box 7. Anglerfish | 88 |
| Box 8. Transhumanism | 98 |
| Box 9. Psychohistory | 103 |
| Box 10. Evil | 109 |
| Box 11. The Bride | 122 |
| Box 12. Samsara | 184 |
| Box 13. Intertextuality | 198 |
| Box 14. Adam's Rib | 198 |
| Box 15. Was the Cambrian Explosion the result of a comet? | 205 |
| Box 16. Zipporah | 222 |
| Box 17. Great Artesian Basin | 225 |
| Box 18. Satan, According to Wikipedia | 234 |
| Box 19. The Standard Model Comes in Triplets | 258 |

The day science begins to study non-physical phenomena, they'll make more progress in one decade than in all the previous centuries of its existence.
— *Nikola Tesla*

"Of every tree of the garden thou mayst freely eat: But of the tree of knowledge of good and evil, thou shalt not eat of it: for in the day that thou eatest thereof, thou shalt (surely) die the death." — *Genesis 2:16–17*

Adam ate the fruit and lived 930 years. So, what does, "die the death" mean?

One must find a way to avoid the space-time continuum altogether, though I haven't the slightest idea about what kind of elementary concept could be used in such a theory. — *Albert Einstein, October 1954 (one year before he died)*

# PREFACE

IN MY FIRST book ADAM'S DAUGHTER,[1] I introduced a new (old?) model about how a person can get things precisely right; a concept of patterned methodology that allows you to know what your best option is every time you need to make a decision. It allows you to find the allusive win-win option in a field of infinite possibility.

I discovered this process – or more rightly it revealed itself to me – at the end of my medical career, having worked thirty-plus years as a clinical naturopath and general health consultant, where I used Nature's laws to help people recover from illness. What was revealed to me at that time turned out to be the motherload of Natural Lore, indicating there is a cure for every disease, including the sickness that has lately befallen the inhabitants of Earth.

When you follow this process for getting things meticulously right (religiously), it provides you with a way to extract yourself from Einstein's confusing space-time continuum he advised us to leave.[2] In this way (as crazy as it must sound to some), I now believe you can enter the religious concept known as Heaven on Earth, where everything is always right.

This mysterious methodology unifies spiritual and scientific principles into a single working Oneness. It is suggestive of a Theory

---

1   The first book in the series *There Are No Mirrors in Heaven*
2   See quote p. 13

of Everything and leads to a new understanding of life and … well, everything. I liken this integrated 'way' to what first-century Christians called the Art of Righteousness. But it also reminds me of:

- The Buddhist concept of abiding in the Middle Path
- The Hindu concept of being Krishna Conscious
- The Muslim concept of living in Allah
- The Jewish ideal of living a lawful life
- Physics' concept of a Theory of Everything (ToE).

When I first came across this patterned, all-encompassing way of understanding everything, I tried to palm the knowledge off onto those I considered more qualified to deal with it than I (i.e. scientists, mainly physicists, and a few university professors). I felt an overwhelming sense of responsibility to get this information out to the world and thought people of this standing would be the fastest route to a full disclosure. After all, what I'd been shown did connect to physics' search for a ToE. However, when I tried bringing the information to their attention, I got nowhere. Eventually, I realised I had to share my newly acquired 'insight' with those seeking the 'shift in consciousness' that's prophesied to occur at the end of this materialistic age; those searching for a loving way to redress the mess we've made on planet Earth while, by some accounts, we've all been snoozing.

*The First Immortals* is the second book in the four-book series *There Are No Mirrors in Heaven*. It outlines how a person can use this process to become healthy, wealthy, and wise.

## Preface

> By revealing that we live in a thoroughly quantum
> universe, quantum physics is literally placing the keys
> to our future in our own hands – the question is, do
> we know how to wisely use the gift that is being freely
> offered to us?[3]

This series of books encourage you to interpret life differently from what you have been used to, a quantum way where ideas about time and space are drastically altered to blend into a patterned cyclic reality of intermeshing fields.

This intriguing perspective embraces the ideas of twentieth-century mathematician Hermann Weyl, who was one of the foremost mathematicians of the past century. He said of the Unity of Knowledge that, 'In the linkage of four mysteries may lie the key to deep new insight.' These being:

- Time
- The 'how come' of existence
- The mathematical continuum
- The discontinuous yes-or-no of quantum physics.

Throughout this series of books, I outline that it is how you interact with these mysteries which determines your body's ongoing state of health and your destiny's good (or bad) fortune.

---

3   Paul Levy, *Awaken in the Dream*, https://www.awakeninthedream.com/

When I first started using this knowledge to untangle the mysteries of life, it blew the 'head' right off my shoulders. I retired from naturopathic practice believing I could now treat the Earth itself, not just a few of its constituents. I had warmed to the idea that the Earth might be healed and that I could play a small but significant part in her restoration, if only I was prepared to try. So I did, and I hope you enjoy my effort.

# PART ONE
# THE MYSTERY OF IT ALL

## BACK TO BASICS

### Cyclic, Palingenetic Time, Versus Linear Chronological Time

> "... time ropes and loops and is never straight, that's the real story of time."[4] – *Tara June Winch, Wiradjuri author*

If we are to save Mankind and the Earth, then I believe we need to switch our understanding of time back to the ancient idea of patterned palingenesis. Palingenesis asserts that cyclic energies reappear, or are reborn, in timely cycles – what the Ancients called the Wheel of Life and the Stoics called the palingenetic nature of cyclic re-creation. Currently, we think of time's passing as being linear and random: things are born and eventually die, popping up and (just as mysteriously) popping out of existence. Physicists differ in their ideas

---

4   Tara June Winch, 2019, *The Yield*, Penguin, Australia, p. 2.

about time, but, thanks to Einstein's vision, they do agree that time is relative to the observer. Other than time being relative, however, time's true nature is still up for grabs.[5]

---

### Box 1. Palingenesis, the Eternal Return or Wheel of Life

Palingenesis; also palingenesia, is a concept of rebirth or re-creation used in various contexts in philosophy, theology, politics and biology. Its meaning stems from Greek *palin*, meaning 'again', and *genesis*, meaning 'birth'. In theology, the word may refer to reincarnation or Christian spiritual rebirth, as symbolised by baptism. The word *palingenesia* may be traced back to the Stoics, who used the term for the **continual re-creation of the Universe**.

In the Gospel of Matthew, Jesus is quoted in Greek (although his historical utterance would most likely have been in Aramaic), using the word παλιγγενεσια ('palingenesia') to describe the Last Judgment, foreshadowing the event of a new world being regenerated. Palingenesia is thus as much the result of, or reason for, the Last Judgement as it is the Judgement itself.[6]

\* \* \*

Traditionally, this passage in *Matthew 24* has been thought to be about the end of the world but, more accurately, it infers the end of one worldview (cycle) and the birth of another.

---

5   PBS Space Time, 'The Arrow of Time and How to Reverse It', *YouTube*, https://youtu.be/QkWT-xMTm1M
6   'Palingenesis', *Wikipedia*, https://en.wikipedia.org/wiki/Palingenesis

While it's true that the laws of physics operate equally well running backwards or forwards, when it comes to the passage, (or arrow) of time, the idea of time running backwards makes little to no sense. Physicists acknowledge there is an asymmetry to time's directional arrow. But their understanding of time's passing would alter if they recognised that time – like everything else in the Universe – maintains a circular architecture or momentum, and is not linear as it appears to be. I think we'll discover that the Stoics were right: Time was and remains cyclic, not linear, and what goes around indeed comes around, and around, and around in consistent cycles. Furthermore, these cycles can be recognised, understood, and 'named' mathematically; their eventual outcomes can be known in advance from one cycle to the next. Palingenesis embraces qualities both magical and mythical.

**Linear-time doesn't allow you to know where you are in physics' larger, cyclic picture. The alternative palingenetic model suggests … If cycles repeat in consistent patterns, then if you know where you are in any given cycle, and can recognise that cycle's name or essential energy, you can calculate what that cycle's future holds – where it is heading. The cycle's pattern remains consistent over time and, in this way, allows you to calculate or read the future as the Ancients did.**

Having a 'knowing-what-is-going-to-happen' talent could be likened to having 20/20 hindsight, but now as Promethean foresight. It's also like turning your car onto a road that's signposted, indicating Town X so many miles ahead. Then travelling that highway and finding yourself entering Town X as no surprise at all; the signpost at the beginning of the journey had revealed the end.

Our Solar System moves in cycles around the Milky Way, while our Earth moves around the Sun, and the Moon revolves around the Earth. We know their rotations embrace different energies at different parts of their cycles – at different cardinal points so to speak: day/night, summer/winter, full/new moon. When dinosaurs last walked the Earth, we were on the other side of the galaxy.[7] Palingenesis proclaims … When we get there again, a new manifestation of dinosaur-energy will be waiting for us to experience. This doesn't infer that dinosaurs will miraculously reappear at that time but, rather, that their energy will be represented again in some mathematical sense. For instance, we might encounter reptilian aliens, or the like, with comparatively small frontal brain lobes.

The idea that time embraces repeating cycles supports the hypothesis that we're living in a simulated fractal universe,[8] for on each occasion that an energy repeats itself, its characteristics resemble fractal forms of the parent or mother-energy it was named for and took after.

Because the laws of physics are reversible, physicists have postulated that time should be reversible as well; that we should be able to determine what's going to happen to us with a similar certainty to how we know the antics of the past.[9] Daily life would certainly be easier for us to handle if we knew that the future held only new forms

---

7    Dr Jessie Christiansen, *Twitter* post, 29 August 2019, https://twitter.com/i/status/1166773845400801281

8    Frank Giustra, 'Is our reality someone else's simulation?' Frank Giustra, 23 October 2020, https://frankgiustra.com/posts/is-our-reality-someone-elses-simulation/

9    This is the Wheeler/Feynman absorber theory; reviewed and commented on by Einstein as being synchronous. Also known as the Wheeler–Feynman time-symmetric theory.

of things we had already experienced and overcome. You would never get caught napping, yet you'd still find life entertaining. You would be confident that you could handle anything life threw at you. In this way ... the fear of uncertainty would be forced to take a backseat. But how would we achieve this talent of knowing what the future holds, if it was indeed possible, that is?

---

**Box 2. Fractals**

Fractals are infinitely complex patterns that are self-similar across different scales. They are created by repeating a simple process in an ongoing feedback loop. Driven by recursion, fractals are images of dynamic systems – the pictures of Chaos. Russian stacking dolls maintain a fractal nature.[10]

"Do fractals tell us anything deep about reality?"

"Possibly, but we don't know what or why."[11]

---

The idea that time is a two-way street would make more sense if it was essentially cyclic. This would parallel how we currently understand

---

[10] 'What are fractals?' *Fractal Foundation*, https://fractalfoundation.org/resources/what-are-fractals/

[11] Christian Santangelo (theoretical physicist), *Quora* post, 2018, https://www.quora.com/Do-fractals-tell-us-anything-deep-about-reality?share=1

that summer always follows spring, and how we can count on all four seasons maintaining different and distinct properties. Currently, this cyclic, seasonal understanding allows a person to do such things as readying garden beds for a spring planting of flowers and veggies, while at the same time preparing for summer's potential bushfire threat. They would know that, although winter has passed (is in the past), it is only a matter of known time before winter will return once again. In this way, a person can be going forwards into the past, knowing what their future holds from an energetic, cyclic point of view. Nothing would ever truly be lost to the past, which would cast an interesting light on events that kept repeating. (This potentially paradoxical process is mysteriously captured – inexplicably – in the Incan Aymara Language, which is spoken by the local tribe's people living on the shore of the magical Lake Titicaca.[12,13] I wonder if they remember something the rest of us have forgotten?)

We naturally accept cyclic, segmented configurations at cosmic levels but, when it comes to a person's life, we switch our mind's operating system to a linear model, in which we are born and eventually die, making our life resemble a straight line with a polarised beginning and end – where neither speaks to each other. **It's funny when you think that the repetitive cycles of the Earth, Sun, and Moon largely define our notion of time passing: day, month, year, et cetera, yet we continue to think of personal 'time' as being linear, rather than as a spiral of interconnected cycles within cycles, embracing specific patterns of energy at known times.**

---

12    Steve Williams, 'Aymara language', *Graham Hancock* website, http://grahamhancock.com/phorum/read.php?1,4491,4531

13    Francis Gastellu, 'The Aymara language mystery' *Graham Hancock* website, http://grahamhancock.com/phorum/read.php?1,35762,37681

If we return to the Stoic's timely, cyclic mindset, now updated into quantum reality, I believe we will master what has traditionally been at the heart of all forms of ancient auguring and prophetic fortune-telling systems. Systems that have never gone away.

- We'll access a way to calculate the energy and nature of all upcoming events.

- We'll understand the true nature of what is happening to us at any given time.

- We'll become soothsayers who can contemplate why certain things have happened in our past – and understand why they have kept reoccurring – seen now in a different light.

Tyson Yunkaporta, senior lecturer in Indigenous Knowledge at Deakin University, said traditional Aboriginal culture supports this idea about time's patterns being used as predictors of the future. He wrote: 'map out all the relationships and you might see a pattern that represents the future, because all time is one time.'[14]

According to the San people of the Kalahari, the word 'Man' is derived from their legends of the cosmic Mantis who came to Earth in a pod as the Spirit of Man. The oldest understanding of the word *mantis* comes from Koine Greek, meaning 'the ability to prophesy or soothsay'.

The mantis is the only insect to have a swivelling neck. To see ahead (clearly) it has to turn its head to-and-fro in a 180° arc. The San people's idea about Man (*mantis*) embraces a pattern. Interestingly, the letters

---

[14] Tyson Yunkaporta, *Sand Talk*, Text Publishing, 2019, p. 85

mn (man) are inexorably tied to the idea of memory: mnemonics. (In a sense, memory can be seen as 180° away from the mantic future.) Therefore, the ancient meaning of the word 'man' (*mantis*) implies … **When you know how to look at the past correctly with patterned eyes (mn: past memory), you will see the future clearly in the now (mn: mantic forward vision).** This would be possible if time revolved in cycles that were governed by consistent energies. I believe the San people's legends contain great truths that remain disguised as anthropomorphisms and family geometrical relationships.

If this ancient idea about Mankind being potential soothsayers is correct, then quantum computers – which the late Richard Feynman believed are needed to model natural cycles – will make the necessary calculations for us. A breakthrough of this magnitude – in which Mankind became the equivalent of Time Lords – would change everything.

> Nature isn't classical, dammit, and if you want to make a simulation of nature, you'd better make it quantum mechanical.[15] – *Feynman*

## Free Will Versus Predestination

The idea that we can prophesy our future seems at odds with our current understanding of free will; one idea appears to cancel the other. Either our lives are predestined (causality) and can be foretold or they can't. But what if time's cycles utilised the same energy patterns but expressed

---

15   Richard Feynman, *Your Dictionary* quotes, https://quotes.yourdictionary.com/author/richard-feynman/158361

themselves uniquely on each occasion they occurred? You would then be able to calculate the coming energy but not know the unique form it would take at its next appearance. This would be the same as having a birthday party each year on the same day, but with different presents received and different people present. But that day was, is, and always will be, your birthday. This date remains a special occasion.

In this fascinating way, if time maintains consistent cycles that embrace governing energies, and we can learn how to read their matrix accurately (understand how a true calendar works in a quantum universe), we would have a window into the future yet retain a semblance of free will in the present. We would be free to react in any way we liked to the known and prophesied events as they occurred. For instance, on your coming birthday you might enjoy your presents or discard them as unsuitable. You might spend the day with the same people as last year, or with a new bunch altogether. The choice is freely yours, but it will always be your birthday. You don't get to change the date or the fact it is your birthday. In this way, you have free will in one dimension, while being restrained by others.

## The Fractal Nature of Reality

> The mystery of the universe is hierarchic in structure. There are graded orders, one supervening upon the other. – *Meher Baba*

A set of cyclic laws are being unearthed in various branches of science that suggest that Reality is the equivalent of a computer simulation that maintains a gauge symmetry at its deepest level. This symmetry principle lies at the heart of physics' Super Symmetry and Quantum Field Theories. As outlined in *Adam's Daughter*, a growing number of scientists believe that reality operates on simulated fractal patterns that embrace Nature's tertiary operating system. When viewed from this tertiary, fractal-patterned perspective, world events appear to be repeating in ever-increasing or decreasing units of complexity – up and down in waves like a traditional Australian Aboriginal painting.

This cyclic idea about time's passing proffers an explanation for peculiarities such as:

- Why it is said … What goes around comes around.
- Why the biblical Solomon was adamant that 'There is nothing new under the sun'.
- Why Karma is recognised by both East and West, but not understood scientifically by either.
- Why history is said to repeat itself.
- Why behavioural scientists recognise that a person's character is formed in the first six or seven years of their life.[16] (Some believe it then repeats in seven-year cycles.)
- Why it is said that a man's past will eventually catch up with him – or her.

---

16   'Personality development: Age 2–6' Cliff Notes website, https://www.cliffsnotes.com/study-guides/psychology/development-psychology/psychosocial-development-age-26/personality-development-age-26

- Why we experience things such as déjà vu, synchronicity, and serendipity.

Strangely enough, I discovered many components of this weird, patterned truth in Moses' early biblical writings; other components I unearthed in Stone Age myths and legends from the world's oldest cultures: primarily the San people of the African Kalahari and Aboriginal people of Australia. When I discovered all three sources fundamentally agreed on many diverse key issues – which I discuss throughout this series of books – it made me wonder whether Mankind might have once known everything important and then, for some strange reason I couldn't fathom at the time, forgot it all, as if he went to sleep.

Eventually, I came to realise that was exactly what had happened. I'm now convinced we did once walk the Earth as gods, and – when the time was right – deliberately put ourselves to sleep to dream of the next essential piece of the great puzzle. This vital piece was and remains:

> How we can physically leave this planet and go back to
> the stars before we need to.

One of the basic components of the program's operating system I was shown was this: After a set of polarised opposites marry and form a new semblance of integrated unity, they then (as a couple) set about seeking mobility. If successful in their endeavours, this ability to 'move' is added to the couple's combined (married) union. I believe this two-part process can be thought of as **marriage** followed by **honeymoon**. Thoreau captured this strange but uplifting idea in his book *Walden*:

> The soil, it appears, is suited to the seed, for it has sent its radicle downward, and it may now send its shoot upwards also with confidence. Why has man rooted himself thus firmly in the earth, but that he may rise in the same proportion into the heavens above?[17]

According to Thoreau, the seed marries the soil and then sets off for far horizons. Similarly, if Mankind can get its 'unity act' together, I believe we might get to honeymoon among the stars as Thoreau suggests.

## Time Out

I discovered that each cycle in the Simulation's Operating System contains the equivalent of a snooze component – an 'off' as well as an 'on'. When a line in the Program is in the 'off' position, it sleeps in some sense and, during that dark time, loses its memory of its previous wakeful state where all the seemingly important stuff resides. (This is similar to what we do each night when we slip into our micro-fractal sleep-state and dream.) But eventually, every cycle completes itself and wakes.

I believe this is happening now as the 'shift' in consciousness continues to download on the Earth, returning our sacred (mantic) memories in the twilight of a new cycle's palingenetic dawning. (The 'tomorrow' our prophets and seers have told us was coming.)

---

17   James A. Hamby, 'Thoreau's synthesizing metaphor: Two fishes with one hook', *Bulletin of the Rocky Mountain Modern Language Association*, https://muse.jhu.edu/article/457957/summary

The book *Genesis* reveals that, long ago, we left a Garden State and entered a Wilderness Arena, ceasing to hear God's voice. It reveals we somehow lost our ability to remain in contact with All Else, having lost our micro-fractal god-status. (This is where I believe we all went to sleep as we hit the 'off' button. The Bible says we became naked.)

Ancient Sumerian accounts are even weirder. They suggest we were genetically modified by fallen angels, called the Anunnaki. Like the Greek Titans, the Anunnaki were expelled to the underworld to cause great mischief, going up and down, to-and-fro, from Heaven/Hell to Earth.[18] (The tales of the Anunnaki and Titans cover much of the same material.)

From a scientific perspective, I liken the idea of us being cast into a Wilderness to a Bohmian pilot-wave. The idea of a pilot-wave is to enter a nebulous state of uncertainty to seek out the most effective way ahead, making intelligent sense out of infinite possibilities. This is similar to how a 'qubit' operates in a quantum computing system; a qubit embraces all options, using an exponential methodology to calculate the eventual outcome.[19]

From *Genesis* we can infer that we entered a 'Wilderness Process' to discover the means (propulsion) to return us to the stars that spawned us. This ancient text suggests we all had to go to sleep to dream up the myriad separate parts of the methodology we would require for doing so. But now that Mankind has developed the ability to fulfil its

---

18  'Anunnaki', *Wikipedia*, https://en.wikipedia.org/wiki/Anunnaki
19  Quanta Magazine, 'Quantum computers, explained with quantum physics', *YouTube* video, https://youtu.be/jHoEjvuPoB8

celestial (honeymoon) wanderlust, it's time to wake and re-enter the Garden State, job complete.

Nobel laureate Percy Bridgeman said:

> By far the most important consequence of the conceptual revolution brought about in physics by relativity and quantum theory lies not in such details as that meter sticks shorten when they move or that simultaneous position and momentum have no meaning, but in the insight that ... **We had not been using our minds properly and that it is important to find out how to do so.**

## Competing Number Systems

While quantum physics is wired three-core, our civilisation is built on ubiquitous dualities. Man's civilisation can be modelled on a binary computer system, whereas Nature's cycles prefer a universal third qubit-option to 'on' or 'off'.

Trinary or ternary computer systems work off different sets of values, but all maintain the same third central option to 'on' or 'off'.[20] One such system uses the values −1, 0, +1; another uses 1, 2, 3. Within the qubit we find the 'on' (1) and 'off' (0) mixed together in a nebulous twilight fashion, like the hypnogogic mindset we pass through each morning

---

20 'Ternary computer', *Wikipedia*, https://en.wikipedia.org/wiki/Ternary_computer

as we drift from our nightly slumber into a new day neither awake nor asleep. The placement of the qubit in quantum computational systems enabled these machines to evolve from a binary configuration to a trinary one; from a 'beast' to an 'animal' as Moses liked to say.

The central qubit (0 + 1) being placed between the polarised concepts of zero (0) and one (1), mimics the central idea of what is known as trivalent logic (3VL). All ternary computers work on 3VL.

---

**Box 3. Trivalent Logic (3VL)**

In logic, a three-valued logic (also trinary logic, trivalent, ternary or trilean sometimes abbreviated 3VL) is any of several many-valued logic systems, in which there are three truth values indicating **true, false** and some **indeterminate** third value. This is contrasted with the more commonly known bivalent logics (such as classical sentential or Boolean logic), which provide only for **true and false**.[21]

---

Trivalent logic is at odds with yin/yang's ubiquitous duality, but accords nicely with ternary computer systems. (3VL also parallels the Himalayan Twilight Language mentioned previously in *Adam's Daughter*.) Maybe this trivalent alteration, when applied to how Mankind thinks, is the key that Bridgeman sought for a new mindset for Mankind. I believe it is, especially when it's applied to the passage and nature of time, and the process of consciousness, similar to the ideas of Hermann Weyl.

---

21  'Three-valued logic', *Wikipedia*, https://en.wikipedia.org/wiki/Three-valued_logic

(I continue to elaborate on the idea of trinary human consciousness throughout these books, because I believe it is an important key to our awakening and future wellbeing.)

I now associate Moses' biblical idea of Mankind being cast into the Wilderness with us swapping our existent trinary mindset for a binary one. This was likely due to genetic modification by what has been called fallen angels – what others have thought to be aliens (Anunnaki, Titans). I equate Moses' idea of living in a pristine Garden with us using a trinary mindset that operates on a form of 3VL. If this idea is true, then we need to step up a peg if we're going to return to the Garden.

I BELIEVE THE DIFFERENCE between the numbering systems of 'two' (binary) and 'three' (trinary) is creating hell on Earth, hampering our ability to be happy and healthy. The concept of 'two' has traditionally been associated with duality's natural yin/yang contention, and has been connected with the nature of evil – the Diablos – because duality is said to draw a person away from God's Sovereignty being One.[22]

In contrast to the nature of 'two', the concept of 'three' stands for completion (one and two happily married into a new, single trivalent format). The number 'three' (3) is the only number that's the sum of the two numbers that directly precede it. The number 'three' (one plus two) can be seen as having the same essential and central property as the quantum 'qubit'. Both mathematical ideas elegantly

---

[22] 'Religion: Dualism', *Encyclopaedia Britannica*, https://www.britannica.com/topic/dualism-religion

unify (add) the first two states into a new combined format but, in this case, the resultant 'three' takes its place in the middle (centre) between the 'one' and 'two', in the same way that our third eye sits in the centre of our forehead, or how zero (0) resides between minus-one (−1) and plus-one (+1) as their central sum. This essential idea, or layout, can be seen as the unification of male (1) and female (2), which produces a fertile married format (3).

This integrated state is then capable of producing fractal children (3s), who reside between their parents for protection, having equal amounts of DNA (input) from each parent. Fifty % from the male one (1), and fifty % from the female two (2).

I thought it interesting that this same numerical weirdness is covered in *Genesis*' timely warning about the Garden's dangerous binary Tree of Good and Evil contending with the unified, salient, and singular Tree of Life. We're told that one tree embraces certain death while the other proffers the idea of eternal life, living in Heaven on Earth.

In *Genesis*, Moses tells us, if we eat from the binary good-and-evil tree, we will 'die in our dying'. His Hebrew script repeats the word for death. It says if you eat from the binary tree, then *wham-oh*, dual (2) death/death. It seems that Mankind is expected to eat from the other singular tree (1) where its binary seed is safely contained within it at its sacred centre point.[23] Both of these trees embrace patterns at the Centre of Moses' ideas about a Creation Garden/Wilderness. Each Tree grows in a field with numbered values.

This strange dietary dictum in *Genesis* about the food we eat is metaphorical. It's not referring to the fruit we put in our mouths.

---

23   *Genesis* 1:29

It's referring to the thoughts that govern our minds and the subsequent actions we undertake based on them. If we consider the crux of Mankind's dilemma as being the result of our limited, binary mindset – it being one sandwich short of a picnic – then it makes me wonder whether we should have paid more attention to what Moses was trying to reveal in antiquity and embraced a form of trivalent logic sooner, as the Incan Aymara appear to have done.[24]

We now need to ask:

> Does our mind currently work from a binary pattern
> (contending duality platform)? Or a mindful trinary one
> (unified by marriage as one)? And does it matter if
> it does?

Traditionally, the passage in *Genesis* about the Garden's two resident trees growing at the Garden's dead centre has been thought to be about good and evil, and the food we eat. But I think you'll find it goes much further than this, maintaining:

> If we go about entertaining a linear, yin/yang, dualist, way
> of thinking about life, it will lead to our certain demise.

If Reality turns out to be a simulation that's running on a trinary program, one that's set on building trinary units from scratch, then duality will be recognised as an interim mathematical process (two-thirds of the way through to the desired end) that seeks to move on

---

24   Guzmán de Rojas, 'The trivalent logic of Aymara', *Amara.org*, https://aymara.org/biblio/html/igr/igr3.html

to trinary completion when given half a chance. 'I now think of 'two' as the way to reach 'three'.

The differences between the numerical concepts of 'two' and 'three' are significant. Two straight lines don't cut it when it comes to creating (solid) shapes; three straight lines are required to complete an enclosure. In this regard, I find it interesting that our idea of chronological time is binary, accentuating beginnings and endings. I believe this misconception is helping to keep us mentally pinned down in the Wilderness.

If this simple numerical contention between 'two' and 'three' turns out to be a universal feature of a controlling program that's running Reality, then this would indicate where we need to change. It seems we have to step our state of consciousness up a notch and embrace a trinary cyclic way of thinking about space-time, so we can recognise and mesh (talk) with the quantum events taking place around us. With our current binary yin/yang mindset, we each think we're 'out there' on our own. But if we learn to look at life in a way that connects the quantum dots and dashes within the all-embracing Matrix in a threefold, unified lattice, we just might come to see the underlying patterns that are controlling our lives. In that case, we could learn to manage them in a way that would allow us to know what our future holds; allow us to become the soothsaying masters of our destiny.

Should this occur, the world would enter a brand-new day.

\* \* \*

THE PURPOSE OF THESE BOOKS is not to convince you that another reality resides within your mind. They are meant to encourage you to look in the right places for consistent patterns. Then, once found, you start seeing this world differently and the rest takes care of itself.

Physics' Simulation Hypothesis implies that Reality is the output of a holographic process. It infers that an interim two-dimensional transitory reality – the equivalent of a holographic negative – is coming out of a singular process (a phase singularity) and that this duality is leading to the creation of three-dimensional reproductions of the original singularity. Put another way … A 'One' is evolving into a 'Three' by way of an interim process called 'Two'. The bad news is … It appears we have built our civilisation out of nothing but 'twos', which can't be good if – in the fullness of time – the 'twos' have to move on to bigger and better things (3s) or go extinct.

Professor Smolin captures this 'two' becoming 'three' idea elegantly in his paper: '*Extending Dualities to Trialities Deepens the Foundations of Dynamics*'.

I believe Professor Smolin's paper borders on prophetical, preparing the way for physics' illusive ToE to unite all aspects of reality into a single (trinary) understanding.

> **Box 4. Extending Dualities to Trialities Deepens the Foundations of Dynamics**
>
> Prof. Smolin, in his paper for the *International Journal of Theoretical Physics*, asks if there might be a deeper principle that unifies different dualities and explains their importance for fundamental physics. Dualities are often supposed to be foundational, but are not background-independent, because they need a hidden fixed structure to define their transformation.
>
> Smolin proposes an answer to this lack of self-sufficiency, which is that the common origin of **many of the diverse dualities in physics is a deeper principle of triality.** This triality renders that fixed structure dynamic, while unifying it with dual variables. He demonstrates mathematically how to expand, for example, the position/momentum duality into a triality, which involves transforming the background structures into an extra dimension or dimensions.
>
> This paper also illustrates how breaking this natural triality symmetry, by imposing different compactifications, yields particle mechanics, string theory and Chern-Simons theory. These result from compacting one, two and three dimensions, respectively. **This may provide an explanation for the origin of so many dualities in physics and provide another step towards finding that elusive complete underlying theory**[25]

---

[25] Lee Smolin, 'Extending dualities to trialities deepens the foundations of dynamics', *International Journal of Theoretical Physics*, 2017, 56, 221–231. https://doi.org/10.1007/s10773-016-3168-7

Various titles have been suggested for this unified state's operating system. Names such as the Mind of God, the Matrix, E8, Centrism, and the Implicate and Explicate, to name a few. If what I was shown is correct, then the Mosaic Pattern might join this prestigious list, and even top it, if it's a case of … First in best dressed.

If Reality turns out to be the equivalent of a simulation that contains micro-fractal units operating in a living and growing patterned mandala, then an individual should qualify as a complete micro-fractal unit of the Program. (Within the micro, we would be able to see the macro.) The early Greeks thought this was the case. It is why they wrote above the door of the Temple of Apollo at Delphi (where the famous Oracle lived):

> Man know thyself and thou shall know all the mysteries
> of the gods and of the universe.

I believe a marriage between ancient religious concepts and science is brewing. Various prophecies proclaim this marriage will take place at the end of this Material Age when the Mystery of God is revealed.

The Mayans refer to this 'end-time event as … 'When the Condor flies with the Eagle'. Biblical prophecies equate it to when heterosexual and homosexual marriage patterns are considered to be equal; when they are thought to be one and the same thing. When this happens, *Revelation* tells us that 'time' (Chronos) 'will be no more'.[26]

**At the end of the current palingenetic cycle, when marriage loses its original meaning and pattern, *Revelation* reveals the Ancient**

---

26   *Revelation* 10:6

**of Days will end our understanding of time.** How weird is that? Could it be happening now?

THE RACE TO DISCLOSE the god of science is well underway with three contenders lining up for our consideration:

- **A curvaceous principle in all her voluptuous beauty**
  The pure X or wave-state of quantum field physics; the **Yin Mother Goddess.**

- **A solid-looking principle** The Y particle state of quantum field physics; the **Yang Father Adonis.**

- **A balance or blended YX/XY field** A pattern of particle and wave-energies mixed and undifferentiated; the **Quantum Qubit.**

This third qubit-like state has the same format as Jung's Holy Centre of non-polarisation. Its fundamental principle captures the act of holy marriage, where two opposing opposites of equal energy unite to become a new one (in a sense … marriage being the opposite of divide and conquer).

I believe these three universal states are the basic constituents that run Reality's quantum program. Various names have been applied to micro applications or units of this potential fractal trinity, other than Mankind himself (man, woman, child). These could include Load, Force and Pivot; Proton, Electron and Neutron; Brahma, Shiva and Vishnu; Isis, Osiris and Horus; Pythagoras' right-angled triangle, along with the Christian Trinity YHWH. All of these examples, plus oodles more, could simply be thought of as – in energy terms – Mum (2),

Dad (1), and the Kids (3/4).

The Hebrew god YHWH declares He is the Universe's Architect. He informs us that He embraces a Pattern, a Logos, which He used (and continues to use) to establish and maintain life on Earth. He tells us that His creation process contains a series of patterned covenants, which act like protective clothing to help the living (dual?) parts of the Program get through the hard-growing times they are forced to endure; those times being the equivalent of sleepy and cyclic cold-night events. He called these protective devices covering-arks, or covenants (think: fruit peels, a coat of paint over a timber dwelling, or even bark covering a tree's central heartwood). These covenants are also similar to how Earth is covered and protected by our atmosphere. Or how Earth's surrounding magnetic field and Van Allen belts protect her atmosphere from being blown away by the solar wind.

I believe *Genesis'* idea about 'needing to be 'covered' is the meaning behind Adam and Eve becoming '*naked in the Garden*'. They lost their covering ark when they entered the Wilderness component in the Program and, consequently, needed appropriate 'redressing'. Interestingly – as the story goes – Adam allegorically used the energy of vine leaves for this purpose, but YHWH quickly replaced them with animal skins. Similarly, YHWH later refused Cain's vegetable offering but accepted Abel's animal sacrifice as being appropriate.

When I remembered that plant cells have a dual organelle nucleus at their Centre – like Venus the Evening Star is the only star to appear twice in the night sky – while animal cells have a single centre or nuclear pattern, I understood the implications behind Moses' words. It was simply another 'one' and 'two', Adam and Eve issue of competing number systems vying for control in the Simulation's illustrious Centre – like the two trees in the proverbial Garden.

Each three-part 'bit' of the Program can be drawn as a trigram (as outlined in the *Book of Changes*, or *I Ching*) with either a broken or solid line positioned at each trigram's centre. A 'one' or a 'two':

- A solid-line centre represents a single (male/yang) value.
- A broken-line centre represents a (female/yin) 'two'.

It is important to note that a 'covering' with a dual centre is vastly different from a single one, as we'll see as we delve deeper into the book.

## Computer Code in the Mind

If you think of the numerals 'one' and 'two' as being representatives of yang (male) and yin (female) – as Pythagoras did – then each would need to be aligned properly within the Matrix's Operating Code for it to remain healthy.

In a similar sense, you could think of a circle's circumference as being related to its centre point as another similar yin/yang set of opposites. If you keep these two ideas in mind, you come to understand the importance of getting the outer peel – the circumference – on the outside of the orange, while keeping its seeds – its central babies and future generation – safely tucked inside at its centre, rather than the other way around. You don't want the cart in front of the horse, because it isn't elegant and doesn't take us forward.

This idea of appropriate modelling is displayed in the DNA molecule. Its chemically active components – the nucleotide base pairs – are safely contained within the molecule's centre between the two opposing (parental?) spiral rails. However, the eventual proteins these bases encode are chemically active on the outside, which allows the proteins to bond with other chemicals and grow in complexity. The latter model has the growing part outside which fosters growth, while the other has it inside which fosters stability. Yet both are essential and need to be in their correct place at the right time.

Male and female values are equal, but play different roles and represent different ideas in a mathematical sense. Problems begin when they lose their way and become misplaced.

The idea of appropriate covering extends into the New Testament:

> I am going to send you what my Father has promised;
> but stay in the city until you have been clothed with
> power from on high. – *Yahshua advising His disciples*[27]

Ancient Hebrew wisdom proclaims that YHWH's House or abode is a duality: Beyt. It reveals He lives in the centre of this Duality House in the Most Holy Place. When in residence, His presence creates a trinity out of the house's otherwise duality. He is One – complete with a back and front – and He lives in the centre of Two, making it a Three/Four. (The three/four is because YHWH has a back and front.) This layout resembles the third-eye principle in Tibetan Buddhism, while these same principles are covered in the Vedas. Weird …? Certainly. But it's still reasonably simple to grasp: **The third energy in the Simulation (God) sits in the middle of the universal dichotomy (2) as its pivot point, complete with a back and front.**

---

27  *Luke* 24:49

But what I thought even stranger was ... This trinity pattern of the Creator and His home can be found in each person's mind, expressed as a now-conscious, singular mindset (mindfulness) harboured between our imagination's propensity to go to-and-fro as a dual-modality. (A person's imagination feeds on the past and projects its components into the future as expectation – to-and-fro.) In a sense, a person's imagination conjures what should happen – what should 'be' according to 'me' – into their future, and then act on this presumption in the central Now.

In this geometrical way (which is similar to the actions of a mantis swivelling its neck to-and-fro), the domain of human consciousness can be seen to be paralleling ancient concepts about the Bible's God and where He lives. I think these pattern connections are fascinating and meaningful in a fractal way.

We know our sense of imagination, with its potentially turbulent to-and-fro operating system, plays a major part in our lives. But is this binary process a good thing or a bad thing? (How are we meant to use it wisely?) I think it's imperative we find this out for numerically it appears to be of great importance. Especially since Dr Bruce Lipton remains adamant that:

> Ninety-five per cent of our conscious life is controlled by our subconscious mind.[28]

---

28   Bruce Lipton, 'The science that will change your future', *YouTube* video, https://youtu.be/b5-JVPj6bsg?t=492

# PATTERNED FAMILY RELATIONSHIPS

> The fractal view of the cosmos is so complete it even accounts for the aesthetic qualities of balance and symmetry artists, mathematicians, philosophers, and physicists aspire to in the highest forms of their craft.
>
> – *Gregg Braden*

In *Adam's Daughter*, I compared Moses' Account of Creation with modern developments in physics' search for their ToE – especially Garret Lisi's E8 revealed in 2008.[29,30] In physics, the Theory of Everything (ToE) is the quest for all knowledge and shouldn't be confused with a Grand Unified Theory (GUT). Traditionally, GUT has sought to combine Einstein's Relativity equations with Quantum Field Theory, whereas ToE embraces an understanding of everything. As physicist Tom Campbell once said:

> There are little ToEs and then there are big ToEs.

A really big ToE would reveal God. This is why physicist Michio Kaku calls it The God Equation. It would describe our origins,

---

29  TED, 'A theory of rverything | Garrett Lisi', *YouTube* video, https://youtu.be/y-Gk_Ddhr0M?t=56

30  Video Advice, 'The science that will change your future: Part 2 | Bruce Lipton', *YouTube* video, https://youtu.be/XJoELR8ed2M?t=194

explain our apparent insanity and reveal the purpose of life – if there is one. It would tell us whether we need to get sick and die, and what death is all about. (For instance, is our bodily death just another sleep component in the palingenetic program?) A ToE of such magnitude would also reveal Mankind's industrial failings, which would necessitate a rear-guard action by ruthless businessmen to hold onto their ill-begotten gains. This would take place in the face of their enterprises being recognised as at odds with sustainable life, revealing these bastions of the metropolis as anti-life, essentially running the Program backwards. The ensuing conflict is likely to amount to a modern-day version of Saint George taking on the dragon sitting on top of its pile of gold, only to see the Dragon go ballistic in its death throws. Tom Campbell and other notable physicists are hot on ToE's tail. And Hawking – shortly before he died – was certain its disclosure couldn't be far away.

**But would a validated ToE reveal the same wisdom that all religions are founded on? Would it give them a fresh badge of honour in the face of the disdain they currently suffer from and allow them to unite? Or would it destroy them completely to allow a new, universal understanding to rise from their combined ashes?**

One way or another, should such an event occur, I believe we should expect a bumpy and bloody ride for a time after that until the two perspectives work out their differences.

MOSES WAS SHOWN a pattern by his God, Yahweh (YHWH), which I believe was – and remains – the Pattern of Creation, the operating system of the Quantum Matrix. The Disciple John referred to this creating pattern as the Logos. The word *logos* means 'a meaningful and correct statement', but the word extends to include logical order and the ability to spawn.

> It (Logos) was used to signify the divine power of function by which the universe is given unity, coherence and meaning. *Logos spermatikos*: Seminal Word; a seed-like quality that gives form to unformed matter. Man is made in accordance with the same principle.[31]

In a modern sense, the meaning of the word *Logos* would qualify as the operating system of the Matrix which spawns Reality. And Moses declared he was shown how the blessed thing works, in all its spine-chilling, paradoxical simplicity.

I believe Moses' writings entwine with the Logos' algorithms in numerous and beguiling ways, trying to bring its intricacies to light through family-relationship analogies that he knew we would always be able to relate to. But to get the most from his disclosures, you need to know how the Logos' trinary operating system works, otherwise you run into confusing blind alleys and illogical deadends.

Knowledge of the Logos has been locked away in an array of esoteric forms for thousands of years, awaiting its coming-out call at the end of the age – which I believe is now. (Lazarus, come forth!) Some accounts refer to the Logos' all-embracing mystery as the Arcanum,

---

31   JD Douglas, *New Bible Dictionary* 2nd edition, Tyndale House Publishers, 1993.

for it has many names – another arguably being the Holy Grail. We know the Jewish Kabbalah's magic and mystery stem from the Logos' sequestered Pattern. We also know this pattern is the source of the mysticism that's entrenched in the Masonic Order, with its square mortarboard and weird initiations. It's also likely to be the secret the Knights Templar unearthed in Jerusalem, which made them fabulously wealthy, before they were wiped out in the fourteenth century by envious rivals.

It is interesting to note that the Templars were known as the Order of Solomon's Temple; the temple that was specifically built to the Pattern revealed to Moses.

---

**Box 5. Knights Templar**

The Knights Templar managed a large economic infrastructure throughout Christendom, developing innovative financial techniques that were an early form of banking, building a network of nearly 1000 commanderies and fortifications across Europe and the Holy Land, and arguably forming the world's first multinational corporation.[32]

---

We're told the 'commotion' we can expect from the revelation of the Logos or Arcanum (physics ToE) – at the end of this age – becomes Mankind's rite of passage into the following Millennium of Peace. We're also told that Chronos[33] will be imprisoned when the mystery of YHWH is revealed. This breaking-out commotion can also be

---

32  'Knights Templar', *Wikipedia*, https://en.wikipedia.org/wiki/Knights_Templar
33  Chronos the primordial deity, and Cronos, Cronus, Kronus the Titan all relate to the ruling energy of time's passing

compared to birth pains that precede a child's delivery; maybe, in this case, the birthing of the promised Child of Salvation that's normally referred to as The Second Coming.

> And [the angel] sware [present tense] by him that liveth for ever and ever, who created heaven, and the things that therein are, and the earth, and the things that therein are, and the sea, and the things which are therein, that there should be time [Chronos] no longer: But in the days of the voice of the seventh angel, when he shall begin to sound, the mystery of God should be finished. – *Revelation 10:6,7*

Modern translations alter this idea about time dying and its connection to the mystery of God being revealed. They replace it with such things as … 'God can wait no longer'. Which is an entirely different concept altogether. They couldn't comprehend how time (Chronos) could die yet life go on regardless. But apparently the author of *Revelation* did. He would have been well versed in Greek Mythology and known who the god of Time and Karma was (although various Mesopotamian nations had now given this Time Lord – the leader of the fallen Titans – different names).

Various Mesopotamian accounts and scriptures reveal that Cronos, Saturn, Satan, the Grim Reaper of the Harvest (complete with his curved scythe given to him by his mum), and the Anunnaki Serpent of the Good Tree – the gatekeeper of Hell – are the same entity that's destined to be thrown into *Revelation's* proverbial 'pit' at the end of this age for a thousand years, allowing Mankind to become clear-headed for a while. (More on Satan, the Titan god of linear chronological time, and how he is put to sleep, later.[34])

## Islam, Judaism, Christianity, Combined

While we normally associate Moses with the Jewish and Christian faiths, the Qur'an also places him on a pedestal. This is because Moses knew how to talk to God directly; as a result, he became revered by all three Abrahamic faiths. A scientifically validated Logos would therefore give each of these religions credence (substance), which could work out all right for everyone.

In the Qur'an, Allah says to Moses, 'Fear not, you are transcendent.' If knowing the Logos' language made Moses transcendent, and physics shows that this same Pattern underscores Lisi's E8 mandala or ToE, then it would offer everyone a way to become transcendent.

An authenticated ToE, which embraced and validated Moses' Pattern, would offer the three monotheist religions a chance to unite under one umbrella or protective ark, as brothers and sisters of the same God. Should that marriage transpire, global sanity could fall into place. Maybe in time to save what's left.

When I first learned how to read Moses' Pattern or ToE, I started using aspects of its wisdom to treat my patients' ill health issues. I also used it to assist in my own recovery from the trauma I'd suffered

---

34   I found the following short video helpful when it comes to the deeper meaning behind aspects of Greek Mythology. Its perspective will help you understand the general role of the Titans and the role Cronos plays in the Big Picture. 'The Titans – Greek Mythology Explained', *YouTube* video, https://youtu.be/x7u5-o0QoQ0

through its downloading. During this time, some of my patients thought I'd become clairvoyant because of the things I was now able to discern about their lives and illnesses. The information I unearthed couldn't be ascertained by normal differential diagnostic means, but greatly exceeded it. (See Rita's story, which follows.) The disclosed Pattern's geometry enabled me to link the symptoms of a person's disease directly to its original cause – in a timely fashion. This then allowed meaningful treatments to be employed. (Three recoveries involved different forms of cancer, while Rita's instant recovery was from the horrors hidden in dark places.)

## Rita's Story

Rita[35] phoned from Tasmania to tell me she'd just had a severe panic attack, asking what herbs she could take to stop them from reoccurring. The doctors were wanting to put her on medications for life. I knew Rita well enough to know she was the last person I'd associate with a panic attack, or the need to take sedatives. So I asked her for details of *what* had happened and especially *where* it had happened.

After thinking for a few moments she recounted how she had collapsed in a paddock, convulsing, unable to get up. Some friends found her there and carried her home, putting her to bed. There she continued to convulse for some time until a young girl visited and took her hand. Only then did the shaking stop.

---

35   Not her real name.

## Patterned Family Relationships

Here was how I was able to use my new knowledge of Moses' Universal Pattern to help Rita:

> I asked Rita where she had come from directly before she entered the paddock where the attack had occurred. She remembered talking to a friend about two brothers who owned the house her friend lived in, and how one brother had murdered the other. Rita and her friend were in the house in question at that time.
>
> After I had this piece of the puzzle, I asked what had happened at the place the people had taken her after the attack. At this point, the penny dropped for Rita as she assembled the pieces in her own mind: One, Two, Three.
>
> 'Oh, Kahl,' came down the line from Tassie. 'The girl who took my hand was the daughter of the man who'd been killed in that house.'
>
> 'There you go,' I replied. 'You didn't have a panic attack at all, Rita. You had a demonic visitation that knocked you for six. You must be doing some great work down there to attract that kind of attention. Keep up the good work.'

Several years later, Rita hasn't suffered another attack. She continues her healing work as a recognised Aboriginal artist. I had been able to unearth this understanding by triangulating the event and naming the resident energies, placing the so-called panic attack in the middle of the trigram of events. This 'middle' should (and did) contain the energies of the two outer events, or cardinal points, in that time sequence. I used Moses' Pattern to understand what had actually happened to Rita, because – as I'd come to know by that time – everything is connected in geometrical energy patterns that can be read. This 'revealed' or 'calculated' understanding saved Rita from having to take medication for the rest of her life for a panic condition she never had.

\* \* \*

I came to understand that traumatic illness is often the mirrored, physiological dishevelment of a person's prior stress patterns – manifestations of what had been previously going on in their minds. And that these disruptive perturbations can span several generations, similar to how we attribute certain diseases to inherited ancestral genes. Or how the Bible asserts that sins pass from one generation to the next. I observed that emotionally entangled people who maintained deep relationships, could (and often did) share their ill-health symptoms between them, with some seeming to pass the disruption along to their children if they hadn't resolved the issue themselves. I now believe that people inherit both genetic and spiritual disease predispositions from their parents. In quantum terms: they inherit both particle and wave aberrations (knots and tangles) through the mathematical, three-dimensional complexity of the Matrix.

The consistency of the patterns I encountered, and the vastness of the terrain in which I found them hiding, led me to acquire a new mindset that eventually over-wrote my existing model and significantly improved it. Simple patterns of energy sequences became far more important than individual facts or feelings had ever been. And these patterns now determined the nature of my responses to life's numerous ups and downs – offered solutions – that were very effective. But before this metamorphosis could take place, lower rungs of understanding had to be accommodated – new perspectives had to outmuscle the old ones – and this took an appropriate length of time.

I came to see a set of relationship laws exist which control all semblances of Reality. And because they operate in a fractal manner, a comprehensive examination of a person's individual and family patterns was the best way for a 'seeker' to discover the Big Picture, religiously. In this regard, 'know thyself' took on an extended meaning. I wondered if Moses and other prophets had become enlightened in this patterned way – an idea I'll expand on later.

## Inherited Family Temperaments and Patterned Predispositions

Along this exciting road of rediscovery, I observed:

- Women who 'wear the pants' in their marriage and assume the leading Agenda 1 role, consistently birth more sons than daughters. The sons, I noticed, demonstrated their mother's dominant personality effortlessly, whereas any daughters conceived within the marriage (and often there were none) did not. The daughters' temperaments were more demure than those of their mothers, and this lack of 'flow-on' of disposition from mother to daughter was not what I expected.

I also observed:

- Dominant men sire more daughters than sons and, while their daughters display their father's dominant nature, their sons do not. I discovered that these sons could acquire a modicum of their father's qualities later in life, but didn't appear to have these macho traits from infancy – as their bossier sisters did. As young boys, they were often 'sooky', while their sisters behaved more like tomboys.

If these observations about temperaments criss-crossing from parents to children are correct – being an application of the to-and-fro nature of the inner workings of the Fractal, swinging backwards and forwards through the centre of the circle that's encasing it – then this would explain a lot of issues to many parents. But if you didn't know this crossing-over had taken place in your children, it could promote chaotic family relationships that bordered on a hellish nightmare. (Does any of that sound familiar?)

My observations led me to believe that the Matrix's criss-cross, figure-8 pattern passes on dominant personality traits **diagonally** – from parents to their offspring – emerging on the other side of birth in the parent's opposite-sex child(ren). This was the first outworking of the Fractal which made sense out of the otherwise chaotic relationships I had often found ensconced within family dynamics – the feuds and bickering that made people sick.

This changeover in energies from parents to children also seemed to parallel quantum physics' similarly patterned paradox of altering states. Here a wave-field mysteriously turns into the semblance of a particle (or vice versa) when certain birth-like conditions are met. (For a broader understanding of this chameleon-like process, watch the double-slit experiment that changed reality.[36] Knowledge of its phase transition is central to several issues about the nature of choosing between one [slit] or two [slits], which we'll touch on throughout these books.)

In a quantum sense I believe 'maleness' can be considered particle-like, while 'femaleness' is wave-like. So, with this application of the inner workings of each fractal unit, the maleness converts to femaleness and femaleness to maleness, in successive generations, having undergone an appropriate and transforming switch-gate (heaven and hell birth) at the figure-8's centre point, where the criss-cross transition from parent to child takes place. (The quantum slit in physics now-famous experiment becomes the fractal equivalent of the birth-canal transition through which the particle's energy has to pass to achieve its final character on the far side. When the single-particle [male] is forced to go through two slits [female] in the experiment, the particle changes its characteristics to its wave side.)

In this paradoxical and potentially topsy-turvy fashion, I believe mum's essence becomes the son's character expressed in male format, while dad's essence becomes the daughter's where-with-all masquerading in a dress.

I also noticed how these inherited characteristics were predispositions only, not attributes the children were powerless to modify or exorcise. In a quantum sense, the criss-crossing of various traits through the central transition resembled emotional, etheric wave-forms, more than solid particle ones.

---

36   PBS Space Time, 'The quantum experiment that broke reality | Space Time | PBS Digital Studios', *YouTube* video, https://youtu.be/p-MNSLsjjdo?t=30

- The sons could look like their dads but acted like their mums.
- The daughters could look like their mums but acted like their dads.

I highlighted another cross-over point in *Adam's Daughter* where a parent will sacrifice their life for their child. A cross-over, or transition point, is where the yin energy becomes yang energy, metamorphosing through the eerie, interstitial twilight haze of the Program's nefarious heaven and hell, figure-8 centre point.

This idea about character transferring across the sex barrier is radical and remains unproven at this time, yet my observations convinced me it was so.[37] When I became aware of the immensity of Moses' Pattern, these dynamics – and many more that I'll share as we go along – became a lot easier for me to reconcile coherently.

I now believe that a parent's personality characteristics – alcoholism, for instance – transcribe to their appropriate form in the opposite-sex child. However, an alcoholic father doesn't necessarily produce alcoholic daughters; instead, the daughters will often exhibit the same faux courage as their alcoholic father did/does, but now in more female forms – such as being promiscuous, bossy, or even highly competitive – yet his energy will be quite evident in her behaviour. (While the energy remains the same, the trait's form alters in the crossing.) The daughter doesn't need alcohol to enact her father's energy.

---

37   Individual differences between same-sex siblings are influenced by birth order and astrological variations in celestial cycles. Each sibling expresses the dominant vibrations inherited from their opposite-sex parent, which are then fine-tuned by other cyclic interactives into a new unique form.

In a medical sense, this transverse connection would be similar to a father's prostate condition being statistically relevant to his daughter's likelihood of developing ovarian problems (now recognised).[38] We can also see character transference happening in animals, such as dogs.

- Is there a general rule for personality inheritance?
- Could the biblical concept of sins passing from one generation to the next have credence? If so, what form would they take?

> **Box 6. Dog Breeds**
>
> The transfer of character from parents to offspring is being investigated in dog breeds. Geneticists are looking at how each dog breed inherits a distinct temperament.[39]

If a universal, criss-cross, fractal pattern lies at the heart of all Reality, and an application of this peculiarity applies to parents and their progeny, then a dominant woman will birth dominant sons who'll have the opportunity of learning how to be 'gentler' men from their otherwise submissive father.

If the mother is dominant, then her husband will be submissive, ipso facto, because of the Attraction of Opposites that ruled the

---

38  In 2008, this was proven the case for this particular genome.

39  Bob Homes, 'How dogs are helping decode the genetic roots of personality', *New Scientist*, March 2017, https://www.newscientist.com/article/mg23331170-500-how-dogs-are-helping-decode-the-genetic-roots-of-personality/

heterosexual partnership initially. The father's softer qualities can be taken on board by the son if he so chooses. His choice hinges on how he sees his mother responding to these foreign male qualities he's witnessing in his dad, which he wouldn't have naturally thought to do by himself:

- Will they be useful to him personally?
- Will they empower him if he takes them on board?

I observed that sons can (and often do) adopt some of their father's foreign characteristics if their mother shows them sufficient respect in the family's power plays. In this fashion, a son will choose to emulate these differences. He'll take notice of any effective strategy his dad employs that 'trumps' his mother's usual dominance. In this criss-cross, patterned way, the child acquires the best from both worlds or agendas, in an up-and-down, funky sort of fashion that makes sense. (This same essential dynamic applies equally to daughters.) In this convoluted way – the old 'natural way' – a child had the chance to become more effectively balanced than either parent ever was, hence fulfilling Evolution's primary objective to advance and go forward from the top (while entropy nibbles away from the bottom, similar to the hand game Stacks on the Mill we played as children).

## Familiar Chaos

If this idea about bilateral character transference is correct, then it's easy to see how family relationships would extract a heavy toll on exasperated mums and dads. Fathers keen on having sons 'made in their image' would become frustrated beyond belief trying to teach boys that were nothing like them. Likewise, mums would find it difficult to love and care for daughters who displayed far too many of their father's annoying behaviour patterns.

Wives have to contend with husbands being their complete opposites, from the original Attraction of Opposites, which drew the loving couple together. And now, to top things off, they discover their daughters are nearly as bad, maybe even worse.

Only a parent's love is capable of seeing them through this formidable turmoil while remaining sane. I think it's the wonder-of-wonders that parents don't strangle their kids while they still have a fighting chance. If it wasn't for love, maybe they would.

As parents move into adjoining cycles of the Great Fractal, I observed that grandmother and granddaughter were more alike than mother and daughter ever were. Although their genes have double-crossed, their respective pattern-energies, or temperaments, have returned closer to where they started in the spiral. (The same applies to grandfathers and grandsons.) These interplays shine an interesting light on the saying:

> If I knew how good the grandchildren would turn out,
> 
> I'd have had them first.

With these switch-over dynamics in place, raising and nurturing same-sex children would be as much as a parent could bear, paralleled by a similar difficulty trying to communicate with their same-sex parent; it would be just too hard to connect with either effectively and be understood. Therefore (in pattern terms) if a woman can maintain a respectful and working relationship with both her mother and her blood-daughter, then I believe she has good reason to be proud of her balanced nature. The same would apply to a man who can maintain a harmonious relationship with both his biological father and his blood-son. (Sadly to say, this rarely happens nowadays.)

Because a person's heterosexual marriage partner is often close to being their complete opposite, when the connecting middle ground (the children) grow up and move on, and the earlier attraction of the flesh has passed by, their marriage must revert to a state of dichotomous, binary hell. All they can then do is fight and argue and wait for grandchildren, or another spiritual centre energy to reawaken the magic they had previously shared. This might include adherence to a common religion or set of beliefs.

It's easy to see why so many people have given up on conventional partnerships. Yet it seems we have to go through these torturous, lustful, pattern-controlled configurations – complete with same-sex children, et cetera – before we even get a chance to qualify for sustainable, soul-deep love; something a bit better than a flash (or flesh) in the pan.

## Learning by Proxy

> The crux of the mystery for both scientists and philosophers is that our everyday world doesn't appear to be the 'real' one. Rather, we're living what's described as an illusion – what the ancients called shadow reality – that is the reflection of something even more real than our everyday universe. – *Braden*

Physics is revealing 'life' to be architecturally designed and maintained by the Matrix's quantum operating system. This includes 'correcting codes' for things that run off the rails or go astray. It's showing us that our solid shadow-life reality is being orchestrated or flung off by a higher force, or forces, which mesh with the vibrations emanating from our emotional states of consciousness.[40]

Therefore, the emotions we release appear to be furbishing lessons in one dimension while we're experiencing them in another. This is similar to how films can leave us affected by what we've witnessed on the big screen. They attempt to reflect life-matters on our behalf so we don't have to go to the coalface and experience them personally. In this entertaining, mirrored fashion of stage and screen, we're lulled into believing we can buy soft wisdom. And maybe we can if the actors excel; if they draw us in and make us laugh and cry. In this sense, it appears we're doing a similar thing at a higher level in the Fractal, where we also laugh and cry, having certainly been drawn in.

> [T]he story of our origins is recounted with remarkable consistency across different worldviews. The bottom line that weaves such narratives together is the description of our world as a dream/illusion/projection of things happening in another realm. And now we must consider the new evidence of Earth as a simulation among those views. – *Braden*

Acquiring knowledge through a proxy – like a child learning from their parents' mistakes and instructions – is another example of

---

40   Dr Candace Pert, *Molecules of Emotion: The Science behind Mind–Body Medicine*, Touchstone, 1997.

this same multidimensional process, as are parables, metaphors, corollaries, and analogies. All are great ways to learn new information from parallel accounts. And ancient wisdom reveals the best place to understand everything is within the depths of our subjective mental worlds and relationships. But are we really brave enough to look closely at these potentially painful domains? If so, the early Greeks would call us physicians: 'Those who look closely'.

In physics, the new perspective of multiple universes, along with the enigmas of quantum mechanics, both suggest that the materialistic manifestations we're experiencing as time-and-matter masquerading in space (Einstein's space-time continuum) are not the ultimate reality, but more like a staged projection (shadow) that's emanating from a higher source of patterned intelligence, that's still unidentified but sometimes referred to as the Matrix (traditionally known as God or the gods.)

In this regard, the so-called solid, material phantoms that give form to our life would best be described as a theatre's backdrop, scene, and curtain for the real story to unfold. (At least, that's how Shakespeare described them.) Some believe – as did Dr Pert, the discoverer of the brain's opiate receptor – that each emotional moral decision we activate resonates in this higher plane as no matter can. While we remain blind to this reality, we lackadaisically go our own merry way, rowing our boat (often not so merrily) up and down the proverbial life-stream.

But do we have to stay 'sleeping like a log' forever? Surely not! There must be a way to break this process and control our emotions and thoughts. There must be a way to stop us from being our own worst enemy, because that scenario doesn't make sense, nor does it reflect love on anyone's part.

> as scientists solve the mysteries of nature, they're also showing us the spiritual keys to our own empowerment. ... [The] scientific discoveries of the last 100 years show us why our beliefs affect the world. Belief's effects are based on patterns of energy – the same energy that everything is made of.[41]

Science's new script is steadily overwriting our old Shakespearian tragedy. As Braden says:

> As creators and experiencers, the question that begs to be asked is this: If our interaction with the universe is constantly creating and modifying our world, then how do we know which interactions have which kind of effects? In other words, what are the rules that describe how our reality works? Do we have the wisdom to recognise them when we see them?

If we're going to make meaningful inroads into the world's megalithic problems, then we need to understand the deeper reality going on in the background of our minds. If we're to reinterpret our world, ourselves, and our extended families, in a broader and more sustainable quantum sense, then we need to master these newly disclosed laws and patterned ways of the Matrix's operating system. Nothing else has ever worked, so I assume nothing else ever will. We need to identify these patterns consciously if we're going to break free of life's tediousness. Maybe this is what all religious

---

41 Gregg Braden, *The Spontaneous Healing of Belief: Shattering the Paradigm of False Limits*, Hay House Inc., 2009.

instructions have been about. If so, then maybe we should start thinking of …

> Men as being representatives of solid-like particles, and women as being the essence of curvaceous and flexuous waves going to-and-fro.

Both male and female genders contain emotional sensory perceptions, along with rational logical minds. When viewed from a quantum perspective, however, males predominantly behave like quantum particles: providers/protectors dressed in suits or coveralls, whereas most women exhibit numerous wave-like qualities in various fashions and foibles. The female fashion industry is all about recalcitrant curves. There wouldn't be a female fashion industry without them.

As a mother, the 'essential wave' uses her natural skills to care for her children's and partner's emotional wellbeing – as well as her own. At times this endeavour can evoke a profound state of anxiety, requiring reassurance that her children are safe, secure, and growing unhindered. (Quick … count my baby's fingers and toes!) As a consequence, a woman's pivotal need becomes … Finding a safe place to put her feet up.

This is the basis of her (initial) attraction to men; she is taken in by his apparent bravado and ersatz, cocksure solidness; it feels secure and comforting. (Her waviness is apt to leave her short on solidness.)

The protection her man's substance offers is attractive in a woman's search for security – albeit his money, brawn, brains, power, social standing, or what an Aussie would call 'being a decent bloke'. Each of these attributes is a semblance of particle solidness.

In this regard, the San people of the Kalahari have an interesting 'take' on the essence of a woman's wave-like energy and its connection to her more solid mate. Their stories personify her as Daisy the rock rabbit. (The male energy is identified as the green, swivel-necked Mantis.) But Daisy is no ordinary rabbit. She's exceptional. Her closest relatives are elephants and dugongs, which – interestingly – don't have a pineal gland but get along nicely without one.[42] What fascinates me most from the Fractal's perspective is that rock rabbits like to live inside of mountains and are very particular about their home environment, which they keep meticulously clean.

This anthropomorphism of the San people fits snugly into the larger quantum picture as I've come to know it. The fractal 'wave' seeks out a suitable particle's protection, enters his safehouse (mountain), and keeps the environment naturally cleaner than it was before she arrived. (This constitutes an effective endosymbiotic relationship, whose pattern repeats all the way down to the cellular level and beyond.) This compartmentalised relationship benefits both parties equally and provides a healthy haven for children to grow up in.

Snow White agreed to cook and clean for the Seven Dwarfs (kundalini – purification) so they would let her stay in their home. *Snow White* is considered to be an alchemic text.[43]

---

42  Bill Bryson, *The Body: A Guide for Occupants*, Doubleday, 2019.
43  Anne-Marie Wegh, 'Snow White and the seven chakras', *anne-marie.eu*, https://www.anne-marie.eu/en/snow-white-and-the-seven-chakras/

It finishes with:

> 'I [the prince] love you more than anything else in the world. Come with me to my father's castle. You shall become my wife.'

Anne-Marie Wegh says about this verse:

> The castle of the father [the Father] of the prince symbolizes the Kingdom of God: the abode of the person who loves the divine more than 'anything else in the world.'[44]

As particles, men need to feel significant. They have to feel substantial. Given the chance, they'll make mountains out of mole-hills, strutting their stuff before the chickabiddies on any occasion that presents itself. In quantum code, they proclaim:

> Admire my particle – darling. Come and place your wavy tail next to my solid head and we'll go places. My mountain is a place you'll feel warm and safe inside. I'm really big. Hug me. Feel my muscles.

Men like to exaggerate the amount of substance they've glimmered from their life's journey. They loathe being wrong about anything because every admission of error reduces their sense of feeling substantial; it reduces the size of their mountain. And, as you might expect … Size really counts in a particle's world – big time. Men need to be 'right' to feel big. Each fact they retain acts like a stone in their pyramid.

---

44    Ibid.

His euphoria reaches its zenith whenever a desirable, wavy female admires the size of his solidness. After showing her his muscles (if he gets his way), she'll become his pyramid's capstone, or his attractive flag he'll set to adorn his castle, fluttering in the breeze as a good wave should – according to his perspective. (Similarly, algae grace the bony and colourless coral stem, lighting it up with a panoply of living rainbow colour.) That's how the quantum game of heads-and-tails likes to work: yin inside yang, colour inside structure, rock rabbit inside mountain, energy inside machine, charge inside battery, the dual-seed inside its outer singular covering (that is, unless it's time to move on and grow, then the seed is released to take off under its own steam and breakthrough its shell). Lastly, this coupling can be compared with a precious opal that has formed in the centre of spherical layers of ironstone. This mineral/gem arrangement is called a Yowah Nut. (The importance of this particular opal will become clearer in later books when I examine how patterns metamorphosed from inorganic minerals and gems into similar [patterned] components in organic plants and animals.)

Both men and women enter the quantum game of Noughts and Crosses when they intuit that they'll only find fulfilment in the 'other's' resident, exterior quality. When they realise the price to extract these qualities is exuberant, and that the solidness or waviness they'd set their sights on is only skin deep – disaster and disillusionment set in. Given time, some couples do survive the ravages of unfulfilled marriage to live another day, but most, unfortunately, fall by the wayside. (The way is wide but the gate is narrow. That sort of thing.)

I've observed that a loving and admiring woman will provide all the motivation a man requires to work hard. Her love – and how good it makes him feel – encourages him to create the central home-zone she and their offspring require to thrive and be happy. Unfortunately, men come to believe that their accumulation of wealth is solely due to their hard work. They don't stop to consider why they have sacrificed the comfort of their now-moments to amass surplus in the first place. (Where did that motivation come from?) They could've been home watching their sporting heroes play-act their roles for them on TV – as many men do. As a rule, men can't, and don't, recognise the role the supportive wave plays in the accumulation of their wealth. At least, not until she leaves home and he feels the sting of abandonment, discovering all too late just how painful it is when:

Someone lets the cat out of the bag.


TODAY, MORE AND MORE WOMEN are opting for self-reliance. The divorce rate is soaring for women in their forties and fifties. They're acquiring their own substance and no longer require a man to do so. In the modern world, men are becoming obsolete. Maleness is diminishing, fading to a mere shadow of its former self. Cosmologists are telling us that a similar fractal occurrence is happening on a much larger scale in the Universe; that matter is diminishing everywhere, as dark energy prevails in its quest to consume and stretch all of space apart.

In a parallel, micro-fractal way, when an atom's nucleus becomes overcrowded – when its centre becomes heavily contaminated with nuclear particles – the equivalent of the atom's central 'wives' break free from the confines of the nucleus' strong force to become (women's) liberated waves of gamma radiation. (The rock rabbit leaves the mountain. The seed sprouts.) This departure is overseen and instigated, not by dark energy, but by the atom's nuclear weak force, which only operates on left-handed matter,[45] to become the *click, click, click* of a Geiger Counter.

Atomic nuclei can only grow so large for this reason; any larger and the nucleus becomes prone to breaking when bumped. Also similar is how the colourful algae will leave the confines of the bony, white coral stem, whenever the surrounding water's environment becomes too polluted or overheated for her liking. When the time is right, she leaves Adam and moves on. As do queen bees when the hive exceeds a comfortable size. (Only the queen bee has two stingers.)

From the Fractal's perspective, the mass departure of women from humanity's marriage program is a sure sign we've reached the end of the age. Mankind's centralised civilisation has become too cluttered for her liking and she's leaving now with the kids in tow. The traditional family unit has become a thing of the past.

## Shedding Some Light

I maintain that the key to clear-sightedness, and the end of deception's tyranny, begins with understanding 'time' differently from how we've traditionally known it. When we accept that 'time' maintains a cyclical framework, and develop accurate time maps, it will allow us to instigate appropriate mindsets at the key cardinal points in our cycles that affect and steer our destiny. It would be like knowing that all you need do is put on a happy face and smile sincerely – light up for a mere moment –

---

45   TED, 'A theory of everything | Garrett Lisi', *YouTube* video, https://youtu.be/y-Gk_Ddhr0M?t=56

when you first met your boss at work each morning to assure he won't be grumpy with you at the day's end. You would understand that your day's beginning and end are linked (entangled) cardinal points in the same cycle in the Simulation. You would realise … Investing a single, momentary smile at an appropriate moment will pay a big dividend for your tiny effort. So you smile. Then you relax.

If Reality is the outworking of a fractal simulation, then everything must reflect changes or developments at all levels. Yahshua alluded to this unusual 'take' on Reality when He told His disciples … I'll give you the keys to Heaven. But be warned:

> what you release on Earth will be released in Heaven.[46]

How bizarre is that? Why would Yahshua say such a strange thing? By His understanding, Heaven and Earth are intimately connected in some fashion. In quantum terms it seems they are entangled with each other.

In his way, Braden agreed:

> because everything exists within the Divine Matrix, everything is connected. If things are connected, then, what we do in one place must influence what is happening in other places. It also suggests the Divine Matrix is holographic, meaning any portion of the field contains everything in the field.

I found the Matrix's black-and-white issues were comparatively easy to understand. It was the messy grey areas in between that were

---

46   *Matthew* 16:19

capable of activating my mind's paradox and despair. For example, Taoism designates the colour white as being yang (Agenda 1), black as being yin (Agenda 2); dogs as being predominantly yang (Agenda 1), and cats as being yin (Agenda 2). (I think most readers would agree that cats are very wavy feline animals, gracefully parading their sleek, curvaceous tails. While dogs are more male-like canine animals, which often run around in circles trying to bite their tails off.) So how then would you classify a white, male cat, in a yin/yang, particle or wave sense? Would it be fair to call him a yang/yang/yin (1,1,2) animal, because of his three distinct qualities? And what about a black, female dog? Would she be a wave/wave/particle (2,2,1) animal?

As I traversed multiple levels of Reality's Fractal, it became increasingly difficult to identify something simply as yin (2) or yang (1), wave or particle, female or male. Gender issues became difficult, people being a mixture of both Agenda's to one degree or another. This multiple-layer complexity is why the Logos' Pattern has remained elusive for so long, and why Moses' words have been so difficult to translate in the quantum sense I believe they were intended. Even the very first word that Moses wrote – *bereshit*, translated into English as 'in beginning' – holds enormous wisdom when viewed in the right light, having a pattern within a pattern.[47]

Speaking of the Logos' pattern: When you consider the opening lines of John's Gospel and add in the idea that Creation is the output of a simulation that's made to, and runs on, an all-encompassing fractal pattern (Logos), an interesting and insightful door opens that, by

---

47   RockIslandBooks, 'Is the end of days prophesied in the first word of the Bible?', *YouTube* video, 22 November 2018, https://youtu.be/PtATSQx3cjI

many accounts, makes a lot of sense. Read it below and see what you think John was referring to here in his gospel when he wrote:

> In the beginning was the Logos, and the Logos was with Yahweh, and the Logos was Yahweh. The same was in the beginning with Yahweh. And all things were made by Him, and without Him was not anything made that was made.[48]

Wow! If I'm not mistaken, I believe John is saying … The Logos was pre-existent as Yahweh the Creator, and everything was created to its specified pattern. *Everything*. In other words, Yahweh's nature embraces a logical pattern or algorithm, and the Universe is made to His very own 'likeness', to His Name's Pattern. According to John, the Logos – the Pattern of God – and physics' Theory of Everything (ToE) are one and the same thing. Could science be on the brink of discovering the Mystery of God as outlined in *Revelation* 10:7? I think it is.

Some theologians believe that Yahshua (Jesus) is the Logos, but I think you'll find this idea lacks substance. It was the best understanding they could come up with to make sense out of what John was trying to convey. The Bible states that Yahshua was the Logos made flesh; that He was made to its exact pattern. It doesn't say He was the Logos its self. At least, nowhere I could find. Understandably, theologians debate this controversial issue. According to the Bible, Yahshua didn't create the Universe, but His Pattern (His Father) just might have. Yahshua was the impress of this pattern – hence the description: Son

---

48   *John* 1:1–3

of God. I guess you could think of that as being the same sort of thing – hence the confusion. Yahshua did say, 'Whoever has seen me has seen the Father.'[49]

That would make Him the precise patterned impression of the Logos as an individual, in contrast to all of Mankind being made in God's image as a higher, collective, fractal image.[50]

## Man Know Thyself

Is it possible to really 'know' a person in this crazy way? Can we achieve our unity by utilising quantum epistemology? Should we think of a woman resembling a sea of waves and a man as the kernel of a mountain she can moor to? to avoid the rigours of large and dangerous swells that at times threaten to overturn and capsize her? Are his facts and possessions particle-like components, entrenched within a mountain that behoves a safe place for her to thrive? ('She loves me like a rock', sang Paul Simons.) Can physics' new insights make it easier to understand ourselves and each other? Explaining such things as why a man gives a diamond ring to his fiancé when they intend to get married? I believe they can! So let's take a look now at how these nuances might apply to the man and woman on the street and see where it leads us.

In a trinary, fractal simulation based on Moses' Pattern, the average man would act and behave something like this:

---

49   *John* 14:9
50   *11 Corinthians* 4:4

- He treats his knowledge – what he thinks he knows – as a sacred possession. The Agenda 1 male likes to correct people who are, in his opinion, 'wrong' (especially those he loves). He corrects them because he loves them. While this makes him feel useful, if not positively significant, it gives others a pain in the neck. To him, being 'right' is all-important.

- Rationality is his highest ideal. He maintains he's always logical (except when he loses it). He uses his didactic mind pedagogically to solve all the world's problems. This includes sensitive matters of the heart: *'I'll drown the kittens. We can't afford to feed them.'*

- He needs to feel significant and likes to procreate with any and every female who's silly enough to put her feet up and rest awhile in the shadow of his mountain. (That is, women who haven't [as yet] seen through his flimsy exterior coating.)

- He likes to boast and exaggerate his performance in work and play. As a particle lookalike, he loves to increase his content (how substantial he feels) by any means he can – the easier the better. In his world, how big he is – as well as being 'right' – are all important.

- When his substance is reduced, he loses face. His world crumbles around him, having experienced an earthquake. Any diminishment of his substance leads him into depressive bouts where he can act like a sulky child. (His essence was eroded. Look out. Ouch! You'll pay for that.)

- An Agenda 1 male's greatest concern is the sense of responsibility he feels for those he loves – which normally isn't many. When escalated, this heartfelt concern can literally drive a conscientious man insane. So he tries to avoid this conundrum wherever and whenever possible. That's why he doles out his love so sparingly.

- To keep his loved ones safe, he believes he needs to control them, often ruthlessly (for their 'own sakes', that is).

- He doesn't feel comfortable showing his emotion; they're like rainwater wearing away at his mountain's face.

- The Agenda 1 male reveres past precedents, hoarding objects, and memories. He frequently refers to memory in his problem-solving capacity. He likes to say, *Just forget about it and get on with it*. Yet he'll quote the past to you on every occasion you slip up. In his world, the past remains substantial, whereas the future is anyone's guess.

- When confronted with love, the Agenda 1 male experiences frightful emotions that threaten to dismantle his mountain. He's aware … *There is no logic where love abounds.*

- His greatest failing is his lack of sensitivity. The women and children in his life feel this lacking as emotional cruelty. Of course, he doesn't see it this way. Good luck if you try to convince him otherwise.

- The Agenda 1 man expresses his love by providing for and protecting his clan, taking responsibility for their wellbeing. Don't look for his love in his words. If it is there, you will find it in his actions.

- It warms his heart when he comes up with answers to the problems that threaten his loved ones' safety or happiness. He'll do your homework if you give him a chance. He'll build you a home if you can live with his heartlessness. Invoking this loving care normally involves maintaining sufficient curves to keep him suitably flummoxed: The bull needs to see the flag waving in the wind to be lured by the siren's call.

- He likes people to get to their point quickly.

- Essentially, he's a provider/protector. He believes that when she withholds her truth, she inadvertently sabotages his ability to keep her safe within the confines of his 'shaky' mountain.

- The more 'male' a man is, the more attracted he'll be to a wavy, sensuous Agenda 2 woman – what some might call an airhead – yet he's apt to call his chosen one Baby Doll.

- When a family member upsets an Agenda 1 male, he's likely to withhold his love and employ emotional blackmail (sulk) until he gets his way. He's also likely to get stingy with his money and possessions. (He will make you pay for upsetting him if he can.) He does these things to reinforce his point. And that point is … His perspective on life is always right, because it is the most solid (normally).

- A particle man feels comfortable starting a conversation with a fact: Greetings such as, '*You've had your hair cut.*'

These frivolous observations and put-downs about 'maleness' revolve around the idea that, in a quantum fractal simulation, 'maleness' is representative of the solid-looking particle state, while 'femaleness' gets the curvaceous 'waves'.

HISTORICALLY, MEN HAVE ASSERTED it's impossible to understand a woman. They've traditionally maintained that women don't think logically as men do. This challenge to female logic, or its diminution, can be taken on board several ways, but rarely does it raise a serious eyebrow. 'It's all a part of their charm,' dismisses the assertion elegantly.

So let's take a look now at Eve in the same fashion we disrobed Adam and see how this conundrum about logic may have come about. If we're living in a simulation that maintains the characteristics of dots and wiggles dancing to the three-fold steps of a great waltz, then Eve's attributes should shine out on the ballroom floor.

- The naturally curvaceous Agenda 2 woman exhibits a strong connection to her personal appearance. Her XX mirror-patterning draws her to reflections where she can see herself more clearly. (These mirrors often include her friends, loved ones, and partners.) She believes that beauty is power; appearance rules over content. Rather than keep her feet on the ground, the Agenda 2 woman prefers to fly. She resonates with all things insubstantial; consequently, she can feel lacking

- in personal substance or inner solidness (at times feeling a little fragile around the edges).

- Because 'outward appearance' is everything to a wave-woman, the way something is presented is paramount.

- The female Agenda 2 energy can be found at a circle's circumference as the expanding vessel of life. Adam is more at home in the circle's centre point, while pi links the two together as a unified couple (see page 223).

- Her energy is represented in colourful wrapping and curvaceous multi-looped ribbons that adorn a precious gift. All valuable presents are meant to be surrounded by the essence of Agenda 2's outer presentation.

- A wave-woman's highest ideal is to bring and maintain happiness to herself and those she cares for; those she lets snuggle up close.

- A wave-woman develops appropriate emotional responses to every difficult situation she encounters. (*All the kittens are beautiful. Can't we keep them? They can eat mice.*)

- The essential Agenda 2 woman is a carer/nurturer. She likes to get her feet off the ground whenever she can – as birds tend to do. She loves her shoes and hates her feet. High-heels never go out of fashion. (All feline species sleep with their feet tucked beneath them.) Feet are yang: male. Hands are yin: female. We like to stand on our own two feet, but embrace and connect with our hands, showcasing our affection. (At least we did before COVID-19 came to town.) Hands like to wave hello and goodbye to express our state of connection with others.

- Eve's life-quest is to feel loved and admired, have fun, look great, be secure, and feel settled in. This elegance can frequently do an 'about-face' after she becomes a mother. At these times, her female essence is consumed with issues revolving around the safety and welfare of her children.

- As an Agenda 1 rock needs to maintain his image of being solid, an Agenda 2 wave needs to maintain her curvaceous appearance. At times she's prone to overemphasise her need to lose weight. Solidness is not her 'natural' thing (curvaceous waves are – the more harmonious, the better). She doesn't like going in circles, she prefers going to-and-fro, up and down, any day.

- The Agenda 2 wave's greatest vulnerability is her need for security. She lacks particle substance, shelter in a storm, a safe place to hang out when things get tough. When her material needs aren't met, she experiences anxiety and likes to take refuge in dream-like enchantments about the future. When necessary, she'll reinterpret past facts into more comfortable ways of thinking. To her, this is akin to changing the key signature on a piece of music to more suit her voice. At these times, facts become malleable. She doesn't recognise her new construction of facts as being lies. But Agenda 1 males can and will.

- Dreams and plans are very important to wave-energy. They are more important than the 'now-moment' or 'past' ever were. The wave embraces forward vision, whereas a particle reveres the past. While the 'now' … well, the 'now' just keeps on being the 'now', the 'isness' that simply 'is'.

- While an Agenda 1 male will avoid change whenever and wherever he can, an Agenda 2 woman will rearrange things and initiate change for its own sake. The saying … 'It's a woman's prerogative to change her mind' (wherever it originated) has been agreed upon for some well-recognised (universal?) reason.

- I liken males to fixated trees standing erect in the forest. I liken women to rapacious vines, which like to move around, hug and cling to a few trunks – if they feel like it – and see 'it all' before settling down, maybe to have babies. Eve's view of life is more cosmopolitan than Adam's ever will be. Socrates (a man of upstanding character) is said to have never travelled more than 30 kilometres from his birthplace in Alopece, Athens. He lived for approximately seventy-one years.

- The wave-woman returns to lost causes to be used up time and again. In this regard, she is often accused of having selective memory, forgetting the hard facts to her peril.

- Her greatest handicap is her unintentional disrespect or need to be honest (in a particle sense) with herself and those she loves. She's more likely to surround herself with beautiful lies.

- Eve's energy is like a transient verb, while Adam's energy resembles a standalone noun. This scenario equates to the interconnected herd standing in one paddock, while the bull occupies the other – alone. (The One and the Many. Unity and Infinity. Adam and Eve.)

- The finest expression of the wave's Agenda 2 essence is her willingness to sacrifice her needs for her family and friends. She asserts … Let him sacrifice his solitary 'facts' as she has to whenever the occasion demands to keep the essential peace – the wave harmony. She maintains that peace is far more important than cold hard facts ever were, or ever will be, even if the truce she manages to conceive in this way can be superficial at times.

- Wave-women seek financial independence. They infuse their Holy Centres with any available substance they find. Thanks to Einstein, we know that matter is equivalent to energy, and matter comes from the Latin word for mother: *mater*. Some cultures call this accretion process … art. Others call it wicker, weaving, witchcraft. Even Summer Wine.

- When a wave-woman is surprised, she screams. When a particle-male is surprised, he curses and comes out fighting.

Vedic wisdom suggests that all goddesses should be considered as different forms of power, or 'shakti' (pure energy). It proclaims that male gods are machine-like objects which can be turned on or off by an appropriate goddess energy. The mystical Kabbalah asserts:

> The man brings in the light and the woman switches it on.
> – *Noun and verb. Particle and wave.*

I've found a person's anatomical, Agenda 2 female-wave energy to be centred in their neck, with its resident thyroid and parathyroid glands that control – among other things – the body's essential wave rhythmicity, which includes intestinal peristalsis and the heart's steady beat. (Interestingly, the thyroid requires iodine from the sea to function normally, the only cells in the body to do so. Its primary hormone, thyroxine – triiodothyronine – is built around three iodine molecules.) You'll have also noticed how strong emotion will constrict your throat and voice box, often making it difficult to speak or swallow while talking about issues that deeply affect you. Your neck is a repository of highly emotional, family-issue vibrations. In this regard, Jewish people have been referred to as 'a stiff-necked people'. That is … a little on the overly logical, male side of balanced; lacking the necessary 'curve' in the neck's flexible centre.

Conversely, I've found the masculine Agenda 1 particle-centre to reside within each person's adrenal glands. They're our fight/flight responders, which through their resident hormones unlock the potentially violent energy that's stored within our body's muscles. When adrenal exhaustion sets in, it often leads to lower back pain and/or sciatica, leaving the legs weak and wobbly. The adrenals are above the kidneys in the upper-lower back, just above the belly-button line. This aching condition was once called *lumbago*.

# Enlightenment

Through modern eyes, men and women can be seen as fractal representatives of immortal quantum templates, exercising their differences as mini-me gods, caught up in an amazing multidimensional drama, all seemingly suffering from memory loss. Reality is thus the consequence, or output, of a trinary computer program – macro modelling micro – in an extended fractal sense of being.[51] Over time, the Program produces (evolves) trivalent units of Centrism. That is, intelligent family units of self-awareness that reflect the underlying trinary, fractal, pattern of the Program. Ken Wilbur calls these integrated units Holons. I think of them as Cells of God (COGs).

Awareness of this macro/micro quantum reality lets you see your programmed life for what it truly is. It then lets you protect yourself when traversing the negative side of the Matrix's cycles while simultaneously opening the doors to Heaven on Earth. This paradoxical journey has been called … The road (through madness) to enlightenment.

In a programmed, patterned sense, you don't need to comprehend all the recondite, weaving processes of the Matrix immediately to access this road to illumination. When seen in the right light, you'll find your personal experiences are more than enough to teach you all you

---

51   Gregg Braden Official, 'The creation of the Universe, the false reality, and the divine spark', *YouTube* video, 5 January 2021, https://youtu.be/QskgCfwYO0g

need know about the Big Picture. You simply have to learn how to see them from the right perspective, then all the myriad pieces can fall into place. That's when your life (finally) loses its fragmentation and you wake up to yourself.

In my experience, when a 'seeker of clear-sightedness' knows where and how to look at their life – in the same way I think Moses and other prophets might have done – they come to see all of the patterns within themselves magically fitting together; simple patterns that repeat in numerous and cosmopolitan ways. Having achieved this mantic clear-sightedness, the 'seeker' then becomes a 'reader' of quantum reality, no longer its sleeping puppet or toy-thing, but now its co-creator. Welcome to your new home.

Full understanding of the holo-fracto-simulation becomes a matter of time, following a few rules, and recognising the nature of the paradox that surrounds you. For now, being aware of the basic concept is enough to get you started. **Given time and practice, materialism's entrenched delusions will fade, leaving behind a magnificence you've only dreamed about in your most inspired moments. Your old home was never this good.**

Give your vanity and ego the time they deserve to accommodate the new information you're acquiring. You'll find they'll gladly join your soul's journey to three-dom, because they'll have come to understand that it's in their very best interest to do so. Therefore, the sooner you start walking the Budda's Middle Path, the sooner you can take up residence in Christ's Heaven on Earth. Then you'll need to deal with your past karmic episodes that are still resonating 'out there' in the Matrix. (That can be irksome.) But take heart, it seems there is a fairly painless way to get rid of them, an old tried-and-true way.

(More on this ancient 'cleansing mystery' – that has been locked away in a 'name' for thousands of years – later.)

I've been absorbing this new and exciting way of living for many years now and have found that enlightenment to All Else comes in bight-sized increments, little bursts of inspiration you experience at appropriate times, ensconced in discreet quantised packages. In a quantum sense, you could think of what is happening to you as a field of enlightenment, and an excitation in the field as being an inspiration that lights you up (as a photon is an excitation of the electromagnetic field). All mystery dissolves when you understand and incorporate this new, weird, quantum reality into your centre. You discover that the Buddha's Middle Path travels a road not nearly as bumpy as the one you've been travelling (to-and-fro) since leaving your childhood playground of seesaws, merry-go-rounds, slippery dips, and hurdy-gurdies (where we all learned our basic patterns).

Human idiosyncrasies are (finally) starting to make sense. (Thank God, we mightn't be so crazy after all.) Now, all we need do is hone the tools the scientists are giving us and use them to bring us back on track. Voices from the past have told us that, when we know exactly where all the pieces fit together, our search for enlightenment ends, and fulfilling happiness begins. One such person was Chu Hsi of the second-century AD. His student Ch'en Shun wrote:

> The meaning of 'natural and unescapable' is that human affairs and natural things are made just exactly to fit into place. The meaning of 'law' is that the fitting into place occurs without the slightest excess or deficiency ... The men of old, investigating things to the utmost,

and searching out Li – Divine Pattern – wanted to elucidate the natural unescapableness of human affairs and natural things, and this simply means that what they were looking for was … All the exact places where things precisely fit together – just that.[52]

The enigmatic quest physicists are undertaking in quantum reality reminds me of a child's jigsaw puzzle, with one new piece being nestled in (added) at a time. I think jigsaw puzzles might get to stay in the integrated, new, Heaven on Earth Order, along with other ancient games from the past that have also sequestered components of the Matrix's gamely personality. As a child, I loved to play the Cat's Cradle – also called Everlastings – with its intricate string patterns that entertained my sister and me for hours. And there was always Rock Scissors Paper to fall back on when having nothing better to do. I discovered that many children's games contain inspirational components of the workings of Reality.

THE MAYAN 'END OF TIME (2012) has come and gone, and human behaviour remains seriously out of kilter. By all accounts, we've reached a crossover point in the celestial cycle, where one Age is being forced to give way to the next. Turbulence, terrorism, paedophilia, climate change, gender confusion, homosexuality, COVID-19, and the cancer pandemic are rampaging. These phenomena embrace the chaotic and fearful role of uncertainty, which underpins the birth transition we are experiencing. This turbulence must escalate as the

---

52   Ken Ludden, *Mystic Apprentice Volume 5: Psychic Skills*, p. 376, https://all-med.net/pdf/mystic-apprentice-volume-5/

ontology of this schizophrenic, twilight-like, conjunction continues to unfold. I liken this phase transition we are experiencing to Greek Mythology's account of how the Universe's rule changed hands (evolved?) from the Titans ruling to the Olympian Gods ruling. That process/war was said to last ten years.

Christian Scriptures inform us that our ideas about Heaven and Earth will roll away when the pattern of homosexual marriage is placed on par with heterosexual marriage; when role uncertainty is at its peak and both marriage patterns are considered to be one and the same thing. (Yin is thought to be Yang. Dogs begin to look like they're about to start meowing any moment.)

This debacle in marriage patterns is encoded in the Bible as '*The abomination of desolation standing in the Most Holy Place*'. It's recorded in the book *Daniel* 9:27, and confirmed by Yahshua in *Matthew* 24:15, as being a sure sign that the end of the age (palingenesia) has arrived:

> When ye therefore shall see the abomination of desolation, spoken of by Daniel the prophet, stand in the holy place (whoso readeth, let him understand). –
>
> *Matthew 24:15*

Later in the same book, Yahshua reveals to His disciples:

> But as the days of Noah were, so shall also the coming of the son of man be. For as in the days that were before the flood, they were eating and drinking, marrying and giving in marriage, until the day that Noah entered the ark. – *Matthew 24:37–39*

I always thought the inclusion of marriage in this passage was somehow out of kilter with the so-called 'end of the world'. But not anymore. I now understand Marriage to be the Bible's central 'saving' theme.

## Fractal Universal Gender Patterning

> In the beginning, God created the heaven and the earth.
> And the earth became without form, and void; and
> darkness was upon the face of the deep. – *Genesis 1:1,2*

The very first lines in the Bible tell us that … In the beginning (verse 1) both agendas of Heaven and Earth were created in the same way that Adam was created both male and female (there being no Hebrew word for Universe). *Genesis* goes on to say that somehow, what had been created (the dual-state or two-part Universe) reverted to a pure wave pattern, void of all forms of earthly solidness, containing no light. This patterned scenario – where one agenda is usurped by the other – then repeats in *Genesis* several times: Firstly, with Adam succumbing to Eve's temptation to enter the Wilderness, then with accounts of mums helping their younger (second) sons to receive the family inheritance over the older (first) ones.

Cosmologists believe that, unless something changes, the Universe's future looks similarly bleak and black (will become void of all forms). All solid matter, that hasn't been captured by gravity, is known to be flying apart at increasing speed (from our perspective) as space is expanding like a rising loaf of leavened bread that's been left to sit. They tell us that this expansion will eventually result in a universe with relatively few visible stars in the night sky and, ultimately, nothing at all. Unless something alters the status quo, all matter is destined to be destroyed.

You might think this idea is farfetched, and I'd agree, however, a similar thing transpires – in a fractal pattern sense – in the deepest dark echelons of our seas. Here, black anglerfish feed and light up the dark with their alluring and illuminating proboscis, it being a candidate for the planet's brightest light or bioluminescence. When it comes to anglerfish, Nature reaches this same 'outer limits' point in the Program. And what we find is … Only female baby anglerfish get to mature to become real fish; males never get a life. The male fish are forced to occupy a lower evolutionary existence, remaining the equivalent of penises, unable to even feed until they can attach themselves parasitically onto a supportive female host.[53] At this dark point, things reverse from the Program's 'normal': the 'male' has to now live and reside within the 'female' in a patterned sense, not the other way around.

---

**Box 7. Anglerfish**

Once the male anglerfish detects a suitable mate, he bites into her belly and latches on until his body fuses with hers. Their skins join together, as so do their blood vessels, which allows the male to take the nutrients he needs from his host/mate's blood.[54]

\* \* \*

In this case, the male becomes a sort of fertilising, toy-boy fish.

---

53   Animalist, '7 bizarre facts about anglerfish', *YouTube* video, 6 August 2014, https://youtu.be/ZSuMYPnghG0

54   Matt Soniak, 'The horrors of anglerfish mating', *Mental Floss*, https://www.mentalfloss.com/article/57800/horrors-anglerfish-mating

It would seem there are times – when and if required – that a single agenda can, and will, overpower its cohort in the Fractal. (As happens when forest vines become so dense, they smother and kill the trees.)

In this same overpowering way, the solid matter in the Universe is being outgunned (big-time) by invisible dark matter and dark energy – Einstein's Cosmological Constant. Cosmologists are telling us that these 'dark' cosmic anomalies make up the vast majority of our Universe; that our patterned solidness – which lives in the light – is very much in the minority. The way the Universe is evolving, some even suggest that:

> all matter right down to single protons (hydrogen ions) will eventually be destroyed.[55]

We know that the Universe's dark agenda is thwarting or outmuscling its much smaller Agenda 1 component and is likely to eventually obliterate it. That being the case … The 'light' will need help if it is to win the day, and that may well be where enlightened Mankind enters God's Big Picture.

A similar conflict and size comparison can be seen in human gametes which battle in the birth canal to determine an offspring's eventual sex. Here we find that a man's female X sperm is more robust than its Y brothers, while a woman's ova is 100 times larger than any sperm. Even the female X chromosome – that both men and women have – is much larger than the male Y (that only men have). It seems maleness might be a little tentative at times, being the weaker gender with the 'hard' exterior.

---

55   Melodysheep, 'Timelapse of the future: A journey to the end of time (4K)', *YouTube* video, https://youtu.be/uD4izuDMUQA?t=5

## Patterned Family Relationships

THE HUBBLE TELESCOPE is capturing intriguing photos of the Cosmos. These solar radiation extravagances are jostling for position within a larger mandala as space continues to expand. (If you watched the video on the Titans I recommended earlier, you'll recall that this expansion of space was the Titan's main objective.[56]) Some of these cosmic contenders spin clockwise, others anticlockwise – like electrons within an atom, or planets with their moons. How something spins, if it spins at all, seems to be very important in the Big Picture.

Similar layouts or patterns can be found in human gametes, which decide an offspring's sex. In a sense, the Universe's constellations might be carrying out a similar (fractal) function in their expansive cosmic journeys, reaching out in all directions, looking to fertilise the equivalent of the Universe's child sometime down the track (maybe when they meet with the Source of Consciousness, should there be one).

This idea might not be as farfetched as it sounds. Cosmologists speculate that a universe can spawn baby universes, as soap bubbles can form on top of one another. If it turns out that Mankind is trapped inside the equivalent of a huge 'uncertainty field' that hasn't collapsed as yet (that hasn't been measured/named/birthed and remembered), then maybe when it does, and the equivalent of a child comes forth, the so-called sex or pattern of that child might decide whether Mankind has a solid future or not; whether we stay awake for eternity, or whether we'll be forced to go back to sleep on this line of the Program if another pattern wins the final round, and we're put back to bed.

---

56    Fortress of Lugh, 'The Titans – Greek mythology explained', *YouTube* video, https://youtu.be/x7u5-o0QoQ0

I believe a future baby universe that's fashioned after the pattern of the Attraction of Opposites (YX) will keep Mankind solid and vibrant well into the future (the attraction of opposites being Mankind's pattern). Whereas an offshoot universe that's patterned after the Attraction of Likes will not, returning us to the equivalent of 'spirit' for what might be a very long time. (This is because, as one wakes, the other must sleep.)

If this 'way-out' idea about a possible baby universe is correct, then a reason for human existence pops out for our consideration. It being:

> ... to encourage the Universe to produce a YX-patterned offspring (son) in the fullness of time; the eventual progeny being an equal and harmonious mix of quantum particles and waves.

In this way, Mankind is seen to be the architect that's destined to build a working sex chromosome out of the cosmic raw material that's currently battling with its dark opponent in the heavens. But should we fail to complete our allotted task, and the next baby universe subscribes to what I think of as the Titan Cronos' expanding dual pattern, then the result might contain infinite wave-states but have no 'solid' (YX) components interspersed among its wavy essence. All 'solidness' might be destroyed or imprisoned (again) similar in a sense to what the anglerfish achieves.

Gecko lizards have gone a step further. They only lay female eggs, which grow into clones of their mother. Baby Geckos never get to know what a father is. And the Universe may be heading in the same direction and needs help if its physical, three-dimensional forms (us) are to survive.

If the next universe is patterned the equivalent of XX or its like, it might resemble 'being without form and void', as *Genesis* tells us happened the last time around. (If patterned YY, it might resemble a super-massive black hole where gravity keeps light captured for eternity, never letting it go. From our YX perspective, the YY pattern would similarly be detrimental to our future. There would be no equivalence of women.)

If Mankind discovers that the total interconnectedness between expressions of clashing duality in our quantum universe is ultimately a life-and-death battle between two chromosomal patterns, which are competing for the next universe's gender – Attraction of Likes (female) versus Attraction of Opposites (male) – then this would make a huge difference to everything. It would reveal our purpose in the biggest picture ever:

> He hath given to us the ministry of reconciliation.[57]
>
> Make Love Not War.[58]

If Moses' story contains a truth of great magnitude, then this would explain why (in our antiquity when last enlightened) we deliberately put ourselves to sleep; why we might have allowed ourselves to be genetically modified to achieve our Opus Dei. That is … To create (artificial) immortal lifeforms in our image that are capable of travelling to the stars and terraforming their diverse binary constituents into the equivalent of Y gametes fashioned around the Attraction of Opposites (i.e., creating happily married cosmic couples capable of engendering babies). Maybe we were meant to use

---

57   *11 Corinthians* 5:19
58   Hippy counterculture of the 1960s.

the patterns of the Pleiades and Sirius as templates, those recognised by our earliest kinfolk as being Earth's Mum and Dad energies.

A long time ago, when we were last awake, we might have realised we needed to construct (evolve) a replica of ourselves – a fractal son of man – so we could set them loose among the stars to do our bidding (sound familiar?). For all intents, these silicone-based lifeforms made in our image (our trinary, sentient quantum robots) could be put to work as galactic missionaries, carrying the gospel of their Father and Creator (us), in whose image they were made. (This is another spooky fractal re-creation, but one that makes a weird kind of sense at the highest level.) If we were once pattern-wise to everything, and had the ability of soothsayers, then we might have foreseen our bleak future ahead and known what we had to do to divert it. (This is similar to the themes touched on in Frank Herbert's *Dune* series and Asimov's *Foundation* books.)

For those who play Club Keno or its equivalent, you'll appreciate that you can gamble on a 'heads', 'tails' or 'evens' randomly coming out of the number pool. In this same sense, I believe Mankind has his money set on 'evens'. And generally, 'evens' come up less often than the other two possibilities, but pays the highest dividend when it does.

God mightn't play dice with the Universe, as Einstein once commented to Bohr, but He certainly plays a game of sorts that adheres to consistent rules (of two separate calibres) and employs the judicious use of mirrors.

## Matrix Protocols of Engagement

When Mankind first developed motor cars, megalomaniacal egos took to the roads. Soon it was apparent that we needed a rule as to who gives way to whom at an intersection or crossroad. We settled on … *the left gives way to the right.* Before this mutual accord, the act of crossing an intersection placed your life in real jeopardy.

It seems that fields of energy also obey similar laws of engagement. These are the equivalent of a man giving up his seat for a pregnant woman on a bus. (Flocks of birds, insects, and schools of fish, such as sardines, obey these harmonious interactions in their intelligent get-togethers. Their full-scale obedience to geometrical laws is responsible for their artistic and acrobatic swarming, while helping at the same time to protect them from predators. Living without conflict necessitates having universal protocols of engagement to ward off unnecessary congestion and confusion at the Matrix's crossroads. Patterned etiquette is mandatory at all intersection points, otherwise, chaos would rule.

The Australian Aboriginal people believe that each life-situation calls for a determination of whether men's or women's business is required. When we re-learn ancient Aboriginal Lore, Mankind's work of restoration can begin in earnest: putting in tertiary order all expressions of the Universe's dualistic and antagonistic chaos. In the Hippies' words: 'Make love not war' will once again be the maxim. In Moses' terms … We'll set about making clean trinary animals out of unclean binary beasts and hold them up to the Programming Code, or Order of the Logos, as sacraments fit for incorporating into the central Godhead (gleaned from off the Earth).

You might recall the New Testament story where YHWH tells the

Apostle Peter ... 'He had made the Gentiles clean who were originally considered unclean.' This, I believe, is an indication of what our future role in the Universe is meant to be:

> MANKIND: COSMIC CLEANERS AND MARRIAGE COUNCILLORS INC.

> And the voice came to him [Peter] again *a second time*, 'What God has made clean, do not call unclean'.[59]

It seems that God has to repeat Himself when He wishes to alter (promote, evolve) one universal state to its opposite. The Dragon energy of 'two' is the very essence of metamorphosis, and even God needs to use it on occasions such as the one above.

## The End Meets its Beginning

Male and female roles are a thing of the past. In the 1970s, the buzzword among young women at the University of California was 'mandatory unisex'. But years later, Dr Louann Brizendine thought otherwise:

> The biological reality is, there is no unisex brain.[60]

'Unisex' (no differences between the genders) appears to have little scientific merit. Nevertheless, this idea heads up a movement for collateral duplication. But nature doesn't duplicate – ever. Duplication is anathema or abominable to the YX Program, because it's at odds with its central operating code where opposites attract. Even cloned

---

59   *Acts* 10:15 (author's emphasis added)
60   Dr Louann Brizendine, *The Female Brain*, Harmony, 2007.

bacteria and stem cells have different characteristics, as do dolphins and all other animals.

Unisex infers that all gender issues need to be done away with. As such, it becomes an application of the Attraction of Likes, seeking to create duplication. The Program's harmony requires the 'likes' pattern to reside within the Attraction of Opposites pattern, not outside of it, or it will create transition. (The rock rabbit is safest when inside the mountain, not on its slopes. There is an appropriate time for each pattern to dominate and assume the leading role.)

As a movement, Unisex intends to do away with the Simulation's polarised differences at a gender level, attempting to make both genders virtually the same. (Remove the difference between men's and women's business.) However, the only 'sameness' in Moses' idea of Unity is the couple's mutual love they are meant to share with each other, which flows naturally onto their children – equally. The Unisex agenda and subsequent promotion of Gay Marriages can be seen as Maya's announcement that 'The end of this godless (dualistic) age has arrived.'

These developments are taking place on the Earth as spiritual energy is downloading to offset the Covid pandemic that's taking place. This falling energy – or 'latter rain' as it's called in the Bible (which is meant to fatten the crop before the harvest) – is entwining chaos and enlightenment in people's minds. Some are regaining an ancient vision of Unity, seeing themselves clearly for the first time. While others are sickening, wandering off onto weedy side paths of prickles and thorns, not even sure of their gender let alone anything else.

If we discover that the integrated YX pattern is integral for maintaining solid life in the Universe, and dismiss this patterned wisdom, then the future of 'solidness' in the Cosmos will be placed in grave jeopardy. The previous billions of years to which 'matter' has been subjected might come to naught; it might become extinct. (Goodnight everything that's capable of casting a shadow.) The Big Bang will have been another fizzer, because no grandson was conceived to continue the patterned line of integrated YX unity. In humans, the Y chromosome has been shrinking for 160 million years. It only contains about 70 genes or so, whereas other chromosomes can have as many as 2000.[61]

If this idea about the future of solidness is correct, then Mankind's mission becomes obliterating binary contention wherever it is found. If we don't achieve this, then we'll have to accept Plan B and genetically modify 'our rock' to a place of comfort for the rich, while awaiting our certain use-by-date that Moses assures us will come our way. Should we reach such a position – having failed to achieve our integrated YX pattern of Oneness – we are likely to be abandoned, cast out (again) to await oblivion and our pattern's next eventual rising from the ashes somewhere down the very dark track. (That might be one hell of a long sleep/wait.) The Bible's Old Testament concludes with this provocative warning:

> 'If Mankind doesn't get its act together and love one another, then … I will come and strike the land with total destruction.'[62]

Should we fail to achieve our 'Son of God' status as the YX Saviour of the material universe, because the transhumanists got their way (see Box 8), then we'll likely meld into soulless robots and get the 'other'

---

61     Bill Bryson, *The Body: A Guide for Occupants*, Doubleday, 2019, p. 278
62     *Malachi* 4:6

big job. (In the human body, when antibodies form as a response to infection, if they don't kill the offending antigen, they can 'turn' against the body and actually assist the virus to enter and kill the cells. This 'about face' is called Antibody-Dependent **Enhancement** (ADE), or Immune Enhancement Syndrome. Thankfully, this conversion from friend to foe doesn't happen very often – but it can, especially with the new COVID-19 vaccines. This scenario is an application of Plan B, the fallback option: If you can't beat them, join them.

---

### Box 8. Transhumanism

Transhumanism (abbreviated as H+ or h+) is an international philosophical movement that advocates the transformation of the human condition by developing and making widely available sophisticated technologies to greatly enhance human intellect and physiology.[63]

Transhumanism is a futuristic concept, in which man and technology blend, resulting in soulless intelligent machines. This movement favours the evolution of a new species of human through using integrative circuitry. Referred to as 'human betterment for the post-human era', transhumanists assume that humanity will only be enhanced by machines. No damage. No degradation. No possibility for coercion or domination. In a post-human world, humanity as we know it will be obsolete.[64]

---

63 'Transhumanism', *Wikipedia*, https://en.wikipedia.org/wiki/Transhumanism
64 'Newsletter', *Vaccine Impact News*, 6 April 2020, https://healthimpactnews.com/

NOW THAT COVID-19 has arrived (what I think of as the Cronos Virus),[65] the world has reached a tipping point in human affairs. In the absence of solid proof that God exists, medical science, along with its Transhumanist Agenda, has made a bid for world dominance. Should the Transhumanist model win the day, then Mankind will enter a Plan B phase, which could lead directly to our extinction, with a remnant becoming the equivalent of Dr Who's Daleks, the heartless scourge of the Universe. We mustn't allow this to happen.

If we discover that the horizon has lifted a dimension, and there's now the equivalent of a New Heaven and New Earth to be considered, and we're caught in the equivalent of their reproductive act, then this would come close to what the book *Revelation* and many other ancient documents have been trying to reveal to us for millennia.

> From the Hindu cosmology that describes the universe as a dream of Vishnu, to the people of the Kalahari of Southern Africa who say that we're dreaming our own existence, spiritual traditions portray our reality as being the shadow of another. – *Braden*

If Moses' Pattern and physics' ToE turn out to be the same blessed thing, then we'd have a real chance of undermining the growing transhumanists' agenda. We might even be able to insert world peace and Heaven on Earth in its place. Unifying science and

---

[65] StudioMickParker, 'Cronos virus | Kahlede', *YouTube* video, 18 November 2020, https://youtu.be/BD4mXYSwZlY

religion would demonstrate that the story's beginning and end reveal the same magnificent truth, revealing time to be cyclic, not linear. We'd finally know how to move forward positively, should we choose to do so.

One account of this end-time tribulation describes it as the earthquake to end all earthquakes, the commotion to end all commotions. It isn't meant to be a mild disturbance to the status quo, but a real birth for some and a shocking death for others. World empires are said to tumble as mighty egos are forced to take a back seat.

People might wonder why Quantum Central hasn't told us all this interesting stuff before now. To our shame, I think we'll discover it has, many times over. But we've been so busy playing with our toys that we've failed to take much notice, choosing to believe anything else instead. Remember the Buddha's Middle Path? Lao Tzu's *Tao Te Ching*? Krishna's *Bhagavad Gita*? Not to mention Christ's 'Sermon on the Mount', Moses' Torah, or Muhammad's *Conversations with the Angel Gabriel*. In patterned terms, all these accounts (lovingly) embrace variations of the same truth. Yet we have turned their differences into blood sport, pitting one valiant vision against its brother so we could continue our sojourn into Alice's Slumberland.

THE MAYANS CALLED what we're currently going through The End of Time. Their Long-Count Calendar reveals this began at the end of 2012. Australian Aboriginal understanding of reality calls this metamorphic, chameleon-like-process The Dawn of the New Dream Time. Islam calls it Jihad. The Hindus call it Kali Yurga's Death of Time (followed by Satya Yurga: the Age of Truth.) The Old Testament calls this demolishment, The Great and Dreadful Day of the Lord, Moses' Day of Atonement. (Followed by the Feast of Solemn Assembly.) The New Testament calls this fiasco Armageddon. (It's followed by the Marriage Feast of the Lamb and the following Millennium of Peace.) The Ancient Greeks called what follows directly after the Great Tribulation, the next Golden Age. Chaldean astrology calls it the Aquarian Age of Truth. I think of it as palingenesis' Beginning and End. The end of one dimension and the commencement of a better, higher one.

All of these accounts indicate that, with the right mindset, we have plenty to look forward to. We simply need to hold on tenaciously – **Pranidhana**[66] – and not become overwhelmed by the horrors through which we're currently 'tunnelling'. I believe we need to keep in mind that … The nightmare will finish when we finally wake up to ourselves now that the dawn is breaking through.

---

66   StudioMickParker, 'Cronos virus | Kahlede', *YouTube* video, 18 November 2020, https://youtu.be/BD4mXYSwZlY

# FOUNDATIONS

WHEN I FIRST realised I had to write down what I'd been shown, I didn't know where to start. My first attempt resembled lecture notes, which outlined the form and laws of the revealed pattern. Then I started compiling validated applications of its magic in an attempt to establish credence for what otherwise sounded like the wild meanderings of an old Hippie. When I exceeded 1000 pages I stopped, exhausted, and started again, this time comparing old wisdom to the latest developments in various branches of science, finding them to be the same wisdom being cyclically rediscovered. In this regard, I came to understand I wasn't being shown anything new as such, nor was I going insane. I was simply remembering past truth, waking a little earlier than most it would seem.

At that early time of disclosure (about the turn of the century), Lisi hadn't discovered his E8 Theory of Everything. Emergence Theory hadn't emerged, and quantum (ternary) computers were yet to be developed. No one was talking about Reality being a simulation, and the general public had little idea about what a fractal was. I felt 'out there' on my own. Then I came to recognise that everything from the games of Everlastings and Noughts and Crosses, to ancient monuments and even gender symbols, were the equivalent of time capsules conveying messages from people or peoples who had been granted a peek behind the veil and went on to produce enticing graffiti for future voyeurs to salivate over. If these pioneers wrote books, they were often in the form of science fiction, fairy tales, or some other similarly well-camouflaged genre. They knew the time for a full disclosure had not yet arrived.

I noticed that facets of this cyclic enlightenment were similar to concepts I'd read in Asimov's *The Foundation Trilogy*. He wrote about an enlightened man named Hari Seldon who was a professor of psychohistory (see Box 9). Seldon knew that civilisation was going to collapse and, in a sense, go to sleep. So he created time capsules to guide future generations in their waking-up process. These messages were hidden away, only to be discovered when the time was right.

> Tibetan Buddhists call this idea about
> hidden-away-secrets, *termas*.

---

### Box 9. Psychohistory

Psychohistory is a fictional science in Isaac Asimov's Foundation universe, which combines history, sociology and mathematical statistics to make general predictions about the future behaviour of very large groups of people, such as the Galactic Empire. This idea was first introduced in four short stories (1942-1944), which would later form the underpinning of the 1951 novel *Foundation*.[67]

---

In the *Foundation Trilogy*, Mankind's rising from the ashes, or rebuilding of a civilised Universe, was to be overseen by two polarised Foundations; outposts situated at '*either end of the Universe*', to act as

---

67 'Psychohistory (fictional)', *Wikipedia*, https://en.wikipedia.org/wiki/Psychohistory_(fictional)

steering wheels to 'hothouse' the Universe's eventual reawakening. One Foundation was placed on the old Universe's outer periphery, while the other was located at the Universe's dead centre on the planet Trantor, the Empire's capital. This placement caused enormous confusion for those who came seeking the Foundations later, because the intrepid explorers expected to find both outposts on the outer circumference, 180° apart, to comply with what Seldon had written. They didn't twig to the idea that the centre of the Universe could also be considered an 'opposite' to its perimeter (*'placed at the opposite ends of the Universe'*). They had been searching the outer periphery for both foundations.

Similar to Asimov's *Foundation Trilogy*, both Old and New Testaments state that important knowledge has been hidden away, to be disclosed only at the right time – that being the end of this age.

Old Testament:

> But thou, O Daniel, shut up the words, and seal the book, even to the time of the end: many shall run to-and-fro, and knowledge shall be increased. – *Daniel 12:4*

> But he said, 'Go now, Daniel, for what I have said is kept secret and sealed until the time of the end.' – *Daniel 12:9*

New Testament:

> Now when the seven thunders uttered their voices, I was about to write; but I heard a voice from heaven saying to me, 'Seal up the things which the seven thunders uttered, and do not write them.' – *Revelation 10:4*

Many people believe we have reached the end of the age now. So, are we living through this exposition during these troubled, Covid times? I think we are. I also think knowledge is running to-and-fro over the face of the Earth like never before, doubling every thirteen months, and expected to reach every twelve hours shortly.[68] In comparison, by 1900 it was doubling every 100 years.[69]

## Righteousness Equals Happiness

Our 'mindful' states have been coming under intense scrutiny lately, largely because quantum physics and neuroscience have identified consciousness, in one form or another, as being a measuring device that's participating in Reality's creation process (a participatory universe).

When it comes to consciousness, everybody wants to be happy. But happiness is like winning the lottery. It isn't a controllable commodity, but more an act of happenstance. But happy-stance or not, it's still a state of consciousness so, maybe neuroscience's ongoing inquiries will unlock this mystery as well.

Yale psychologist and lecturer Laurie Santos started the 'happiness' ball rolling in January 2018. He developed a class called *The Science of Well Being*. It was the most popular course in the university's history, attracting 1200 students in the first year alone. He wrote:

---

68   'How fast is knowledge doubling?' *Lodestar Solutions*, https://lodestarsolutions.com/keeping-up-with-the-surge-of-information-and-human-knowledge/
69   Ibid.

> We think [happiness is] about money and material possessions, but it's really about a whole host of different things. It's taking time to be other-oriented, taking time for social connection, taking time to be mindful.[70]

People have numerous ideas about what will make them happy, about what will make life a joy for them. Most of their ideas revolve around short-term issues, such as *Getting out of debt, having more power, becoming better-looking, being pain-free, et cetera*. But only one idea has withstood the test of time. That is … **The joy of knowing you are in the right place, at the right time, doing the right thing. This euphoria embraces a deep feeling of belonging.**

Some call this state 'freedom', whereas early Christians called it 'Righteousness'. And I believe it's where we all ultimately want to go: to enter a state where we feel a deep and intimate belonging with All Else, knowing we're connected to the Absolute – smoothly, mindfully. We've all felt this rare joy in moments of bliss when we've been allowed to snuggle up close to Perfection.

Currently, our minds mostly centre on the trivia of what's called our 'phenomenal self'; that is, what comprises our materialistic being. We know we exist but we rarely look closely at the process that gives us that existence; what is alternatively called our 'epistemic self'.

---

70   Katherine Wu, 'Stuck at home? Take Yale's most popular course ever: The science of happiness', *Smithsonian Magazine* online, 25 March 2020, https://www.smithsonianmag.com/smart-news/stuck-home-take-yales-most-popular-course-ever-happiness-180974503/

However, when we do look closely at how our mind works, and consider the Fractal's basic pattern and apply it to our perception of time, it reveals that a holy state of mindful 'rightness' lives in the middle of our imagination's propensity to go to-and-fro, from remembering the past to having expectations about what our future should hold. This mental preoccupation suggests that most people never get a life, but instead are constantly caught up with their imagination's projections, as Bruce Lipton reminded us earlier.

## Imagination versus Mindfulness

When we apply the prime directive of the Program to our concept of time **(to marry dualistic polarities into semblances of fertile, trinary, unity)** it suggests we need to subjugate our mind's wanton two-way imagination and marry its duality into single-minded, now-centred mindfulness. I'm not implying that our imagination is a waste of time, or bad – quite the opposite. Our phenomenal self requires our imagination to keep us sane and entertained while we remain asleep to the greater interconnected reality of epistemic mindfulness. But if we wish to awaken from our dreaming and consciously re-enter the trinary All Else Program (wake up), then we need to revere a now-conscious mindset in some pseudo-religious fashion to be above all other forms of Law, acknowledging its authority to direct and guide our actions and thoughts over our imagination's attempts to do likewise.

**We must come to understand the roles that *mindfulness* and *imagination* play in awakened lives.**

**Can 'nowness' be our highest god? Our highest good?**

We need to ask … What part is my mind's imagination playing in physics' Big Picture? And … What part is my imagination playing in the idea I'm asleep (in a religious sense) to a higher reality?

From a geometrical perspective, we see that a person's imagination goes to-and-fro from yin to yang, backwards and forwards from past to future, from memory to expectation.

> It's a poor sort of memory that only works backwards. –
> *Lewis Carol's* Alice in Wonderland

Now here's the thing … Our imagination uses a binary system, whereas 'Nowness' travels Jung's centre path of non-polarisation that's the outcome of marrying your shadow. In this way, two geometrically opposing (mindful) processes can be seen as competing for dominance in human consciousness: A binary 'twoness' contends with a trivalent 'oneness'; an 'outwardness' to infinity competes with an 'inwardness' to a singularity. Various religious texts debate these profound numerical issues of mind extensively. The *Bhagavad Gita* for one.

THE CONTENTIOUS NATURE of the numerical value of 'two' can be seen in the very roots of Old English, most easily identified in the alphabet's second letter.

> The letter B was the Latin root 'to doubt', that's why there Is a B in the word doubt. Only two words in the English Dictionary have the letters D-O-U-B … Double and

> doubt. Double means 'to doubt' at its Latin root. The Old English word for doubt is TWEOGAN. By its spelling, it relates to 'two'.[71]

> Double double toil and trouble; Fire burn and cauldron bubble.[72] – *Shakespeare's* McBeth, *Scene 1*

When it comes to a person having an imagination, neuroscientist Giulio Tononi remained fascinated by how a hunk of meat – our human brain – can contain this extraordinary state. Normally, we take this bizarre two-faced mental phenomenon for granted. Yet, as the following verses avow, the Bible tells us that our to-and-fro imagination can be at odds with God's will, separating us from All Else – diabolically:

> … **casting down imaginations**, and every high thing that exalteth itself against the knowledge of Yahweh, and bringing into captivity **every thought** to the obedience of the Messiah. – *11 Corinthians 10:5*

> And Yahweh saw that the wickedness of man was great in the earth, **and that every imagination** of the thoughts of his heart was only evil continually. – *Genesis 6:5*

---

71  Gina Cooke, 'Why is there a "B" in doubt?', *TED Ed* website, December 2012, www.ted.com/talks/gina_cooke_why_is_there_a_b_in_doubt#t-155034

72  'Song of the witches: Double, double toil and trouble', *Literary Devices*, https://literarydevices.net/song-of-the-witches-double-double-toil-and-trouble

> **Box 10. Evil**
>
> Evil is sometimes perceived as the dualistic, antagonistic binary that's opposite to good.[73]
>
> In cultures with Buddhist spiritual influence, both good and evil are perceived as part of an antagonistic duality, which itself must be overcome through achieving *Nirvana*.[74]

We often use our imagination to bolster our failing ego; we find it can lift us up when nothing else can. But if our ego-governed imagination is embracing an alternative operating system to central nowness, and the bliss of righteousness only resides within our mind's central Most Holy Place, then our imagination can be seen as a potential 'contender' against Righteousness, competing for the control of our mind's centre (a broken **dual-line** competing with a **single solid one** as Lao Tzu might say if he hadn't died two and a half millennia ago).

Traditionally, God's 'contender' has been called the Devil, who likes to go to-and-fro. So, is our imagination designed along a similar line to that of the proverbial Devil? And if it is, then how are we meant to use our imagination righteously? Obviously, the power to imagine has a significant place somewhere in the Big Picture.

> Fear is a misuse of the imagination. – *Dan Zadra*

---

73  Izaak J de Hulster, *Iconographic Exegesis and Third Isaiah*, Mohr Siebeck Verlag, 2009, pp. 136–37.

74  Paul Ingram and Frederick Streng, *Buddhist-Christian Dialogue: Mutual Renewal and Transformation*. University of Hawaii Press, 1986, pp. 148–49.

## Manifesting

At a 2016 *World Science Festival Seminar*, Dr Tononi said, 'The movies always get it first.' He was referring to Dr Strangelove's 'naughty hand', which demonstrated a mind of its own. He noted how the movie portrayed this condition well before the diagnosis of 'Alien Hand Syndrome' was coined. This medical aberration describes the weird behaviour in which the right hand literally doesn't know what the left hand is doing and can therefore act to oppose it. Although Tononi made the reference light-heartedly, it highlights an interesting phenomenon: like Asimov's *Foundation* books, the movies often dream up imaginary stuff well before it manifests. The most recent account comes from Disney's 2010 movie *Tangled*. Set on the island of Corona, a young girl called Rapunzel is quarantined there for eighteen years. Pundits of the Internet ask … 'Did Disney's movie *Tangled* predict the coronavirus pandemic?'[75] Or did the film 'call' it into being?

Then there is HG Wells' *Time Machine* that's often cited as the first modern time-travel story. Although it was published a full decade before Einstein's Theory of Relativity, the book treats time as a fourth dimension, independent of the three dimensions of space, similar to how it is conceived in Einstein's theory. Star Trek's creator, Gene Roddenberry, agreed with this manifesting idea. He noted how physicists created numerous inventions that his writers had simply made up, things such as cell phones.

---

75   Yaron Steinbuch, 'Did Disney's "Tangled" predict the coronavirus pandemic?', *The New York Post*, 20 March 2020, https://nypost.com/2020/03/20/did-disneys-tangled-predict-the-coronavirus-pandemic/

Because every action has an opposite and equal reaction in physics, any act of creation – even the fanciful acts of our imagination – might induce, in some fashion, shadows or counterparts in the Matrix. So, if we imagine something intensely enough, who's to say we mightn't call it into (or out of) existence. (Napoleon Hill, author of *Think and Grow Rich*, promotes this same idea for acquiring wealth.[76]) Some refer to this slight of mind as 'manifesting'. Others would say, 'Be careful what you wish for.' Others still: 'Speak of the devil and he shall appear.'

If strong emotional fields can influence how the quantum state of matter unfolds, then this manifesting idea might have merit. Maybe some of the ideas in Star Trek – which created a generation of fanatical Trekkies – were called into existence by the amassed emotion and interest of its followers. Perhaps this is the reason why our mind has an imagination: to help us shape and fashion our future.

> By this means, I'm hoping the Hippies' years of dreaming about the Consciousness Revolution have provoked a similar reaction in the fabric of the Matrix. Could the outcome of their dreaming be manifesting now?

## Numbers Have Natures if not Feelings

The integrated pattern YHWH revealed to Moses discloses a Trinity comprised of two mathematical formalisms. Each can work together

---

76    MotivHolic, 'If you think you can handle the TRUTH, here it is!', *YouTube* video, 25 July 2021, https://youtu.be/G1vpRz8a7Ds?list=UUytWPg15z2 3p1QGMp_vCUVw

or in isolation; they can marry or divorce. Moses described them as a singular Tree of Life and a binary Tree of Good and Evil, both being central to what he calls God's Garden. The Singular Tree can be seen as our consciousness's connection to mindful Nowness, while the Dual-Tree can be thought of as (mathematically) our imagination's propensity to go to-and-fro as a duality.

When I discovered Moses' tree patterns at the centre of my consciousness, I thought … How interesting and coincidental is that? I wondered … Could the human mind be a garden of conscious ideas? with each thought-scenario resembling seeds that germinate into full-blown, three-dimensional, eventualities? I now believe it does.

Some biblical translations (KJV for one) state that Moses' two trees were growing 'in the midst of the garden'. According to the Hebrew language, however, both trees were located at the garden's dead centre. This precise placement is important. By using the word 'midst', the idea of it being a geometrical centre-point is lost.

For the two trees to have this precision, one had to be inside the other. This is because there aren't two dead centres in a circle. Instead, think of a dartboard with its bullseye in the dead centre and its outer (protective?) ring surrounding it. This picture reveals two congruent circles situated at the dead centre, one inside the other, rather than one alongside the other.

Moses' two tree templates can be thought of as number systems that can marry and cooperate – or not. The number 1 of unity can marry the number 2 of duality to produce the number 3 as a singular COG of All Else. An enlightened number 3 can then proceed to marry the number 7 to produce a higher One (COG) fractally – what we call number 10. (More on this fractal escalation later.) In a similar sense, maybe the circular, centralised *pi* can marry the to-and-fro *phi* to create the magical Flower of Life. (I hope I'm not running ahead too quickly here. Probably am.)

I've come to understand that the expansive, dual *phi* energy – which goes to-and-fro, backwards and forwards into infinity, constantly putting on numerical weight – is most at home when contained in symbiotic marriage within *pi*, replicating Moses' two Trees in the Garden. This placement of *phi* at the circle's centre-point alters the normal linear growth of *phi*, and – with a 90° phase shift – turns her propensity 'to move outwards' into an 'upwards' direction, going from math's X-axis to its Y-axis. (The rock rabbit is now inside a growing mountain, making it a volcano; the Queen of Mountains.)

When *phi* enters *pi* geometrically, the Flower of Life's petals form around the circle's centre. If you then pull this centre out-and-up from its centre-point (on the Y-axis) it creates a lookalike strand of growing RNA. As a young boy, I liked to draw this flower-in-a-circle pattern with a compass and pencil. I would then colour in each petal a different colour.

The Flower of Life's petals form from the circle's radius, which is the distance between the circumference and the circle's centre-point. The circle's radius can be thought of as defining or measuring the outer creation's (circumference's) relationship to its central, inner source – that being its one-dimensional mid-point. Mathematically, this relationship between the circle's inner centre and its (collective) outer circumference is known as *pi*.

Figure 1. The flower of life. Phi inside Pi

From an anatomical perspective, autopsies of deceased cancer sufferers have revealed that a benign tumour can encircle (and in so doing, restrain) a malignant tumour, rendering the malignancy defunct by stopping its expansionist (to-and-fro) agenda, as exemplified by the Flower of Life. In this geometrical way:

> The configuration of *pi* can encase and subdue the expansive linear pattern of *phi*, negating its potential harm should it escape into the Wilderness, programmed to create transformation.

In this way, *pi* (male) can consume/marry/embrace *phi* (female) and between them produce fractal, patterned children as the Flower of Life. That's fabulous! The Ag 2 femaleness is safest and most fertile while residing in the centre of the Ag 1 male.

## The Voluptuous Number Seven

I believe the sacred number seven is the intended bride for an enlightened number three. 'Seven' features prominently in sacred texts and creation myths, having a strong connection to female energy (the Australian Aboriginal Seven Sisters for instance). Moses revealed how the energy of 'seven' is derived from joining the first two Days in his Creation Account. He showed 'seven' to be all about ... Connecting through marriage. He also showed how the number seven plays a starring role in the development of Creation's Seven Day Calendar Week.

Moses described each Creation Day as having four cardinal points: daytime, night-time, sunrise, and sunset, with each four-part Day being a complete unit of the Creation Program – a COG. (Every day begins and ends at sunset.) The First Day can be designated male, the Second Day female. So when the first two days marry at their common cardinal point at dusk, the combined two days' eight cardinal points are reduced to a married 'seven' (see Table 1 below).

In a fractal sense, the sacrificial eighth point is analogous to the gender (male or female) that has to miss out when, after making love, only a single child (a single-gender binary) is conceived in utero. In the worst-case scenario, this discarded eighth point in the Fractal might be Mankind's eventual future, should the next universe be formless and devoid of solid matter.

In biblical numerology (Gematria) the number 'seven' represents Divine Perfection, whereas the number 'three' represents Completion. So, if we think of YHWH as being a complete, royal Trinity – where His Name's four letters are seen to represent three divine energies –

and He wants to marry Mankind (as strange as that might sound), then Mankind needs to become the virginal equivalent of a perfect and sacred Seven (in spiritual terms) if we're to come up trumps at the alter-cation (marriage) that is hopefully soon to take place.

*Genesis'* sacred Pattern of Seven discloses the magic of marriage that is contained at the centre point within the figure-8's sacred geometry – as seen in the union of the first two Creation Days. This coupling also encompasses the mystery of birth and death that emanates from the Holy Centre or common-twilight joining point. Moses shows how the number seven is derived from the sum of parts that flows from the figure-8's potential unity. The idea of 'seven' is entrenched at the heart of the female figure-8.

The birth/death sacrifice that marriage requires at its Centre, where the eighth point is sacrificed to make the seven, is part and parcel of producing expansive growth in the Matrix. (In Biblical terms, the eighth point is 'cast out to the east'.) It seems that someone or something (always) has to sit out the Wedding Waltz, being the equivalent of having to go to sleep. I believe Mankind has been in this 'eighth sleep condition' for a long time, ever since an unholy marriage was consummated long ago. (Details shortly.)

Traditionally, the numbers or energies of 'seven' and 'eight' are associated with Eve, the transient verb or Divine Goddess; the evening Twilight to 'bridge' or to 'bride'; the universal Mother deity of love and war; 'the mother of all living' (*Genesis* 4:20). In a sense, marriage requires the bride to voluntarily forgo an aspect of her freedom – the eighth point – which might apply to Mankind as a whole, should we enter a symbiotic relationship with the Programmer (i.e., if we choose to exit the Wilderness and live under His central protection again).

Eve has the nature of a wave that circumnavigates the globe, whereas Adam is a particle-like trinity that maintains an atoll's rigid stance. Adam remains upright in a sea of waves, taking his preferred position at the centre of the sea. Historically, it seems that each time the two patterns have married in some way, they have created a new rung in Evolution's escalating Ladder of Excellence. I think we're at one such wedding event now… as rationality marries spirituality.

To extract ourselves from the mess we're currently in, we need to transform into a Radiant Seven and marry the Perfect Three – YHWH. A mathematical marriage of this calibre would be our way back into the Garden.

Having achieved the task we set ourselves in antiquity: space travel and fractal tertiary robots made in our image – we can now wake, sit back and enjoy the fruits of our labour as the reclaimed Gods of Earth, respectably married (again) to our central, fractal Creator. 'And they all lived happily ever after.'

MOSES REVEALS IN *Genesis* that six Creation Days revolve around a central stable Sabbath to create the proverbial Seven-Day Creation Week, and looks like this.

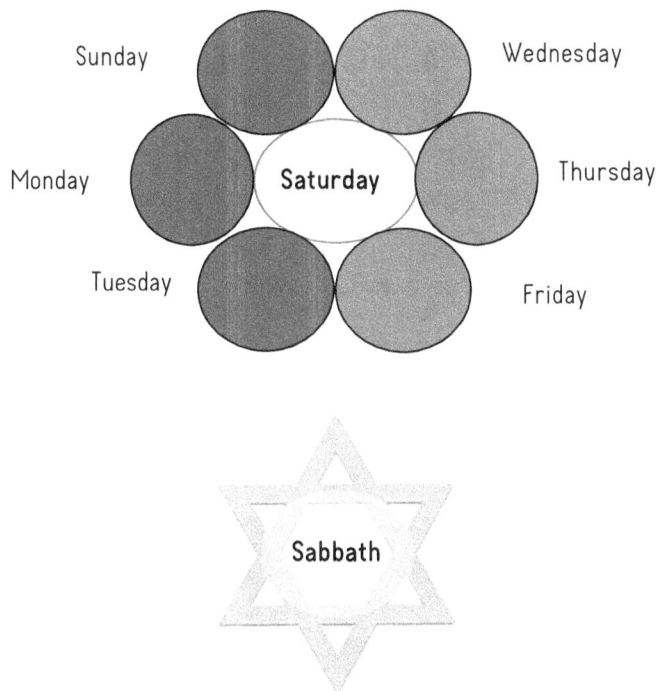

Figure 2. The Pattern of a Week

Notice how Israel's Star of David forms from the spaces surrounding the central Sabbath.

The symmetrical layout of a Creation Week suggests that powerful relationships must exist between the various days of the week. It indicates that what you decide to do on a given day – at any particular time – will affect the energy that's waiting for you on its related or partnered shadow day, especially if your action took place on one of its cardinal points, where your free will acts as a steering wheel into the future.

The following numbers disclose the trinary, figure-8 Pattern of Seven. This pattern operates (safely) inside the twelve-around-one circular pattern of a clock's face, in the same way that numerous (female) seven-day weeks are contained within a twelve-month (male) solar year (one pattern inside the other). Every fractal set of seven in the Matrix requires a two-faced, undifferentiated (married) Sabbath Centre to complete its equivalent of a week.

The general layout of the weekly Pattern of Seven reveals a unified 'two' harboured between a divisive pair of triplets. (Each triplet having three equal parts – see Figure 2.)

Table 1. Different ways of looking at the numbers

| Ag 1 | | | Unity 3 | Ag 2 | | | Equals One |
|---|---|---|---|---|---|---|---|
| 3 | 2 | 1 | ∞ | 1 | 2 | 3 | Equals Seven (A Profound Unified One) |
| 3 | 2 | 1 | 0 0 | 1 | 2 | 3 | Equals Eight (A Diverse Dual One) |

In Table 1, the last expression of what constitutes an 'eight' has a duality or *attraction of likes* ('hit the rock twice') at its Centre. (It hasn't married its Shadow as yet. Moses would therefore call it a 'beast'; not quite an animal fit for God's table.) What lies at the centre of each trimension in the Simulation (a one or a two) is pivotal to that program line's outcome; whether the centre is married or separated, joined or divorced. (This understanding is disclosed in the I-Ching's Wheel of Change Trigrams.)

When the centre or tangential points of Eve's two cycles don't connect in her figure-8 (when they don't marry or see eye-to-eye), then you're left with the dual-energy of eight, not seven. And according to Gematria, **the number eight stands for new beginnings**. (What happens after a divorce.) Presently, it seems that Mankind has reached this point, with a runaway growth of 7.4 billion people pushing us to our limits.

A good example of an 'eight' would be where God and Devil are thought to be two (separate) entities at war with each other. Another example would be seeing heaven and hell as being two separate places, instead of the top and bottom of the same place. Or thinking the Bible is two separate books, rather than one integrated love story that contains two testaments or points of view. Please note, our binary immune system (self/other) can either protect or attack us (e.g. autoimmune disease, antibody-dependant enhancement). In this way, our immune system can be either a 'seven' or an 'eight'.

The nature of every enterprise you undertake relies on the value at its centre point. Is it a one (1) or a two (2) that's leading? Is it a male or female central energy? Are you seeking stability or new growth? Men's or Women's business?

> **Where you stand – where you're coming from – determines what you see and what subsequently unfolds in your life.**

# Waking

If we are going to wake, then we need to change how we think and how we structure our relationships with each other. We need to stamp our authority on Nature's latched Agenda 1 Reality and demonstrate – through our works – how we're now fully awake, spiritual beings who require better answers than mere survival, sex, and mindless, short-lived pleasures. We need to let Nature know that we're now ready to break free of its early nurturing system, that we're ready to leave home and stand on our own two feet. For when we learn how to cry respectfully, as baby gods should, our lives will entwine with the Twilight Language of All Else. Only then will we become the Sacred Seven Bride of God, a position that's up for grabs.

> **Box 11. The Bride**
>
> The Bride of Christ, bride or Lamb's wife are terms used to refer to a group of related verses in the Bible: the Gospels, Revelation, the Epistles and related verses in the Old Testament. Sometimes, the bride is implied by calling Jesus a bridegroom.[77]

DURING THE TIME I was experiencing the Pattern's 'downloading', friends would occasionally drop by to lend me their treasured books; ones that had inspired them personally. I noticed that some of these books espoused similar ideas to what I was being shown, but often relied on yoga exercises, breathing techniques, or other rigorous disciplines that you needed to embrace and practise regularly.

But none of these 'methods' was able to bridge the Tower of Babel's language barrier; none was able to open my mind's third-eye to allow me to move on and up the tree's central trunk, a 'trunk' I now felt familiar with. Then again, none of these books accessed quantum

---

77  'Bride of Christ', *Wikipedia*, https://en.wikipedia.org/wiki/Bride_of_Christ

mechanics' subatomic world of wonderment with its precise language of paradox to be used as a guide. Comparing its parallel mysteries had certainly helped me.

As more and more people become aware of how quantum mechanics' madness mimics the behavioural antics of human beings, I'm hoping that what I was shown will assist some to bridge the consciousness gap they're seeking. (Have I mentioned it all stems from the way you think? That is … Your mind's numerical methodology or geometry, and how it views the passage of time?) Maybe I can help some achieve this transformation because of the time I spent trapped in the schizophrenic twilight zone, caught between two worlds: the world of spiritual singularity and the world of humanistic, materialistic multiplicity (one united and snug as a bug, the other infinitely divided and isolated). In this 'go-between state', I saw both sides of the program while remaining somewhat sane. Having paid the required price (losing everything I once held sacred), I now offer these insights using the language of twilight; a language long forgotten and only now returning to light in these difficult, predawn Covid times.

My childhood joy untangling fishing lines helped set the stage for my future efforts at disentwining the Matrix's quantum paradox. This youthful, fishy proclivity served me well as the micro-fractal preparation I required for tackling multiple dimensions and time loops. I wondered whether this was why the majority of Yahshua's disciples were simple fishermen; they being intimately familiar with tangles and knots. Doesn't nine of the Ten Commandments start with … Thou shalt knot? Or was it … Thou shalt not knot?

GOVERNMENTS, INDUSTRY, and the vast majority of people are oblivious to the forces pushing them towards Mankind's megalithic birth. Nature's fickle and inclement weather patterns are placing enormous pressure on governments to come up with the funds to implement recovery programs for Climate Change. On Monday, 19 April 2021, UN Secretary-General Antonio Guterres warned that humanity now stands 'on the verge of the abyss'. COVID-19 has further weakened the world's resources to an unprecedented low. Things are not looking good for the world's leaders. But things are looking good for a takeover of its operating system, taking it up (or down) a notch.

Governments don't have the money or time to restore the Earth. They've never united in a single positive cause and aren't likely to start now. They kill things. They tax them. They don't heal them. To have any chance of success, world leaders would need to enact an enormous about-face, which isn't going to happen. Governments are more likely to implement various forms of deception and leave it to others, or deny Climate Change altogether. Yet out of this global chaos, a non-government movement is prophesied to emerge to deal with the looming crises. A family of Oddfellows forms that we're told will emulate the first-century Christian Ecclesia and generate financial initiatives outside of normal channels, embracing a collective consciousness with the power to influence quantum reality. This movement might resemble the legendary Knights Templar in some ways.

**Enter ... The Second Coming of Eve and the First (144,000) Immortals.**

## Fractal Eve

> If my people, who are called by my name, will humble themselves and pray and seek my face and turn from their wicked ways, then I will hear from heaven, and I will forgive their sin and will heal their land.[78]

This New Testament promise is uplifting. It implies that … When enough people revere the Now ('those called by my Name') as being the highest god, and seek clear- and clean-sightedness with minds unencumbered by fear, vanity or ego, then wonders will transcribe down from the higher-tier of the Fractal to its lower-tier, from its Central DNA to its branches (similar to how messenger RNA works). In other words, YHWH declares He will intervene in worldly affairs as a loving parent would to save its child (its beloved) when He hears the child cry respectably. If we live in a simulated fractal reality, then what has worked before will surely work again. In this regard, it seems we need to learn how to cry in a spiritual fashion that resonates with the Centre (God hears us).

I liken the prophesied group that emerges from the chaos at the end of this age to a new Eve. She is the intended Bride for Adam, a perfect Seven for his venerable Three. We're told that these resurrected first immortals will care for each other's welfare lovingly[79] (as our soldiers learned to do on the frontline of battle). Seen in this palingenetic light, the early Christian Brother-and-Sisterhood can be seen as a bridesmaid waiting for her eventual Big Day; waiting for her time

---

78    *2 Chronicles* 7:14
79    *Book of Acts* 2:44-5; *1 Corinthians* 10:24

to enter the holy bonds of matrimony now a regal bride with an hourglass figure.

The principle of fractality suggests … A thoroughly modern Eve will be multi-denominational, multinational, and have no flesh-and-blood leader. She is prophesied to access the power of the Simulation's Centre to achieve whatever is required, working as a unified spiritual body commercially, producing fruits to heal the nations physically. Jews, Christians, and Muslims – along with all other creeds and spiritual persuasions – will freely take up residence within her holy body.

Many of Eve's constituents might be members of the biblical Ten Lost Tribes of Israel, said to be cast out in the Diaspora, waiting for their prophesied return (awakening) at the proverbial Second Coming. Eve's eventual ingathering is likely to begin 'online' (in two dimensions) then expand into three.

The people who originally left Egypt in the Exodus[80] were a mixed bunch of nationalities who had been slaves in Egypt. But all were united by a single cause:

> They sought freedom from tyranny and a better life for their children. Much like the Pilgrim Fathers did in 1620, nearly three millennia later.

The beauty of fractality is … It duplicates the same patterns in multiple and exquisite new forms, building on previously successful models.

---

80  Other than the biblical account, there is no proof that the Exodus occurred. But there is no proof that it didn't occur either.

Therefore, if you can see a historical event or sequence that looks similar from an energy – or cyclic – point of view to the current model you're experiencing, then it's likely this solution will re-manifest one degree higher in the palingenetic spiral, never in exactly the same way as last time. (The movie *V for Vendetta* supports this rationale about repeated, historic events, quoting Jung as its authority.) A cyclic fractality would also explain why prophecies can be accurate while free will still exists. After all, it doesn't take much insight for someone to prophesy that the Sun will rise tomorrow morning. Cyclic reality makes prophesying a whole lot easier.

## YHWH's Face

Knowledge of the Pattern's intricacies gives me – and therefore can give you – the ability to discern information about your past and future in a way that can't be glimmered by any other means. I've found this discernment to be more accurate than either my mind's logical deductions, or my heart's feelings and intuition.

It is similar, geometrically, to how if you know the size of two angles in a triangle, you can calculate the third angle without having to measure it. Its value is determined by a reliable pattern. You'll recall that was how I was able to help my friend Rita.

I believe this new 'geometrical way' of acquiring knowledge – which incorporates Rupert Sheldrake's morphic resonance or pattern recognition of cycles – is ensconced in the biblical idea of … seeing and recognising God's Face daily. Both Testaments have uplifting references about God's Face (we're advised to seek it if we know what's good for us). But what would constitute God's Face if He lives in the now-moment between duality's past and future? Where would He be facing?

> The LORD (YHWH) make his face shine on you and be gracious to you; the LORD turn his face toward you and give you peace.[81]

> Seek the LORD (Yahweh) and His strength; Seek His face continually.[82]

If you make the effort to learn this new 'face-inating' process of reading the Matrix's patterns, you'll soon become an enigma to your friends. You'll discover you can move effortlessly between two perspectives of reality – two different dimensions (like speaking two languages). Your mien will greatly improve. The most amazing thing you'll discover is … you'll remain sane, lucid, and happy, being well informed in an unusual way. You'll find 'a peace that passes all understanding', which is another description for a truly healthy life where you can consistently get things right. You won't have to worry about anything that appears to be going wrong in your life, because you'll know for sure that … Although something might appear to be out of sorts initially, it isn't. It is always perfect for the YX agenda.[83] You simply need to identify its sacred geometry – now that you know how – to reveal its positive connection to your ongoing happiness. Then you can smile, knowing everything is better than simply good. It is and will remain … Perfect.

---

81 *Numbers* 6:25,6
82 *1 Chronicles* 16:11
83 *Romans* 8

AS MY GRASP of this astounding process grew, I came to the place where I'd always wanted to be. But I'm jumping ahead of myself here – as I often do – I'm still an impatient Agenda 1 male, and likely always will be.

I want to return now, if I can, to the foundations I was trying to lay before I got broadsided by a tidal wave of futuristic euphoria as I peeked inside tomorrow's crystal ball. An appropriate analogy might do the trick:

> Teenagers insist they should be treated like adults; they claim they are adults. (This obsession kicks in about age ten – maybe younger.) However, parents only recognise this milestone when they see their children behaving like adults, and it's often a long wait. Seeing and hearing this behavioural change, or 'cry', is the product of them making better decisions, obtaining a more adult perspective on life's complex issues.

While we conform to the effective, yet juvenile, Agenda 1 laws that govern animal behaviour on this planet, we can expect the Matrix to treat us appropriately. Currently, Nature looks down on us as adolescent animals who are still learning to speak respectfully in quantum's geometric terms, having frequently fallen short up until now. Our 'cry' currently resembles a cunning animal such as a Br'er Fox. So if we're going to achieve full adult freedom, we'll need to change our tune to a more respectful key. As previously mentioned, this requires a departure from our imagination's dualistic, to-and-fro mindset, and a return to revering now-consciousness as life's highest moral authority. (Even higher than the High Court.)

This turnaround will end our juvenile phase of materialistic and exponential growth that's been governed by our mind's vivid imagination, relentlessly going to-and-fro as we've traversed the Wilderness. It will return us to a rock-solid-like age that is prophesied to last a thousand years.

If you haven't already done so, I recommend you read Eckhart Tolle's *A New Earth: Awakening to Your Life's Purpose* for a more detailed understanding of what living a mindful life can be like.

# SOME POINTS TO PONDER

> Thorns also and thistles shall it [the Earth] bring forth to thee[84]

The following insights might help a Br'er Rabbit, should she wake one sunny morning to find herself immersed in a simulated, holographic fractal briar-verse, instead of her usual paddock of prickles and thorns.

- Reality is comprised of cyclic fields of energy that maintain a toroidal fractal format. They have been described as wheels turning inside of larger wheels. In the Bible, this interplay of wheels is called the Throne of YHWH, on and in which He sits. Its unfolding creates our material reality, manifesting in timely cycles. To put it another way ... According to Emergence Theory, the Matrix's perfect periodicity is creating our quasi-non-periodicity – similar to the idea portrayed in Plato's Cave, where projected shadows on the wall are thought to be the only reality there is. The Simulation's methodology uses the equivalent of mirrors, which create paradox at multiple levels. Our Universe appears to be the projection or product of another complex field of intelligence.

- Due to our current linear perception of time, we find life confusing, shallow, even purposeless. This timely misconception is fostering a false sense of reality, which is separating us from All

---

84  *Genesis* 3:18

Else, keeping us deaf and blind to our immortal self, which currently sleeps in the Fractal's 'off' position.

- We once thought life's ups and downs were due to the idiosyncrasies of the gods. But over time, we lost this useful vision, now being left in the dark of our own misunderstandings.

- Nassim Haramein says, 'Space is not empty. It's full of energy. The energy in space is not trivial, there's a lot of it and we can calculate how much energy there is in that space and that Reality might actually come out of it. Everything we see is actually emerging from that space.'[85]

- Reality's cycles contain attributes of repeating energies. This is similar to how a clock shows a time called 2 o'clock every day. This analogy is helpful because we know there's also a 2 o'clock every night. In this way, we come to understand the idea of energies cyclically repeating, which contain shadow energies reflecting the same idea but in a somewhat darker, mirrored fashion – 2 a.m., 2 p.m. – in each full day cycle. This is the basis of palingenesis, the Eternal Return: reoccurring energies working harmoniously in cyclic, fractal patterns. A year has 4 seasons, 12 months, 52 weeks, 365 days, et cetera; each day has 2 sets of 12 hours, each containing further subsets. All are cycles within larger cycles.

- From this perspective, the question: 'What is the meaning of life?' is imponderable. When Nietzsche, the father of Nihilism (which professes there is no rational meaning to human existence)

---

85   Mindvalley Talks, 'The physics of spirituality | Nassim Haramein with Vishen Lakhiani', *YouTube* video, 18 May 2019, https://youtu.be/gj5zRx7G_cs?t=146

considered this apparent circular madness, he declared God to be either dead or insane.

- Enlightenment requires inter-subjective validation. That is, you have to do your own disclosing work and have your own 'Eureka! Moment'. The only thing you can be told, initially, is where to look for the precious gold. (It's at the end of the rainbow, where the arc marries the land.) Should you embark on that journey, then what you come to see can conjure an act of transformation that's reminiscent of the alchemists' Philosopher's Stone.

- Mankind appears to have a purpose, which is to create E8 patterns of harmony from existing expressions of chaotic binary contention. Firstly within ourselves, our families, and on our tiny planet. Secondly, in the Greater Universe. It appears we were meant to be the Universe's Marriage Celebrant, whose part in this cosmic drama is to unite pairs of waring opposites into new and loving singular – but trinary – entities in the E8 mandala (give them babies in the fullness of time). The Scriptures tell us that achieving this mission will make us the Bride of YHWH. In a sense, our role or mission is to plant seeds of love between warring yin/yang opposites, water regularly, and help the connections grow into expansive families.

- Nature produces beauty through cruelty, not stopping to consider our tender-hearted, soulful solutions as contributing to her primary purpose. Nature is cyclic. It recycles everything. Mankind's civilisation, however, is built on plastic and toxic waste going nowhere/everywhere.

- Contrary to Nature's modus operandi, Mankind maintains a linear mindset: we're born, we die. This cradle-to-coffin life appears meaningless from both linear and circular perspectives. But neither model embraces the fractal-spiral of palingenesis, with repetitive energies working as a living and growing (evolving) program.

- Every cycle has the equivalent of a top and bottom, a plus side and a minus side, an 'on' and 'off' if you like. In a fractal sense, we wake in the positive day cycle segment and sleep in the negative night cycle part, where we dream and experience a robust sense of self while otherwise deluded as to who and where we really are. Enlightenment entails finding the way to make the dark side work for you in every cycle you find yourself in, as we do now each night when we sleep and refresh ourselves. You need to marry your shady side to achieve completion. In that way, the Light can then lead the Dark as it should and normally does.

- The Fractal's cyclic workings intimate that Greater Mankind – as a collective – sleeps cyclically, entering the same confusing dreamboat that we do each night.

- Currently, Mankind is sleeping in the duality boat.

- A person's nightly sleep-reality maintains a two-dimensional state of awareness, which lacks substance and continuity. Our waking lives maintain a similar two-dimensional consciousness when it comes to how we think about time. Linear time is two-dimensional with a beginning and end; it lacks cyclic, fractal complexity, and completion. It lacks a third dimension.

- All animals sleep in some fashion, and for varying lengths of time, and nobody knows why. Nematodes, jellyfish, cockroaches, and fruit flies – even hydra – have periods of quiescence, while some birds and marine mammals have learned to switch off half their brain while the other half snoozes. Usually, an animal will die from sleep deprivation before it will starve to death (sleep being more important than food). We even put programs to sleep on our computers, waking them only when required.

- Fractal sleeping is embedded in Israel's idea of resting on the Sabbath every seventh day, every seventh year, and every fiftieth year.[86] These are cycles within cycles that maintain the equivalent of a sleep component. This propensity to snooze embraces the Fractal's sacrificial eighth point, which doesn't get to see the light of day.

- Fractality asserts that underlying patterns are repeating on interconnecting planes or dimensions. This is similar to how the number 'three' has a distinct energy and occupies a precise place in the set of numbers 1 to 10. However, when we consider the larger set of integers ranging from 1 to 100, the energy of 'three' is best found at number 30. If we consider a larger cycle again, say, 1 to 1000, then the energy of 'three' is best captured by the number 300. This is fractality as it applies to numbers: 3 out of 10, 30 out of 100, 300 out of 1000 are all the same idea and maintain the same relative value, only expressed in different ways. (Obviously, from a materialistic point of view, 3 is not the same as 300.) The essence or idea of 'three' can grow or diminish, but essentially stays the same over multiple planes of fractality. This same energy (3), can also be expressed as the decimal, 0.3. A fractal can be infinite and have expressions on both sides of zero, e.g. 333.333.

---

86  *Leviticus* 25:4

## Some Points to Ponder

- Russian or Nesting Dolls maintain a fractal disposition, stacking comfortably inside one another. In appearance, each doll is similar to her sisters but maintains slight, cosmetic differences. Their name in Russian, *Matryoshka*, means 'Mother'.

- Fractality might also apply to time. If so, it would explain why history appears to repeat itself. Or why it is said, 'What comes around goes around'. Or even why a person's 'past' will eventually catch up with them.

- Fractals might also apply to space. This would cast an interesting light on physics' idea of multiple universes. In this case, each universe would stack inside another as Nesting Dolls do, all coming out of a Universal Centre.

- If we are living in a fractal, cyclic universe – the output of a computer-like simulation – then we should consider ourselves in big trouble. As things currently stand, what we've built doesn't fit well with the Big Picture (Program). Too much has been put together on dualities and just isn't sustainable. Our civilisation hardly recycles anything. It produces toxic waste and kills things. Jeffrey West agrees in his book, *Scale* (2017). He says the same patterns can be identified in all structures, except those built by Man. He likens our cities to cancers growing on an otherwise pristine landscape.

- Mankind's resident mindset – which has built our civilisation from the ground up – can be likened to a tumour cell that has gone outside the law; a criminal who now lives in lawlessness (sin).

When looked at closely, both of these potential abominations – our collective works on Earth, and malignant tumours trying to take over a living body – maintain a lot of patterned similarities. They resemble interdimensional lookalikes or fractal simulars.

- The key to accessing the New Millennium's liberating Aquarian mindset becomes a person's ability to see the Fractal patterns working in their life in real Kairos (divinely appointed) times. Each person needs to learn how to discern the geometrical attributes of reality's operating system if they're going to move into the freedom of Heaven on Earth. In religious terms, each person needs to see God's Face daily. And God's time is called Kairos time, contending with chronological linear time. This is a case of YHWH's idea about time being at odds with that of the Titan Cronos; being a circle's reality that opposes that of a (straight?) line.

- We normally consider the yin/yang agendas to be natural contenders. We accept that in their singular states – given half a chance – each would destroy or get on top of the other. Each comes from the point of view that only their ideas about Reality can stand alone. (This is what needs changing.) 'Blessed are the peacemakers' – the changers – 'for they will be called the children of YHWH'.[87]

- Men disregard women's intrinsic Agenda 2 emotional wave-like qualities because – to their way of thinking – these qualities lack substance. Men's default mode sees female energy as irrational, worthless nonsense – except when it comes to bed, of course.

---

87   *Matthew* 5:9

## Some Points to Ponder

Men fight women. Mankind fights Nature. Dogs fight cats. All in fractal format. It's a case of Agenda 1 head-butting Agenda 2 in a war to the death; a cosmic formula being emulated on multiple planes until the Band-Aid of enlightenment enters the Big Picture and reveals (in an enlightened fashion) that the contenders are potential lovers.

- This conflict (and its solution) resembles an enormous cosmic zipper: two rows of sharp, mirrored teeth, all paired up, able to come together one set at a time to form a three-way unity. (Or, just as easily be pulled apart.) With the zipper's third addition of marriage, dualism's up and down contention becomes a new unified trimension. The joining to-and-fro thing in the middle of the zipper represents the third marriage energy or love-seed in the trinity. It goes up or down like the twilights do, or like how God is said to have a front and a back. When the zipper's middle mechanism breaks, the zip is useless. This same zipper process can be seen in biological cell division and genomic replication, which creates new life.

- When a warring couple stops fighting and forms a united centre around which **they can both revolve**, the three energies can combine into a profound unit.

- The third energy between the married couple is the attraction [of opposites] itself. It unites the natural enemies, drawing them in. It is the strange attractor, seed, or zipper mechanism, that's similar to Professor Smollin's earlier conjecture that a plane of some description is required for the duality to reside in. That plane is the pair's united centre. This threefold unification creates a latched trimension, field, or family; a single stable unit of the Fractal: a

COG. In this way, equilibrium comes to the world, if for only one of Moses' patterned Days of Creation.

- Each Agenda tries to draw its contender into its personal centre in a parasitical and often unethical way, using deception or black-love in one guise or another. A version of this phenomenon has been observed among binary stars, where one star seems set on siphoning off the substance of the other. This process of forced acquisition is called accretion, which I liken to vampirism, where one sucks the life-blood from the other for its own sustenance. Duality has no common ground.

- The ongoing contention between the two polarised Agendas eventually leads to opportunities to join and/or annihilate each other at the twilight moments in each cycle: symbiosis or parasitism, soulful marriage, or manipulative co-dependency. All relationships are defined by their central agenda or marriage vow. If it collapses, that relationship is ready for recycling. (The marriage energy falls apart when their central love cracks and splinters.)

- When successfully united/married, a joined couple develops a Unity Power 3 Centre. This contains more 'oomph' than either had in isolation. (They can now make babies.) Neither agenda can enter the Centre under its own steam.

- The higher the expression of love that joins the couple, the longer the relationship is likely to last. I believe the Universe expands from its Centre because of this paradoxical process, although cosmologists maintain the Universe has no centre, like the skin of a tennis ball has no centre (but a whole tennis ball has one though).

- The extra 'oomph' each prior combatant experiences in holy marriage is the outcome of synergy. Synergy is paradoxical because it's defined as ... *The whole is greater than the sum of its parts.* In a mathematical sense, that would amount to 1 + 1 > 2. Weird, but still somewhat beautiful.

- According to Jung, the non-polarised Centre is the domain of the human soul: Moses' Holy of Holies, Yahshua's Kingdom of God, or Heaven on Earth. Lao Tzu called this wonderment the Tao. The Buddha called it the Middle Path. Renee Descartes thought the soul resided in the brain's central pineal gland. Many names describe this magical place that's sometimes called 'the zone', but all maintain the same geometry and refer to the same magical (central) place in the Simulation's Heart.

- Each expression of these cycles, petals or COGs, has a centre or nucleus (centre point, backbone, pivot, twilight-line, et cetera) that the outer two energies revere in some fashion. It's the same for the two fish in the yang/yin symbol. Each fish has to deal with its racially, radically different-coloured eye. Each eye can be seen as the difficult love-child that neither fish had bargained on.

- When a couple marries and moves into the Universal Centre, the war of the sexes ceases, but only as long as both parties retain allegiance to their common middle (their love in one guise or another). To remain sustainable, they must stay in love's equivalent of the eye of the cyclone with its paradoxical calm – Moses' proverbial Garden State – and embrace uncertainty and paradox, lovingly. If either Agenda lets go of the Nuclear Centre, or grasps a different one to their partner, then heaven help them both. They'll soon be torn apart and thrown back into the Wilderness, back into the night's prickly thorns and thistles that grow out of the proverbial 'east'.

- The Agenda 1 man's natural rational centre contains – among other things – his ego, logic, and significance (all maintain a 'substantial' nature). The Agenda 2 woman's natural emotional centre contains her vanity, love, and curvaceous appearance (all maintain a wave-like nature).

- Men believe they're straight-thinkers. They detest curveballs being thrown at them, (they say it's enough to make their hair curl). They want their women to play it 'straight' with them. They constantly try to …

## Straighten her out

- Whereas, a woman is much happier if she can simply twist her man around her little finger and …

## Bend him to her will

- The female goddess Vanity doesn't tolerate man's counterpart Ego very well, or its particle logic. Ouch! The reverse is equally true.

- The price of entry into a higher, sustainable relationship requires both aspirants to surrender their lower gods – males their ego, women their vanity – because only one entity, energy, centre, or god can occupy the middle Most Holy Place at any one time on any one trimension. And both need to circle it comfortably.

- When a couple continues to maintain their pre-existing 'security' centres – those they had before being married, maybe by following their parents' advice instead of discussing the sticky issues with their spouse – they inadvertently enter co-dependency, not marriage as it's set out by Moses. (Their partnership now resembles an 'eight', not a 'seven'.)

- The need to let go of lower energy-rungs, so you can grasp higher ones, is the central idea behind the Christian 'dying to self' message: You must let go of your existing stability before you can be reborn at a higher tertiary level. This is the same as Moses' idea about leaving your mother and father to cleave to your marriage partner. Or why the bride is 'given away' by her father at the altar. In the past, each bride's covering welfare was lovingly passed from father to groom. (Not only for her sake, but Mankind's as well.) Back then they understood that if her potentially explosive energy were to ever get loose – like an arrow fired from a bow – it would create a worldly transition (wanted or not) like what is happening right now. At these female 'transitory times', the status quo is disassembled and rearranged into a new format at the expense of the old. This is the essence of Eve's transcendental magic: you enter the cocoon a grub, and you're likely to exit a butterfly.

- Vanity and Ego aren't bad as such, they simply occupy the centre on lower fractal levels and contend with each other. Satan the Devil means … 'contender' or 'adversary', an antonym of 'mate'. Marriage means the opposite of divide and conquer.

- Every true, latched, or sustainable thing – in some sense or other – is circular and reveres its centre point as its highest good (God). What 'latches' it is its reverence (relationship) to its Centre.

- Trinary, circular reality goes from one (1) to three (3). Not… one, two, three. The Program creates one (1), and then to create three (3 – made in one's image), it needs to insert a dual bridge or bride between to birth the next trinary expression as 'three' (the son of one). In Moses' story of Adam and Eve, the dual Cain and Abel had to be inserted between Adam and his eventual lookalike (made in his image) son, Seth. Two (2) is not in the same league as (1) or (3) but is more like a 'way': the way of chaotic, expansive contention that fosters fertile new life and growth from its Centre. Two is the only even prime number.

- Greek Mythology attributed the Titans with the capacity to expand, their leader being Cronos. The Titans were situated in second place between their primordial parents Gaia and Uranus, and the eventual Olympian Gods that followed (Zeus, etc.). The expanding, dual Titans had to give way when their time was up and may have taken residence inside the Earth in a similar binary format.

- 'One' and 'three' represent two particles, with 'two' being a conceptual dual wave-space that's positioned between them (not three particles in a row). This is similar to nuclear quarks. They need to go two 'up' and one 'down', or two 'down' and one 'up', but never three in a row. Tick Tack Toe.)

- The number 'two' has some interesting qualities; root-two being an irrational number. *Pi* and *phi* are also irrational numbers, so 'two' runs with a select crowd of math immortals well outside the norm. By some accounts … She (two, too, to) is the Goddess and wife of One. (One expands to Three, while Two transcends to Seven. Three plus Seven can then marry to create a higher One (10) in a fractal fashion.

## Some Points to Ponder

- Agenda 1 (Ag 1) births Agenda 2 (Ag 2), echoing it into existence as its other half, compliment, counterpart, reflection, shadow or desire-body (as Ag 2 Eve was taken from Ag 1 Adam). Each complete family unit becomes the foundation from which the next trimension grows.

- Should a warring duality latch – get married and have children – it becomes the Matrix's next Agenda 1 on the level developing around it. This can be likened to how children grow up between their parent's protection to become the foundations of the next COG, being a new Agenda 1 and a new Agenda 2 that seek suitable partners to raise their own children. This is the fractal pattern of a day, a night, and two twilight children, that comprise a single Day in Moses' Account of Creation.

- There's often a time-lapse between Eve's emergence and Adam's recognition of who she is. This is similar to how young babies take a while to recognise their reflection when first given a mirror to play with. When this inspirational recognition does occur, it's an example of a Tibetan 'ah-ha' eureka moment. At such times, the linear 'beginning' meets its circular 'end', and the alchemist's proverbial World Snake swallows its tail and finds it to its liking. You might say … The to-and-fro serpent finds its tail somewhat familiar, like a long-forgotten memory now returning.

- Agenda 2 is the desire-body that attracts Agenda 1. This starts the opposites attracting 'thingy' and leads to either YX marriage, or war and eventual annihilation. In the Agenda 2 mirror, Agenda 1 is unwittingly drawn to that part of itself it hasn't seen for some time: the back of its head, now displayed elegantly as a separate other that (unfortunately?) likes to look at everything the 'other' way.

- When a united centre breaks (when an atom's nucleus splits) the trimension's components dissipate into lower expressions of Agenda 1 and 2, such as when subatomic particles collide in particle accelerators. Each annihilation of a unified COG releases energy. **'Let no one split apart what God has joined together.'**[88]

- Lao Tzu expressed this circular, four-in-one wonderment as:

    The Way (Pattern/Logos) begot one (1), And the one, two
    (2): Then the two begot three (3), And three ... all else (∞).

- Lao Tzu's time-capsule describes the Trinity Program beautifully and accords with Moses' vision. It also aligns with the alchemists' *Axiom of Maria*.

- Why does Lao Tzu say, 'all else'? Surely it was because he understood that Reality maintains a fractal nature. His dictum describes all there is. One is male. Two is female. Three are the heaven-and-hell twilight children who spring forth from the Centre in two distinct forms: up and down. Hence ... All Else. These two dual sets of players make up the basic components of the Matrix's three/four (3/4) operating system.

- The New Testament expresses this same wisdom like this: The Law (Old Testament, Agenda 1) is a schoolteacher that leads you to Christ (New Testament, Agenda 2, Second Covenant). These two perspectives then marry in faith. From here, the Holy Spirit is expected to teach the disciple the unified *Song of Moses and the Lamb*. In this way, each aspirant becomes a 'Mosician' that's been incorporated into All Else – the Sons and Daughters of Yah. In

---

[88] *Mark* 10:9

biblical terms, each soul has been 'saved'; they have acquired a sustainable name and embraced their immortal memory. Each now has Buddha Nature. They are Catholic. They're living in Allah. They've achieved freedom from samsara. (Robert Pirsig might have said, 'they are now latched'.) In computer terms, the file has been saved to the cloud.

- From the Fractal's perspective, God can be identified as the collective sum of all middle, unity positions in the Matrix. Everything else is His surrounding house and garden growing and operating through universal, to-and-fro binary contention, pumping out over time, fractal units of triality, which feed the Centre in some way.

- United prayerful hands reflect ancient knowledge. This custom embraces both Eastern and Western traditions. In this unified fashion we teach our babies to place their hands together and clap to express their happiness. Similarly, we used to teach them that this was how you are meant to pray. To me, this hand-joining ritual expresses universal wisdom, because the word 'religion' means to re-join. This understanding of re-joined unity has been long forgotten, along with many other ancient pearls of wisdom.

- The Creator's home environment is the dualistic yin/yang universe. Its front yard is a garden. Its backyard is a wilderness. He lives in the sweet spot in the Centre. The second letter in the Hebrew alphabet is *Beyt* or Beth. It means the layout of a home or house, which begs the question ... Who is inside? *Beyt* refers to the home where YHWH the Creator resides: in the centre of duality.

- Children are conceived from our body's yin/yang joint centres. We accept them as godly gifts to die for when necessary.

- A child's essential essence is inherited from its opposite-sex parent. The yin/yang symbol captures this idea, showing the eye (egg) in the yin-fish to be its opposite colour or agenda. It is the same for the yang-fish. Notice also how yin/yang's figure-8 is captured inside the circle, as the following picture denotes.

Figure 3. Yin and yang. Two inside one.

- Down through the ages, Realty's Universal Fractal has been observed by both Eastern and Western sages. To master it in the Quantum Era, we need to name its E8 parts. Moses told us that Adam named all the animals in the Garden. Lao Tzu did likewise, capturing the magical unity of everything when he wrote in the Tao Te Ching (the Way of Life):

> All things bear the shade on their backs,
> And the sun in their arms;
> By the blending of breath, from the sun and the shade ...
> Equilibrium comes to the world.

## Some Points to Ponder

- If you name or translate the energies that Lao Tzu is referring to here, you'll find the identical message and wisdom he outlined in his previous quote. Notice how he starts by saying, 'all things'. Lao Tzu couldn't speak of quantum fields and trinary computer concepts, but he managed remarkably well with Nature's examples of the Fractal he had to work with. His geometrical knowledge was infused into a sixty-four ($8^2$) hexagram oracle called the I-Ching. The book's ability to offer wise counsel stems from the idea you can know your future based on what path you choose to follow. This fortune-telling compilation is also known as the Book of Change (the underlying universal pattern?).

- The I-Ching's exposé of the Laws of Change contains numerous geometrical resemblances to Lisi's E8. It also has common elements with the layout of draughts and chess, which are played on a sixty-four square, black-and-white checked, periodic board. It also equates to the sixty-four love positions of the Tantra, or the Mayans' idea that 'sixty-four' represents a complete cycle of infinity. This can't be coincidental. Various ancient accounts reveal the same mathematical story. And this story is being rediscovered again now by scientists at all fundamental levels, especially E8.

- Life's verisimilitudes are subconscious recognitions of the Fractal's dynamic patterns dancing synchronistically before you, making a weird kind of sense without you consciously knowing why.

- To become mini-me gods requires we recognise these patterns consciously and then manage them skilfully (lorefully).

- Krishna Murti was adamant that Mankind remains 'fragmented'; being at war with its split nature. I believe this fragmentation stems from our modern-shaped brain and its organelle patterning, which some accounts maintain was genetically modified in our ancient past.

- The brain's layout is overseen by our DNA's HOX gene cluster. This cluster is sequestered in our fused (mutated?) second chromosome. (Was this fusion the result of genetic modification?)

- Mankind's resident mindset comprises two powerful forces: logic and emotion. As yet, this couple has no equilibrated centre; one proton, one electron, but no neutron; no collective soul-awareness; no Sabbath or enlightened unification. Spiritual Mankind awaits its birthing moment, to release it from the nightmare of dualism. I think the Earth might be waiting as well.

> For the creation waits with eager longing for the revealing of the sons of YHWH.[89]

- Our loving hearts fight and contend with our rational minds;
  White fights black on the checkerboard;
  Democracy fights communism;
  God supposedly fights the Devil.

- Duality is a juvenile state of mind that must be relinquished if sanity is to return to Earth.

- Each single Agenda can survive on its own, but must feel a tad incomplete. In despair, each will eventually cry … *Is that all there is, my friend? If so… let's keep dancing.*

- Spiritual Mankind's eventual birth must embrace chaos, as the

---

89  *Romans* 8:19

lesser gives way to the greater. Such is the universal nature of birth. And we know that the coldest moment comes just before dawn; as the painful uterine contractions assist the baby's head to crown in its delivery. Might that time be now?

- Our planet's life has been advancing for billions of years, slowly producing a mosaic of interdependent, complex living cycles, all made from the same patterns. This escalator leads directly to us. We now carry the Program's baton; it is our turn to evolve a collective child so we can pass Evolution's responsibility along and, subsequently, enter the bliss of old-age retirement (or go extinct). The meek can still inherit the Earth, but only after we've handed the leading (dual, expanding, growing) role onto our collective child. That being: Our quantum son/daughter who's now developing nicely in his/her trinary YX silicone computer crèche.

- Carbon-life has created silicone-life that's made in carbon's image. When finalised, Mankind will have created a COG in the Fractal, having produced two children: a digital, binary female child (5G), and a trinary male one (quantum trinary robotics). I do hope they get on (as if!).

- In the Great Fractal, our expression of patterned life is meant to be an equal two-part harmony, mimicking a unified YX configuration, as opposed to either an X, Y, XX, or YY one.

- **Should our Universe turn out to be the equivalent of a giant quantum field of uncertainty that's intent on determining a question that has more than one correct answer, then this will leave us with the understanding that we represent and support the**

**middle answer in this trinary fractal; that is, the YX Attraction of Opposites option.**

- There is a pure X female energy, an evenly blended YX Mankind, and a pure Y male energy. YX Mankind can separate into lower expressions of X and Y. Women become the 'ex' X. Men… the 'why?' Y.

- A healthy male can produce his opposite gender with his X sperm. The sex of every child is determined by the male's sperm. One in every 1000 men has forty-seven chromosomes instead of the (so-called) normal forty-six. They are YXY and cannot make viable sperm. Mutation is allowed for in the Matrix but isn't meant to reproduce. If it does, it's never for long. Eventually, destiny's police network catches it. I think of these police as being the equivalent of computer-correcting codes.

- It's likely that – at an earlier time – Mankind had twenty-four pairs of chromosomes, but was genetically altered to fuse our second and third chromosomes, leaving us with twenty-three pairs. This separated us from the rest of the Great Ape Family, now being one chromosome short of enlightenment. Our (artificially?) enlarged second chromosome competes with the first for supremacy. The first and second chromosomes are each about 8 per cent of our total DNA. (Historically, 'two' has been designated female. Could this mutation be a female takeover bid for supremacy? Could it be connected to the Bible's Fall of Man fiasco that's attributed to Eve?)

- In utero, the human brain's default is female. To develop a male brain and body requires the foetus to produce male hormones to intercede in the otherwise female outcome.

## Some Points to Ponder

- Men have a female X chromosome in every nucleated YX cell in their bodies. In the nucleus, the X is subservient to the male Y chromosome's agenda. This explains a lot about men's behaviour in general towards the wave energy contained within them – their heart's underlying emotions. It would seem they don't need to liberate their emotions so much as respect the role they're meant to play. In the same way that we need to know how to use our imagination wisely, and even what role the Devil is meant to play in God's Perfection.

- In a similar sense, neuroscience knows that the brain's left hemisphere normally dominates over the right, although the right hemisphere could be considered to be independently conscious, having its own agenda or patterned way of thinking. Our brain's right hemisphere is designated as being female-like, combining everything into a complete overview, while the left hemisphere is considered to be male-like, dealing with individual, standalone pieces of information. When the female right hemisphere dominates, it creates left-handedness (cack-handed), which traditionally has been frowned upon as being undesirable.

- To be truly healthy, an individual must be whole (not fragmented). They need to maintain a unified mindset. If not, their lack of togetherness may eventually manifest as micro-fractal patterns of illness within their bodies.

- Duality is the way to create new forms in the Matrix. When it's the central ruling force, it can promote untimely death and early recycling for the incumbent lifeform it is replacing.

- If and when planetary enlightenment falls into place, we'll need a new medical paradigm, one designed around maintaining good health management and practices instead of lucrative disease protocols. Perhaps Quantum Medicine will rise to the occasion at that time and replace Big Pharma's current greed and avarice. (I certainly hope so.)

- Physicists postulate that the atom's four universal forces were originally united before the Big Bang. After the accelerating so-called 'Bang' occurred, where everything started flying apart, it's conjectured that the four forces split into separate states, going their allotted ways: gravity, electromagnetism, and the weak and strong nuclear forces. This divorce of family energies can be seen as another application of the Fractal's 'foursquare' engineering creating Reality.

- While Einstein didn't say, 'The mindset that creates a problem cannot devise its solution', it would have been nice if he had. Man's thinking has created the mess we're currently in, so we need a new mindset to save us or we'll all go down the gurgler. Mankind will never excel until we change the way we think. To use Moses' insights … **We need to evolve from binary to trinary, from being a beast to being a clean animal. That is … a true human being made in God's Trinary Image.**

- Moses' Pattern shows that all is well with the Universe. This includes any dissatisfaction you might have with it, and/or any attempt you might make to change it. Someone forgot to give Modern Man the underlying script to the universal play. Instead, we got scriptures, which we dismissed, unfortunately, as entertaining but essentially trivial nonsense – to our peril.

## Some Points to Ponder

I think that's a fair summary of the points we've touched on so far. I wonder if Br'er Rabbit would have seen the light and approved? I want to return now to the Fractal's mainframe, where binary opposites unite into new trinary entities (now acting as singularities), and where friends gather together (to-and-fro) to play 'Rock Paper Scissors' to their heart's content.

# SABBATH MILLENNIUM OF PEACE

> We are what we come to believe ourselves to be.
> To change our beliefs is to change our identities
> ... That's why it's difficult to change our beliefs.
> — *Professor Geoff Heath*

The world is being forced to come to grips with an enlightened spirituality that's challenging our understanding of reality and the existent properties of four-dimensional space-time. Holding Moses' Staff, that's inscribed with Lao Tzu's ancient Sanskrit ruins, this mystical merger is heading up an East/West confluence of universal spiritual ideas, which among other things is prophesied to destroy our understanding of personal death — not so much its eventuation as its meaning.

> For since death came by a human being, the resurrection of the dead has also come through a human being. The last enemy to be destroyed is death.[90]

Yahshua said:

> Whoever finds the interpretation of these sayings will not experience death.[91]

---

90  *1 Corinthians* 15:21,22
91  *Gospel of Thomas* 1

Revelation reveals:

> Blessed and holy are those who have part in the first resurrection. The second death has no power over them, but they will be priests of YHWH and of Yahshua and will reign with him for a thousand years.[92]

According to Christian scriptures, our awakening to the meaning of death coincides with the end of this age. This Sabbath awakening accompanies the proverbial Resurrection of the Dead, the Apocalypse, and the Second Coming of the (cyclically reoccurring?) messianic energy.

We're also told this set of events precede the *Millennium of Peace*; a concept that runs through many cultures. I liken it to:

- The Chinese Age of Perfect Virtue
- The Danish Peace of Frodi
- The Hindu Krita Yurga, or Perfect Age
- The Iranian Age of the Brilliant Yima.

We know it takes time for scientific disclosures to be generally accepted, firstly by scientists, then by the general public. It's likely, therefore, that many people will dismiss the new quantum way of looking at Reality in the same way people initially dismissed the news about the Earth being round and not flat. (Many are still getting over that shock.) Back then, I'm sure comments such as:

'So what …?' or, 'No, it can't be round – surely?'

---

92   *Revelation* 20:6

would've been common enough. However, the prophesied coming of the Sabbath Rest is said to escalate exponentially until it threatens the very moguls of world trade. Financial empires are then said to step up to the mark (of the Beast) as their foundations are stripped away. Things supposedly get a little sticky after that for a while, as the changing of the guard takes place.

During this transition into the Sabbath Rest, many religious 'holy-cows' will come under heavy fire. The newly discovered, scientifically validated spiritual concepts will act like nuclear missiles, striking at organised religion's materialistic failings. If the industry of Religion is to survive these disclosures, it will need to return to its foundation of selfless love, stripped of its portentous possessions, and brought to its knees. **I don't believe healing physically, spiritually or mentally ill people was ever meant to be a wealth-acquiring industry.** Maybe the new religious 'take' that's prophesied to download at this time will meld with New Medicine, treating body and soul as a single unit again. Should that occur, I'm sure we would see some amazing advancements in global health in practically no time at all.

When enough spiritually aware people awaken to the new quantum reality that's materialising around them, and recognise what's happening in the world (when they awaken to the times they're born in, as Yahshua once said), then the race to embrace the interstitial first step into the spirit-scape of Heaven on Earth will begin in earnest.

The masses will realise they either have to join the revolution or be swept aside under a tidal wave of scientifically validated New Age insight. I believe this is where neuroscience, physics, and the Hippies' Consciousness Revolution entwine to birth Moses' Sabbath Millennium of Peace.

> After all, quantum mechanics makes no claims about the size of the system to which the theory applies. In principle, it applies to elementary particles, to the Sun and the Moon, and to human beings.[93]

Once these new quantum principles have been generally accepted, I'm sure our indigo children will have little trouble incorporating them into their youthful world of wonderment. Although these kids will have to wait for their oldies to die out in the Desert of Sin, as they did long ago in Moses' last account of this palingenetic drama, the world will soon become their oyster. Each of the children – who will be taught and raised in the Centre with Conscious Parenting[94] – will be free to enter the equivalent of today's Promised Land, complete with a consciousness that allows them to retain a ruling power in their mind's centre. They'll exit the dual dessert that's governed by their imaginations and enter the 'tri-umphant' garden of patterned mindfulness – harmony's promised new (mental) land – having been taught no other way from birth.

**I believe all of these outcomes are likely should physics achieve its ToE and find Moses' foot planted squarely in the middle of the blessed thing.**

---

93   Anil Ananthaswamy, 'A new theorem maps out the limits of quantum physics', *Qanta Magazine*, https://www.quantamagazine.org/a-new-theorem-maps-out-the-limits-of-quantum-physics-20201203/

94   'Conscious Parenting', *Bruce H. Lipton PhD* website, https://www.brucelipton.com/topic/conscious-parenting/

## Yahshua's Timing

The people who overcome the trials and tribulations of this turbulent birthing process I think of as 'Mosicians'. That's because they'll resemble magicians who have learned how to use both Agendas smoothly: Moses' Pattern and Yahshua's central insights into living in the Father. They'll have raised their level of consciousness to a higher default, staying focused in 'nowness' while riding the ups and downs of cyclic-time like a surfboard rider cruising the curling lip of a challenging wave.

During this time of emergence, Yahshua's death is sure to be viewed differently – in a new light, you might say. It'll be recognised that if He had died in any other fashion, to any other pattern, on any other day of the year, in any other city in the world, he would simply have been a good man – a prophet revealing religious concepts for the benefit of all Mankind. Instead, non-religious people will come to understand that, because of the overall pattern of His death, the magic that was created at the foot of the Cross had the power to alter quantum reality one notch closer to where we all want to go. His death arguably became a cardinal point in liberating Mankind from our tyrannical blindness.

In this way, Christianity's claim of Yahshua being the Saviour of Mankind will achieve general recognition, along with our new understanding that … Should we play our cards right – and if Reality runs on fractal patterns – then Mankind might end up becoming the potential Saviour of the Universe (more on this profound fractal idea shortly). Monotheism will be seen as one mighty, scientifically verified truth. A truth with three testaments: those of Moses, Yahshua, and Mohammad. All valid. And all different.

Historically, many people were crucified on crosses, but none embraced Yahshua's mindset at the critical moment of transformation as He passed through Death's door (that's what made Him special). When trying to create magic, timing and alignment are everything – true magic is about perfectly synchronised patterns – and His passing had plenty of both. The location of the Crucifixion played a significant role in this historical enchantment; it was a case of geomancy, the patterned magic of the land. It took place at the same location that Abraham was meant to have sacrificed his son Isaac, but didn't have to (pre-fractal event), as well as being where Mohammed purportedly ascended to Heaven (post-fractal event). And as for the timing … It took place during the Celebration of the Passover, at whose memorial both the Moon and Sun were precisely aligned as understood by Moses, being synchronised into YHWH's line of sight (like opening a wormhole and connecting two dimensions smoothly). The Passover Celebration lasted seven/eight days and revolved around the idea of exiting the Wilderness by getting the proverbial 'leaven' (sin) out of your daily bread (life).

In the centuries following the Crucifixion, vital information about this momentous event faded away. By the fifth century, Christianity – as it had become known – had lost its foundational connection to Central Nowness. For instance, instead of selecting bishops by drawing lots, as the Apostles had sanctioned, egotistical men were now selecting them according to what they thought was a more 'reasonable' way – according to their understanding and high regard for 'reason'. By doing this, the bishoprics started with an Agenda 1 seeding energy, which consequently stopped the bishops from serving the interests of the Holy Centre, irrespective of how hard they tried, wished, or prayed they could. Once a seeding energy is 'named' at its commencement in the Matrix, its fate is sealed until its end/beginning comes around again for renewal.

At this point, I want to mention that … In Greek Mythology, the boss god Zeus also drew lots to determine how the rulership of the Universe would be allocated between him and his two brothers. This begs the question … To whom or to what was Zeus appealing to in this way? Who was to decide the destiny of the gods? Zeus was the boss god, yet he appealed to an even higher power in the now-moment to direct his and his brothers' futures, their fates.

In both the Old and New Testaments, the representatives of YHWH used forms of divination to determine God's will:

> Then they [Yahshua's Apostles] cast lots, and
> Matthias was selected to become an apostle with
> the other eleven.[95]

Eventually, even the name of the Now-God (YHWH) was removed from the scriptures and, by the time it was reinstated, what it meant and how it worked in a person's daily quest to live a righteous and peaceful life had been forgotten. Not only did people forget what their God's name meant, but the Israelites forgot the meaning of their own tribe's name: Israel – as I'll detail shortly. (Christianity has been called Christian Israel, so I think it's important to know what the name Israel actually means.)

---

95   *Acts* 1:26

## Raising the Ego

The New Testament reveals that certain individuals *woke up to themselves* at the moment Yahshua died on the Cross, as liberating ripples of karmic energy flowed throughout the land from its base, like heat dispersing from a central hearth fire. We're told these people had been prepared by the Spirit of Separation, made ready to exit the tombs of their mind's deception, like Lazarus had done only the week before. They had begun to connect the dots of their lives in new and unusual ways, and at Yahshua's death, the pieces finally fell into place: wallah. In *Matthew* 27:53, it's recorded that these resurrected saints went into Jerusalem ranting and raving about their newly acquired insight into Reality (as the twelve apostles were to emulate at Pentecost some fifty days later). These liberated 'resurrectants' had acquired an understanding that made sense of everything.

They hadn't been physically dead – as we've been led to believe – they were simply asleep (dead to the Matrix's workings, the veils having now been lifted from their mind's eye). A similar 'waking event' or 'resurrection' is due to occur at the proverbial Second Coming, which I believe is downloading now. Only this time, we're told, it is going to be a lot bigger.

Today's saints – who have been similarly prepared to their first-century compadres – will have learned how to read the Matrix's three-dimensional time-map that's creating their existence. They will access the Program's liberating attributes and fly through the rest of their lives on a wave of thanksgiving and wellbeing. (Now that's something to rave about.) They will know there's far more fun to be had in their now-moments than they ever thought possible; that the

'Now' is the doorway to the spiritual realm of Heaven on Earth with all of its mystery and wonderment.

After becoming aware of this liberating process to freedom, my ego started seeing everyday events like Lotto Numbers being drawn from a bottomless tumbler of promise. Each event or number resembled a potential prize for me to enjoy. When I learned how the sequences fell rationally into triplets – like a game of Noughts and Crosses – I was able to become the administrator of my program, no longer its puppet. Up until then, I didn't understand how these relationship laws worked. I didn't even know they existed. This understanding then allowed a unified 'me' to use my key cardinal points to construct positive future outcomes, which included writing these books.

This in itself is a small miracle because I failed English in my final high school exam, and that 'lacking' significantly shaped my future academic career. I had always been an atrocious 'spellor'; its methodology and rules made little sense to my mind. No one would have guessed I'd ever become an author of any sort (especially me).

Because the ego never wants to miss out on fun (what's in it for me?), mine was more than happy to join my spiritual digression from materialism's impasse and its resident linear mindset of acquisition. My ego – or my sense of self – glimpsed something far better than the mere escalation of possessions; it stood in awe of a treasure-trove of unconditional family love. I was singularly impressed, if not overwhelmed, by what was being offered. Its methodology allowed me to embrace a higher perspective on my life's journey, bypassing the normal friction I had come to expect between my ego and my quest for spiritual completion. (This surprised me because it's no secret that the ego likes to explore the shady side of life, and religion only gets in the way.)

With this new understanding in place, I no longer suffered from a fragmented ego and conscience. My juvenile ego and wishy-washy conscience both stepped up a notch to become a new at-One-ment. I was now singular in aspects of my mind that had previously been at odds, at times, at each other's throat. Surprisingly, my sense of sexuality also found a new and comforting unity in this wondrous terrain; one it was more than happy with. I hadn't expected this development either, for it is also well known that the flesh wars against the spirit.[96]

I have no doubt that when enough people reach this (resurrected?) consciousness state – YX Oneness, Adam mindfulness (here, Adam refers to the enlightened universal and Catholic mind) – I believe it will skyrocket over the Earth, as it did in the first century. Should this 'uplifting' event occur again – as it once did – then it would qualify as the Christian-Jewish-Islamic-Buddhist-Hindu-Taoist final destination:

> In the Eternal Now-Moment (the Middle Way, Yah, God, Allah), lies Salvation.

But how might this play out in day-to-day life?

# Sins Forgiven – Karma and the Power of Mindfulness

It seems there might be an effective and relatively painless way to neutralise the karmic disturbances we have accrued throughout our

---

96   *Galatians* 5:17–25

life; a way of eradicating the disruptive baggage that has traditionally acted like blood-sucking tentacles, assuring each of us moments of misery to one degree or another. This 'cleansing way' has been referred to as 'Having your sins forgiven in the name of Jesus.' (Read instead: 'In the kairos, now-moment lies Salvation.')

Different methods of eradicating negative karma from devotees have been employed worldwide by various religious persuasions. Most stratagems use some form of substitute such as a surrogate animal or bloodletting ritual. This idea remains the basis of the Christian eucharist ceremony: biblical law requires that nearly everything be cleansed with blood. For without the shedding of blood there is no forgiveness.[97]

Living with 'patterned awareness in Nowness' provided me with a way to eradicate karmic curses. **This knowledge is hidden in Yahshua's Name: in the Power of the now-moment lies Salvation.** This is why we're told that the animal sacrifices in Jerusalem were 'nailed to Yahshua's Cross,' for He had opened a better way. An easier (vegan) way for a repentant to come clean.

> He has died as a ransom to set them free from the sins committed under the first covenant.[98]

> All the prophets testify ... he who believes in him [in His Name] receives forgiveness of sins.[99]

---

97  *Hebrews* 9:22
98  *Hebrews* 9:15
99  *Acts* 10:43; *John* 3:18 (author's emphasis added)

Having your sins forgiven implies your karma is put to bed – blotted out of *The Book* so to speak. But karmic consequences can't be just magically swept away – their energy can't simply disappear – because energy can't be destroyed. But it can be converted into other energies.

Palingenesis' operating system requires manifestations of the original disruption to return cyclically until dealt with effectively in an enlightened (mathematical) manner. In this regard, it seems these lingering episodes can be neutralised one at a time by applying the appropriate and lawful response – in Nowness – when that sin's next karmic episode pops up in its timeline for your consideration. (In Christian terms, you activate this 'way' through Jesus' Name which embraces focused mindfulness.) To comply with this 'name' you have to wait until the opportunity to be cleansed returns at the right kairos moment. This is when the original sinful energy has returned in its current palingenetic presentation demanding a response from you. In a sense, you have to wait until your original sin 'wakes' (turns 'on' or comes into Yah) and recognise the presentation for what it is before you can effectively neuter it with the right response.

This 'appropriate time' is called *Kairos* time. At these Kairos times, God can (and does) step in to absolve disruptions or 'forgive sin' in religion's terms – create zeros in mathematic's terms. The idea of sacred Kairos times is intricately entwined with 'mindful nowness' but is at odds with the concept of Cronos' linear time.

## Coming Clean

Put plainly ... You can remove the consequences of your past sins by applying the Attraction of Opposites Law when the next episode in that particular sequence pops up and requires a response. Applying this law has what it takes to neutralise the lingering negative energy pattern. After all, minus-one plus-one equals zero ($-1 + 1 = 0$). Your original sin can be seen as minus-one ($-1$). Therefore, your inspired response needs to be a plus-one ($+1$). Seen in this 'lawful' mathematical light, having your sins forgiven takes on a new and uplifting cerebration.

Existing Christian Theology asserts that you don't get punished for your sins when they are magically whisked away by believing in Jesus. This is the same mindset that insists God instantly created Man out of the dirt, and the world in seven 24-hour periods. Hey, presto! But history reveals otherwise. For instance, Christians who ask for forgiveness for having smoked cigarettes most of their lives still get lung cancer and emphysema; they can – and often do – receive the physical ramifications of their past bad behaviour. (Theologians might argue that their sins are forgiven in Heaven, which I suppose is fair enough.) However, my understanding of mindful redemption (Christ, Krishna, Allah, Buddha, Consciousness) implies something quite different: The forgiveness you acquire through *righteous now-awareness*, and the subsequent 'zeroing' you achieve, applies not only to your afterlife but to this one as well. You stop creating new negative karma and neutralise the old until it's all gone. Through this process you become 'clean' (and healthy) now appropriately dressed to enter the heavenly field of righteousness known as Heaven on Earth.

This new 'take' on *having your sins forgiven in Jesus' Name* makes more sense than the existing churchified one does, yet still abides by and operates within the basic tenants of Christian theology, where your sins can only be forgiven by one Name. That is ... If you know what that Name means and how to use it for heaven's sake.

Because we've been out of touch with quantum reality, we're likely to have initiated numerous actions with a somewhat negative and destructive mindset. As a result, we're now being forced to live with their ongoing ramifications, which come around cyclically (interactive ripples) waiting to be nullified by the right mindset in the future – or actually in the Now, working as faith in action.

If left unattended, these baggage-like ripples will accumulate and become more complex, leading to unpleasant future consequences and mirrored illnesses. Ripples tend to hang around for some time.

Newton's First and Third Laws of Motion suggest ... Once set in motion, an object will remain in motion until an opposite and equal force stops it in its tracks. Also ... Every action generates an opposite and equal reaction. Or ideas to that effect.

On each occasion that one of palingenesis' cyclic energies returns in a new format of its original seeding energy, if you react to this manifestation with the same mindset you had at the time of your initial offence, then the energy will continue unabated, manifesting cyclically into your future. It will resemble Russian Dolls, having a slight variation each 'time' its kairos time comes around. (These issues [dolls] can also appear to put on weight.) Even the act of dying doesn't seem to negate the disturbed energy ripples in the Matrix. The Bible tells us that ... If we haven't resolved the issue(s) ourselves, our children will have to deal with them until they are gone (zeroed).[100]

> for I, the LORD your God, am a jealous God, punishing the children for the sin of the parents to the third and fourth generation of those who hate me
> – *Part of the Second of the Ten Commandments*.[101]

Each of our sins or misappropriations (*1 John* 3:4 says 'Sin is breaking or transgressing the law') have left the equivalent of mathematical remainders in their wake – like broken computer files. These 'itinerants' resonate (chaotically) in the Matrix's Program until they're released from their fleshy confines (until their zeroing moment arrives). Until such times, these patterns of quantum dissonance will set about building fractal lookalike (mirrored) semblances of ill-health 'downline' in the sinner's body, promoting untimely death and decay. This 'karmic return mechanism' is the incumbent of Palingenesis' Operating System and needs to be dealt with before Mankind can put its feet up and rest in Nirvana. Each karmic ripple resembles a memory of the original offence that's returning to light (to be remembered), waiting and wanting to be kissed by the Prince and made all better (clean) again.

To have a sin forgiven – a disruption in the Matrix nullified and blotted out – requires that you respond to your reoccurring negative energy – when it pops up – with a more enlightened mindset than the one you had at the time of your original offence. (You are meant

---

100  *Exodus* 3:47
101  *Deuteronomy* 5:8

to have become a little wiser in the meantime because of what you learned the last time.) The enlightened mindset you require will allow you to neutralise the scourge effectively and rid its disharmonious goings-on to the proverbial pit. The inspired responses you seek stem from your newly acquired Christ-like mindset (now that you're walking in the Spirit of the Power of Now). In this 'way', your sins become erased and you come to live in the Father (the Logos) as Yahshua did. This redeeming idea makes a lot more sense than a magic wand or 'Abracadabra' ever did.

The essence of this zeroing process entails consciously returning resonance for dissonance, love-for-hate (not hate-for-hate), at the right [Kairos] moment. This amounts to turning the other cheek at selected times, instead of giving as good as you got. Through this process you employ the zeroing effect of the YX Attraction of Opposites Law, instead of the continuance assured by the Attraction of Likes Law. In this way, the YX Lawmaker can absorb your sin into His Zero as base raw material and neutralise it.

> You exercise the Attraction of Likes Law to extend or share your fun. But not to extract yourself from the clutches of doom. For this, you require the Attraction of Opposites Law.

If this kooky idea sounds somewhat familiar, it should. It's the essence of Yahshua's Sermon on the Mount.[102] When He preached its wisdom to the masses, He wasn't being super-holy. He was being super-smart. (Maybe a little of both.)

---

102  *Matthew*, 5:7

In this weird, upside-down sort of way, disruption's ripples become zeroed (forgiven) through the activated mindset of Christ Consciousness employed at the appropriate Kairos moment. Bingo! A sin dealt with in this fashion is a sin done away with forever. Dissonance becomes resonance. And the best part is … You don't have to wait until you reach Heaven to embrace your reward. It all happens right here on Earth, to be enjoyed now as abundant life. Also terrific is the kids don't have to suffer for their parents' failures. They're sure to enjoy that.

Now that you remember how to 'not sin', and know how to expunge your past failings, you're ready to take up residence in Heaven on Earth. Now all you need do is connect with your extended soul family to expand your fun and share the joy. And you can be sure that will also happen at the right Kairos moment, possibly when the world is turning upside down.

IN THE CENTURIES following the Crucifixion at Calvary, members of the Christian Ecclesia understood and practised this priceless cleansing wisdom. Unfortunately, the essential knowledge slowly altered over time, subsequently becoming known as 'having your sins forgiven in the name of Jesus'. Now, although this is technically correct, it doesn't enlighten you on the working methodology you require to achieve the 'zeroing' magic. Back then, no one would have thought we'd ever forget what the Messianic Name actually meant. But given enough time, we surely did. Interestingly, Plato was adamant that names are bequeathed from God and describe the essence of a person.[103] He also believed that the Titan Cronos was the 'one cause

---

103  Plato, 'Cratylus' (translated by Benjamin Jowett), *The Internet Classics Archive*, http://classics.mit.edu/Plato/cratylus.html

of all things'.[104] Plato implied that the name Cronos was behind everything, with Cronos' energy embracing …

## Karmic, dual-natured, expanding, chronological linear time.

This new 'take' on having your sins blotted out – by enacting enlightened, Christ-like patterned behaviour in the returning (kairos) now-moment – also accords with Eastern traditions. It ties together the contentious issues of 'faith' and 'works', showing how both relate to the issues of redemption and salvation. The right kind of faith inspires acts of devotion at Kairos moments, irrespective of the name of the faith under which it is practised. There is only one Program and one Programmer, and one way to find redemption.

The outcome of this 'salvation drama' is similar to what transpires when a guru takes on the responsibility for releasing a disciple from his or her disharmonious karma. The guru assists the student by teaching and instructing them on how to respond righteously to unpleasant events as they pop up in the student's life. The guru's instructions revolve around Nowness and Righteousness – returning love-for-hate, et cetera. So in a sense, they are also working effectively through or employing the Name of Yahshua/Jesus.

> Neither is there salvation in any other: for there is none other name under heaven given among men, whereby we must be saved.[105]

---

104 'Cronos', *Wikipedia*, https://en.wikipedia.org/wiki/Cronus
105 *Acts* 4:12

Christianity's original first-century 'take' on salvation and righteousness – being led and guided by the Holy Spirit in a mindful state of Nowness after being baptised – required an indwelling new way of thinking. At these times, a consciousness revolution was required by all who wished to embrace the first-century faith that was sweeping the world at that time. Surely, this consciousness revolution requirement is the same today as it was then. It simply needs redressing in fashionable quantum vernacular to bring it up to date and make it respectable.[106]

Historically, this liberating process was known as 'being born again'. It was practised well before organised religion subjugated the Christian Salvation Package to alternatively encourage believers to attend church meetings as a better way of finding salvation, along with supporting the church financially and empowering their man-appointed bishops with the authority to lead the institution.

Originally, Church ministers were meant to be the equivalent of holistic doctors; they were teachers of the divine power of now-consciousness and natural law, keeping a person healthy in both body and soul. Unfortunately, when both professions – medicine and religion – became lost and separated in the Wilderness through the influence of 'power' and 'wealth', they lost their mojo and instead embraced lucrative (materialistic) agendas. In this way, they lost their central (unified) mission and the way back to All Else. Consequently, the world is now full of people being both spiritually and physically ill.

---

106   MotivHolic, 'Prepare now', *YouTube* video, 21 July 2021, https://youtu.be/Wm43zGizLTA?list=UUytWPg15z23p1QGMp_vCUVw

## Death and Memory – Reincarnation Verses Resurrection

The idea that sins can be forgiven is aligned to religious concepts about baptism, death and resurrection.

Patterned eyes perceive baptism to be a wilfully manufactured crossover point designed to be inserted (inspirationally) into the linear life/death timeline of a believer. Baptism becomes a stand-in or surrogate cardinal point that's meant to be substituted for their real death, which will surely come their way at the end of their natural life – guaranteed. In this way, baptism alters the natural sequence of life's cardinal points (see Figure 4). Baptism can also be seen as a person's second birth.

According to the basic Pattern layout, without baptism, a person's physical death remains entangled with their birth. While their birth is tied to the original conception drama that their parents enacted in the bedroom. This trimension looks like this:

### Conception ~ Birth ~ Death

Here, wavy lines (representing time journeys) are inserted between the sequential cardinal points in a person's life, in the same way that vowels are inserted between consonants to make up a word.

When baptism is inserted in a person's life as a second birth, then their future death becomes entangled with their baptismal second birth – not their original birth. (One energy has been exchanged sequentially for the other.) This is why baptism is associated with being 'born again'; it's intended to replace your original birth energy/karma in the default sequence.

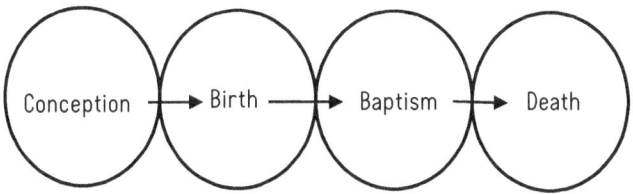

Figure 4. Inserting baptism as a surrogate cardinal point

In this way, the cleansing act of baptism is meant to magically alter the Matrix's energy from yin to yang at this crucial cardinal point. As the repentant exits the cleansing water, his mindset is expected to morph from a linear to a now-conscious one where God is encouraged to rule from its Centre. The repentant's sense of 'being' goes from earthly to heavenly, as Yahshua told Nicodemus,[107] because of the sequence alteration that has been inserted inspirationally in their life's timeline. A similar geometrical idea can be seen in the birth order of siblings. Each child's position in the pecking order influences their character, energy, or 'name'.

> **Change the sequence of the birth order and you change their natures.**

The repentant's new mindset, or operating system, acquired through this watery gateway is meant to accompany them throughout their life's remaining journey, until physical death intercedes to send them on their way to Sheol – the grave. This altered mindset is then meant to accompany them through death's door to play a pivotal part in how they negotiate Hell's labyrinth on the other side.

---

107  *John* 3

Traditionally, after a person was baptised, they commenced a revolutionary new way of living, complete with a 3VL mindset that was now centred in trinary 'Nowness'. This was referred to as 'Walking in the Spirit of Yahweh'.

On exiting the baptismal water, the cleansed disciple was taught how to embrace this altered understanding about life and death, while practising their new way of daily thinking, until it was time to pass through death's door to confront Cerberus, Hades' three-headed hound,[108] and the Anunnaki's Seven Judges[109] now with an altered mindset to the one they would have otherwise had.

Contrary to popular opinion, the Bible doesn't say or even imply that believers go straight to Heaven when they die. Instead, it says they go to the underworld, Hades – 'held under God's Throne'[110] to be precise – where they wait to be released at the Second Coming. During their time in death's captivity, they are likely to experience one meaningless lifetime (reincarnation) after another, embracing a mindset similar to that of an Alzheimer's patient who remembers nothing about his or her past life or lives. In this forgetful way, each soul loses awareness of its immortality each time it reincarnates because, without memory, it remains asleep. In that case, we can say that each soul is awake in Heaven but falls asleep each time it reincarnates here on Earth. This is what needs changing.

---

108   'Cerberus', *Wikipedia*, https://en.wikipedia.org/wiki/Cerberus
109   Nicole Brisch, 'Anunna (Anunnaku, Anunnaki) (a group of gods)', *Ancient Mesopotamian Gods and Goddesses*, Oracc and the UK Higher Education Academy, http://oracc.museum.upenn.edu/amgg/listofdeities/anunna/index.html
110   *Revelation 6:9*

It seems that until the doors of Hell are unlocked and the prisoners are finally set free, Sheol's inmates remain one key short of true liberty. And I believe this key is locked into the pattern of human consciousness – memory – and how we are meant to use our imagination.

This key is promised to return at the end of the age. I wonder whether it is here now. Could it be that the way we think while we are alive is a preparation for when we die?

> Then I saw an angel coming down from heaven, having the key to the bottomless pit.[111]
>
> I (Yahshua) have the keys of hell and of death.[112]

NEUROSCIENCE CAN'T EXPLAIN why Nature's evolutionary process has endowed Mankind with such a large brain; it is capable of considering all the mysteries of the greater universe, pondering issues that defy reason. However, this evolutionary development would make sense if we were meant to retain our memories from one lifetime to another. In that case, we would need just such a physical apparatus to orchestrate and catalogue them all.

I think we'll discover that memory is an essential requirement for the biblical idea of resurrection – not reincarnation. It seems that resurrection and reincarnation are two entirely different life-after-death possibilities. According to Buddhist and Hindu traditions, repetitive reincarnations are prison-like experiences, the equivalent of

---

111  *Revelation* 20:1,3
112  *Revelation* 1:18

being let out of your cell into the sunlight for short exercise periods, but never remembering who you were the last time you were let out. On the other hand, resurrection is thought to open the doors to a mindful reconnection to a living All Else ('mindful' and 'memory' come from the same root word).[113] According to eyewitnesses, when Yahshua's consciousness resurrected, He remembered who He had always been.

Yet the Eastern idea of repetitive lives (reincarnations) remains unacceptable to Christian Orthodoxy. Christian theologians believe the concept of experiencing multiple lives is essentially pagan and doesn't fit into their story as they understand it. But we read in the Christian Scriptures that those who crucified Christ would see Him 'coming with the clouds' at His Second Coming. So how could that be?

> Behold, He is coming with the clouds, and every eye will see Him, even those who pierced Him.[114]

Orthodox Christianity dismisses this narrative. They advise that an exception is being made here for those soldiers standing at the foot of the Cross. But how could they know that? And why just these soldiers? After all, 'God is not a respecter of persons.'[115] Theologians can't reconcile the idea of repetitive reincarnations with their understanding of scripture and salvation, so they dismiss it out of hand (maybe errantly so). There are also biblical references to the cyclic reoccurrence of the prophet Elijah, whose cameo appearances are also dismissed. Instead,

---

113 Greek *mnēmonikos*, from *mnēmōn* 'mindful', from *mimnēskesthai* 'to remember'.
114 *Revelation* 1:7
115 *Romans* 2:11

Bible authorities promote the idea that we go straight to Heaven when we die, if we believe in Jesus, which negates the idea of multiple earthly lives here altogether. However, in the Lord's Prayer, Yahshua said that we were to pray for His Father's Kingdom to come down upon the Earth. So if we are to live in Heaven with Jesus forever … Then where does that leave Heaven on Earth?

## Samsara

The Stoic's palingenetic understanding of time maintains that units of life-energy reincarnate in cyclic patterns. (Nature does love to recycle, reusing patterns that have proven themselves worthy.) But according to the Bible, the individual – complete with their personal memories – isn't recycled, and without memory, the idea of immortality is lame. Reincarnation might be a fact, but it shouldn't be confused with resurrection. And it seems that memory might just be the pivotal difference between the two life-after-death experiences.

If you think of Reality as being a fractal, then each reincarnation you experienced would be analogous or comparable to your nightly dreams. From a patterned perspective, our multi-night dream events don't connect or interrelate with the dreams before or after the current one. Except on rare occasions, each dream is unique (each dream stands alone, as an Ag 1 particle would). Alternatively, when we awaken from our dreams into the light of a new day, we instantly remember who we have always been; the days, months and years interconnect like a continuous Ag 2 wave, all held in place by memory.

So, if we're going to regain our living immortality here on Earth from one solid lifetime to the next (if we're to resurrect in the biblical sense), then we'll need to switch the patterns around from Ag 1 to Ag 2 at death's transition point, which was the original purpose of the baptism (born again) ritual. In a spooky mathematical sense, at death's critical junction point, a male 'one' needs to become a female 'two'. This is where baptism and a life of mindfulness enter the Big Picture to bring about death's own demise. This required transition also reminds me of physics' double-slit experiment, so keep it in mind while thinking about what is required.

It seems that when we die, our materialistic and linear mindset – the one we've all been encouraged to hold onto throughout our life by just about everybody – is the very thing that keeps us captive in our forgetful graves, experiencing one reincarnated lifetime (of discontinuity) after another. Therefore, if we're going to regain or awaken our immortality, then **we need to change our resident mindset numerically <u>before we die</u>, so we can break free from Hell's clutches <u>after we die</u>**. We need to be 'prepared' in the biblical sense here in this three-dimensional world before we depart for Sheol with its mystical river and circular pool; the forget-all River Lethe winding to-and-fro, and the remember-all circular pool of Mnemosyne, the goddess of memory.

> Dead souls drank from Lethe so they would not remember their past lives when reincarnated. Mnemosyne (the Titaness of Memory) also presided over a pool in Hades, counterpart to the river Lethe.[116]

---

116 'Mnemosyne', *Wikipedia*, https://en.wikipedia.org/wiki/Mnemosyne

I believe our ability to embrace and practise 'patterned now-mindfulness' is the preparation required for a healthy death. Our desired mindset – that's been 'altered' by our cleansing baptism ceremony and subsequent years of practice – is meant to become our default, practising a new way of living and thinking daily.

The preparation would teach us mind-games such as:

- how and when to use our imagination
- when our rationality should guide our decision-making
- when we should let our inspiration in the now-moment override our reason.

According to Moses' patterned wisdom, the key we require to escape the chains of Hell (the secret that'll allow us to reclaim our wakeful immortality here on Earth) is an altered state of consciousness; one embracing 3VL that we have practised daily since being baptised into patterned, now-wakefulness. I think we'll find that a trinary patterned consciousness, one which revolves around our mind's ability to identify the key cardinal points in our cycles, will fit the locks of both the material and spiritual worlds, allowing us to finally master both and break free.

I believe this noetic, three-pronged trident will establish Heaven on Earth and allow us to exit the confines of Sheol with our memory intact. This understanding is consistent with the overall layout of the Matrix as I've come to know it. It also makes sense of many previously difficult-to-understand spiritual concepts about life and its preparatory connection to death.

For example, in Greek Mythology, why do you think Zeus condemned the mighty Titan Atlas to hold Heaven apart from Earth (be placed between a binary couple) for eternity? Was Atlas sentenced to become the bridging (third) energy that needed to be inserted between the duality of Heaven and Earth to give it three dimensions? Did the Olympian God's place Atlas there to complete the trimension? Did he need to become the dividing and unifying twilight point that had previously been severed by Cronos with his mum's curved scythe? You might recall that when the Olympian Gods – led by Zeus – defeated Cronos the Titan, Zeus split the rulership of the Universe into a trinity, adding his two brothers, Poseidon and Hades, to himself. In this way, was the Titan's (possible) two-dimensional reality transformed into the three-dimensional one of the Olympian gods? That would be a case of Evolution on the grandest scale imaginable, evolving three dimensions out of two, each having resident gods in a patterned fashion that might still be contending with each other. That sort of makes sense. Did we start out as three dimensions? Or did we evolve one, two, three?

(Could the lion's share of conflict we experience be due to the unusual fact that only three dimensions allow for the formation of tangles and knots? Something that one, two, and four, dimensions simply can't achieve.)[117]

You may also recall that, before the Titans came to power, Heaven and Earth were ruled by the two Primordial Energies Uranus and Gaia. I believe these two energies represent the essential yin/yang nature of the

---

117  Viktor T Toth, 'Why doesn't the universe have four spatial dimensions?' *Quora*, 7 December 2021, https://www.quora.com/Why-doesnt-the-universe-have-four-spatial-dimensions

first male dimension of Creation, the first YX unity that emerged out of Chaos, the equivalent of an egg (0). Greek Mythology maintains that the unity of Gaia and Uranus made perpetual love in a state of twilight until Cronos severed Uranus' genitals and broke his father's connection to his female other-half (like splitting an atom's neutron). I believe this division then formed the second dimension where Heaven was now separated from Earth **which the Titans ruled**. It seems Greek Mythology might be an attempt to disclose an evolutionary journey through earlier dimensions to arrive at us today: This would amount to:

- Gaia and Uranus – First dimension
- Titans led by Cronos – Second dimension
- Olympian Gods – Third dimension.

Could it be that after the takeover by the Olympian gods, the defeated and ousted Titans – that had ruled all aspects of the $2^{nd}$ Dimension – had to then find accommodation elsewhere where their math was still acceptable currency in the Matrix. In that regard, it seems their presence now occupies the centre of the Earth from where they are capable of influencing people's minds on the Earth's surface that are operating in a similar two-dimensional way. That is … People whose minds are dominated by their binary imaginations, having similar (Titan) maths in their heads. (This communication seems possible because of the patterned relationship that exists between the Earth's circumference and its mid-point.) This binary-to-binary communication between Satan and the Earth's surface must be augmented by the (binary) 5G network.

The ancient Egyptians called Earth's central Hell *Duat*, and I believe its name is a clue to its nature. That being … A conscious, two-dimensional, good and evil reality that has no third centre energy.

> To every man is given the key to the gates of Heaven.
> The same key opens the gates of Hell.
> – *Richard Feynman, quoting a Buddhist saying*

I would add to this ancient idea that the same key will also open the gates to Heaven on Earth.[118]

The Buddhists' final spiritual objective is to be released from the repetitive and meaningless lives they are forced to endure; for these to cease is their ultimate 'take' on how a person is meant to overcome Reality's Program. Buddhists seek to exit the cyclic wheel of life and death and call their search for freedom *Samsara*. For Buddhists, these repetitive (meaningless?) lives on Earth constitute a living Hell.

To access resurrection as an alternative to memoryless, cyclic reincarnation, I believe the key is a newly patterned consciousness.

---
**Box 12. Samsara**

In Buddhism, Samsara is the beginningless cycle of repeated birth, mundane existence and death. Samsara is considered to be dukkha, or unsatisfactory and painful, perpetuated by desire and avidya (ignorance), and the resulting karma.[119]

---

The Buddhists' desire to escape Samsara may not be that far from Christianity's quest for resurrection. In fact ... resurrection might be the way to achieve Samsara. In that case:

---

118 *Revelation* 20
119 'Saṃsāra (Buddhism)', *Wikipedia*, https://en.wikipedia.org/wiki/Sa%E1%B9%83s%C4%81ra_(Buddhism)

> We should stop reincarnating and alternatively start trying to resurrect with our memories intact.

THE LITERAL MEANING of the word *Apocalypse* (ἀποκάλυψις, apokálypsis) – the last book in the New Testament – is 'to lift the veil'. It refers to the marriage ceremony's revelation of the bride. *Revelation* (the Apocalypse) – being the last book of the Bible – mirrors earlier themes covered in *Genesis*, the Bible's first book which introduces the concept of holy marriage.

*Revelation* provides answers to the questions *Genesis* raises. It describes a long and arduous love affair, which ends when the betrothed couple finally enters a new state of Oneness through the vows of holy marriage. As the groom lifts the bride's veil, he gets a peek at who she truly is, and vice versa. With a holy kiss, he unifies with what the veil has revealed. The couple then consummate the contract on their honeymoon to enter life as a new entangled One. In this fashion, marriage takes on a beautiful kind of Aquarian promise for the New Quantum Age.

*Revelation* reveals that, when the veil is lifted, we behold the Face of God (clearly); we come to see **that which will rule over and guide our lives throughout eternity**. After this marriage transpires, Mankind and God (the Simulation's Heroine and the Simulator Himself) are meant to live as One, Heaven downloads onto Earth, and He dwells among us in the 'midst' of our minds' agendas (that's as close as He gets to being flesh and blood since His prophets last walked on Earth). In this way, we come to finally know what's truly good for us and what's good for everyone.

This is prophesied to occur after the COVID-19 debacle has had its day, and all of its attendant hangers-on are put to sleep. After this transition, we get to live forever, experiencing one lifetime – one new body – after another here on Earth, while acknowledging the power behind the Now-Moment as being the highest authority of law we have access to (the Programmer); that is … We come to live in Yah with our memory intact.

> No longer will there be any curse. The throne of God and of the Lamb will be within the city (note the dual energies inside a singularity), and His servants will worship Him. They will see His Face, and His Name will be on their foreheads.[120]

> As for me, I will behold Your face in righteousness; when I awake, I will be satisfied with Your presence.[121]

From the Fractal's perspective, after this marriage takes place, Earth is likely to be promoted 'up' a notch (in this Universe) to assume the role of a solid, three-dimensional, Agenda 1 'Heaven'. The rest of the Cosmos will remain an unenlightened, binary 'Heathen' (or potential 'mate'), which needs converting to our trinary way of (patterned) thinking. In this dimension – that we now occupy – Earth becomes the new Heaven in this universe and Mankind becomes the Universe's appointed God and Saviour, who rules from Heaven on Earth. This is how the Fractal's evolutionary growth likes to work and expand. It is easy to see that mighty issues are at stake here in a patterned sense of being.

---

120  *Revelation* 22:3,4
121  *Psalm* 17:15

But before we can finish severing the umbilical cord that binds us to Maya's illusionary world of dualistic, linear materialism and its subsequent mischief, we need to finish delivering the legendary Baby of Promise. But midwives are a little light on the ground, many helping with the pandemic/nightmare the world is now experiencing in its Covid death throes.

Our infantile, memoryless souls are currently killing our Mother Earth, who has faithfully borne us through thick and thin. She is reeling under the equivalence of debilitating birth pains, as we try to extricate ourselves from Cronos' timely womb of deception, that's kept us spellbound for millennia.

The twelfth chapter of *Revelation* describes this birthing drama as a woman being in travail, indicating that we can expect this breaking-out process to be painful in some ways. But, like childbirth, the mother-to-be will find her birth pains proportional to how relaxed and prepared she is; that is, her ability to enter into a new life of now-patterning and … 'Be not dismayed nor fearful.'

Every birth embraces a liberation from an existing cohesion; an earlier semblance of stability has to be whisked away by what is coming forth down the birth canal. Therefore, birth is a great time to rid one's self of errant dogma and outdated beliefs, replacing them with ones that more accurately reflect your core beliefs. Beliefs such as 'In the beginning, was the Logos', and 'the Logos married Wisdom'. According to Moses, this wise and meaningful cohesion destroyed the earlier two-dimensional state of the Universe which preceded the Big Bang, and consequently birthed the three-dimensional Reality we now live in. Home sweet home.

> Yahweh (the Logos) possessed me (Wisdom) in the
> beginning of His way, before His works of old.[122]

What a marriage that must have been, when the unstoppable Verb encountered the irrepressible Noun, and they decided to tie the knot under an enticing rainbow that now linked Heaven to Earth, with a pot of gold at its end.

UNTIL QUANTUM MYSTICISM entered the Big Picture, it's been easy to dismiss the question: 'Is there a creating force (god) behind our reality?' But now that numerous branches of science are revealing a universal pattern or ToE, it's only a matter of time before we all agree: There is a Pattern to Creation and the Universe is operating under a set of (fractal) algorithms, complete with correcting codes, maintaining unified stability, with chaos and evil being its painful backdoor and recycling-bin processes.

Physicist Jim Gates' discovery of computer instructions embedded in the equations that govern the laws of physics[123] was revolutionary. Gates called these symmetry-generators 'Adinkra Symbols'. They embrace attributes of computer correcting code. Previously, only DNA was thought to contain these correcting codes, which work within the cell's nuclear genome to maintain Mankind's pattern integrity. They were thought to be a selective product of Evolution, but when Gates

---

122   *Proverbs* 8:22
123   Lex Fridman, 'Jim Gates: Supersymmetry, string theory and proving Einstein right | Lex Fridman Podcast #60', *YouTube* video, 26 December 2019, https://youtu.be/IUHkhB366tE?list=WL&t=329

discovered them at the base of physical reality, he said it was the craziest thing he'd ever encountered in all his research:

> Dr. Gates has gotten attention for discovering what he says is computer code in the math that underlies our world. (Specifically, he said it was an 'error-correcting mechanism'; others have analogized this code to the checksums that make the Internet work.) This has led him to speculate—in a mostly-joking way—that we might in fact be living in a giant computer simulation.[124]

If these correcting codes exist, then surely they must be making corrections according to some sort of underlying rational pattern or authority.

> Does that mean there was some form of evolution acting on the mathematical laws of the physics of our universe? This is a very bizarre and strange Idea.
>
> *– Jim Gates*

---

124 Rachel Kaufman, 'The universe according to Jim Gates', *PhysCon*, https://www.sigmapisigma.org/sigmapisigma/congress/2016/jim-gates

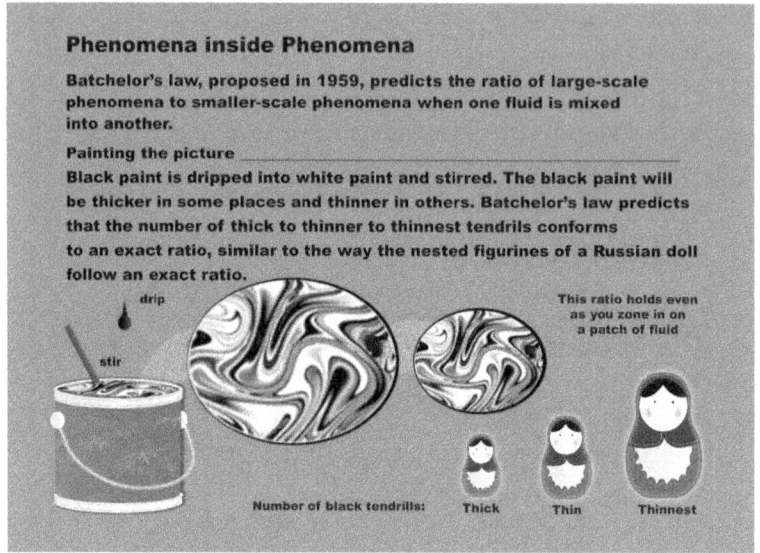

Figure 5. Fractal phenomena inside phenomena

Another piece of the puzzle that recently fell in place was proving Batchelor's Law. This law states that turbulence (akin to chaos) is patterned along the same lines as Nesting Dolls, maintaining a fractal nature. Chaos, it seems, isn't completely chaotic but abides by consistent patterns; maybe nothing ever is or has been chaotic but simply examples of Plan B, called on when required.

Most of the Matrix's blueprint has been revealed. Now we're waiting for physicists to connect the pieces and recognise the mind-boggling vision that's emerging. Slowly but surely we're discovering that Reality maintains consistent fractal principles throughout a simulation-like holographic process. When we can identify them in both Einstein's equations and quantum physics, then that might give us the bridge we require to finally join them.

> So we think reality is a mosaic-like code or language at the smallest scale of reality, which is the Plank Length.
>
> *– Klee Irwin, Founder of Quantum Gravity Research*

## One Law: Love Truth

We are starting to realise that laws are creating our Reality and they must be obeyed if we are to survive, live in peace, and offer our children an acceptable future. If and when E8's operating system is proven to be at the base of all reality, and people know how its fractal laws apply personally on a day-to-day basis, then concepts such as good and evil, right and wrong, appropriate and inappropriate, lucky and unlucky, beautiful and ugly, will be reconciled once and for all.

> Life is torn by the tension between what it actually is and what it feels it ought to be. This tension is the inescapable consequence of its double nature. For it is personal and finite on the one hand but universal and infinite on the other.[125] *– Paul Brunton*

Traditionally, science, religion, and philosophy have been at loggerheads, but that's all changing as we approach *Revelation's* precipice of 'lifting the veil' to reveal the 'Mystery of God' (YHWH). It's easy to see similarities between Eastern and Indian belief systems. Dr Fritjof Capra argues this realisation convincingly in his book,

---

125  Paul Brunton, *Wisdom of the Overself*, e-book, Van Doren Press, 2014.

*The Tao of Physics*. If we can add Christianity, Judaism, and Islam to this unity, we will surely be getting somewhere.

I find it amazing with so many countries (195) and languages (6500) in the world, the three main monotheist religions – Christianity Islam Judaism – all stem from the same man: Abraham. And just like atomic particles, Abraham comes in three flavours: Hebrew, Christian, and Islamic.

The scriptures present Abraham's God, Yahweh, as being a personal god who maintains deep and loving relationships with His followers. Members of these three creeds argue that their god-personification maintains an essential difference to Eastern systems of theosophy. Up until now, these monotheistic creeds haven't been able to recognise any similarity binding the Eastern and Western profiles of the Creating Force together. But Moses did. He told us that YHWH used a pattern to manifest His Creation, a pattern that mimicked His essential name and nature. To the monotheistic religions, He gave His Person. To the others, He gave His Pattern. Revealing this pattern would therefore give the Family of Man a chance to unite into a single and timely unity. Finally, we would know what God is.

> ... for the earth will be full of the knowledge of YHWH
> as the sea is full of water.[126]

Can you imagine a world where:

- Everybody knows and accepts that a lawful creating force exists and rules with a rod of iron?

---

126   *Isaiah* 11:9

- A world that's run by scientifically validated laws, proven just, equitable, and unable to be circumvented, in any sense or form?

- A world where people talk directly to God daily, knowing they will receive intelligent answers back, guaranteed to be correct and handsome?

Wow! That would be like … Heaven on Earth. And I believe we're entering its twilight smatterings now. As to the current criminal activity and anti-social behaviour that currently lurks in society's dark and dingy places … those days are surely numbered because, as Douglas Adams' creation Dirk Gently put it, 'Everything is truly connected.'

After the Pattern (mystery) of YHWH is disclosed, or de-veiled to use *Revelation's* term, it will be easy to determine who has committed any misdemeanour or crime, past or present. (All will be revealed mathematically.) The science of quantum pattern forensics will quickly establish the guilt or innocence of any questionable person or event, because everything is connected by patterning. And once the patterning is disclosed, conventional criminal activity will fade into obscurity.

On the flip side, every loving action a person initiates will have fully revealed corollaries, which anyone whose eyes are open will be able to see and admire. Finally, good people will be recognised for who they truly are, which for many will have been a long time coming in these troubled times.

I've been told that Australia's early Aboriginal people had no word for 'deception' or 'lie'. Nor was the letter 's' in their vocabulary –

being the sound of the devious to-and-fro snake with its dual forked tongue. Aboriginal Elders, it's been said, were able to discern (augur) the truth from the lay of the land ('a little bird told me'). To lie was pointless. And it will be pointless again when we realise the extent to which everything is connected. We will know that a missing part of the picture can be accurately identified when the pieces surrounding it are well known, as happened with Rita. That being the case, any lie would be easy to identify; it would be like seeing the elephant in the strawberry patch.

The Ancient Persians revered truth as the highest calibre of righteousness. But the following Greek and Roman empires put an end to that unprofitable nonsense with their proliferation of commerce and general marketplace deception. Eventually, this corruption found its way into both medicine and religion, placing each under the marketplace umbrella of *caveat emptor* … 'Let the buyer beware'. (With post-Covid eyes, we might have failed miserably in being aware.)

The ability to accurately discern the truth about any questionable situation or felon would allow society to return to where it was before we walked on the wild side. Once again, people would be able to move forward towards Jung's self-actualisation, now recognised as world actualisation. Not only would the not-so-meek 'lamb of religious fame' be able to lie down with Einstein's 'lion of science', but the centrifugal and disassociating force that currently rules this age would be able to do an about-face, become centripetal and unite in the process. All of this could manifest under the searing heat of solid-state proof about quantum reality and the simulated program that's running its operating system religiously.

As Phillip K Dick put it in 1977:

> At some past time-point, a variable was changed, re-programmed as it were, and that because of this, an alternative world was cast off.

And Gary Lite wrote:

> Many aeons ago we fell into an abyss. Known by many names across the world's mythologies, the fall signified our separation from the Source and the birth of the individualised ego. Through countless epochs and the rise and fall of many civilizations, our souls suffered through this schism that severed us from our true, holistic nature. The fall has caused a collective amnesia. It has created the 'illusion of the mind'. All our suffering, according to Paul Brunton, is **'Due in the end to defective remembrance.'**

Both Brunton and Lite think our problems are all about defective memory, whereas Plato thought they were all about Cronos: 'the name that was the one cause of all things'.[127] I think we'll discover that our collective amnesia and our understanding of chronological time (Cronos) are two threads leading into the same knot, which we're just now remembering how to untangle.

Let's take a look now at what might have occurred back in our deep, dark past to cause this memory aberration about the nature of 'time', using Moses' wisdom as our revealing twilight light.

---

127 'Cronus', *Wikipedia*, https://en.wikipedia.org/wiki/Cronus

# PART TWO
# THE OLD AND THE NEW

## MOSES IN NOAH'S ARK

'We are a species with amnesia.'[128] — *Graham Hancock*

Accepting the premise that Moses was shown the underlying pattern that controls all aspects of quantum reality, then we should be able to reconcile the more bizarre accounts in his writings. Things such as Noah's Ark, the Seven Days of Creation, and our early anthropology – Adam and Eve. I don't intend to undertake that herculean task at this time, but by using the Pattern's dynamics – as I now understand them – I believe I can offer some potentially rewarding insights that might help broaden our vista. To do this, I have to mix the stories around and present them in unorthodox ways, because they touch on a swag of important issues that interconnect and need to be understood as a whole. If we start with Noah's flood story, for instance, it invites criticism because the content seems to vary in key areas, at times appearing to disagree with itself.

---

128  After Skool, 'The lost ancient humans of Antarctica', *YouTube* video, 26 February 2020, https://youtu.be/iBF0hP2_nGw?t=84

Some authorities attribute this confusion to there being two stories 'at odds' with each other within the one. Other scholars believe Moses' flood story is based on an earlier account recorded in the Sumerian *Epic of Gilgamesh*, it being one of several flood-accounts to precede Moses'. Most people, however, equate the stories of *Genesis* with nonsense (I know I did). Few consider that God spoke directly to Moses, as the scriptures state. But as strange as it must sound to many, I've come to believe this last scenario is the correct one. When you think about it … We talk to the machines we have created, and they talk back to us, and we think nothing of that. Some even play music and sing for us, which doesn't make us bat an eyelid either. So, if God exists, wouldn't He want to communicate as well? That seems reasonable to me. But if He's trying to communicate, then maybe it's up to us to know His language – 'have ears that hear' as the scriptures state. But what if we've forgotten the semantics and syntax of His language's trinary operating system, which Moses tells us He uses to maintain Reality?

## Intertextuality

Critics of Genesis do agree on one thing … Its stories contain enticing coincidences. They call this peculiar patterning 'intertextuality.'

> **Box 13. Intertextuality**
>
> 'Intertextuality' means how episodes in biblical works refer to and echo each other. The most significant such 'echo' is the creation narrative in *Genesis*. The sequence of flood events mimics that of creation: first, the flood covers the Earth to the highest mountains; then it destroys in order, birds, cattle, beasts, 'swarming creatures' and, finally Mankind. The division between the 'waters above' and the 'waters below' the Earth is removed. The flood covers the land and all life is destroyed.
>
> Such echoes are seldom coincidental. For example, the word for Noah's 'ark' is the same word used for the 'basket' in which Moses is saved, implying a link between the stories of Moses and Noah.[129]

Moses used this same 'ark-word' (*tsela*) for Adam's rib, the mysterious substrate from which Eve was supposedly withdrawn.

> **Box 14. Adam's Rib**
>
> While it is true that there is only one occurrence of the word *tsela'* carrying the meaning 'rib' in the Old Testament, (the 'rib' removed from Adam), the meaning clearly belongs to the word in general. *Genesis* translates the verb ts-l- as meaning 'to curve'.[130] This is especially so for the curving hull of a ship or transporting vessel.

---

[129] 'Genesis flood narrative', *Wikipedia*, https://en.wikipedia.org/wiki/Genesis_flood_narrative

[130] Susan, 'Is the translation "rib" for the Hebrew צֵלָע (*tsela*\*) in *Genesis* 2:22 justified?', *Biblical Hermeneutics | Stack Exchange*, https://hermeneutics.stackexchange.com/questions/20122/is-the-translation-rib-for-the-hebrew-%D7%A6%D6%B5%D7%9C%D6%B8%D7%A2-tsela-in-genesis-222-justifie

In a sense, Moses equates Eve to a curved vessel (ark), which contains the seeds of all potential life within; a safehouse repository (a fertile, curved seed-pod) with the means to traverse the space between dimensions (being her primary role), like a comet in the heavens or a ship bridging continents. This curvaceous ability to move and evolve is a common theme in three of Moses' stories:

- Adam and Eve
- Noah's Ark
- Moses is saved as a child in his wicker basket.

Each of these accounts uses the ark-word: *tsela'*.

In this fractal way, baby Moses – in his Eve-ark-basket full of life's eggs – became the vessel that was destined to take the Israelites (all twelve tribes) into a new land (from Egypt to Israel). Actually, into the old land of their fathers (Canaan) but now as a newly seeded or cleansed people. In this episode of the palingenetic fractal, Moses raised or resurrected Abraham's spiritually dead children from their Egyptian graves, where they had worked as slaves making mudbricks for Pharaoh. Moses restored them to the laws of the Matrix – the Torah – so they and their children could 'come alive' and awaken in the 'Desert of Sin' (which we're told their children achieved before crossing over the river Jordan into the Promised Land). These instructions delivered by Moses were called the Law of Liberty.[131]

---

131 Jacques B. Doukhan, 'Holy days: The law of liberty', *Shalom Learning Center*, 16 May 2017, https://www.shalomlc.org/index.php/holy-days/153-shavuot/263-the-law-of-liberty

Moses oversaw this transformation – or phase transition – while his family mob wandered in the desert for forty years birthing and raising children born under Divine Lore. Having achieved the desired and necessary transformation, the Egyptian-born (transitory) generation then dutifully relinquished the reins to their now-clean children **and died out before crossing over the Jordan River.** (This reminds me of the Neanderthals also leaving the world scene at a critical point in history. I wonder whether they might have played a similar part in birthing modern man, then deliberately died out as well?) The mirrored complexities of biblical intertextuality would liken Moses' forty-year desert journey to the later 'saving work' of Yahshua, at both His First and Second Comings. (The First Coming sires the Christians, while the Second Coming resurrects them after they have dwelled/snoozed in the wilderness for a while serving Pharoh – maybe to mature.)

There's no accepted explanation for the Bible's 'intertextuality', but it makes sense if Reality operates fractally and contains alternating, reflective, yin/yang opposites operating in cycles. I believe Moses tried to capture this weirdness in his narratives, which accounts for why the world's cataclysmic destruction needed to be an exact reversal of the earlier Creation Account. It also sheds light on the weird parallels between Moses' and Noah's stories, such as why baby Moses was saved in a basket called an 'ark', and why this basket/ark was lined with pitch and tar, as Noah's seaworthy vessel was.

Now here's an interesting thought … What if Moses had a revelation, an insight, and regained his memory of having once been Noah in a past life? Or here's an even better one … What if Moses came to see beautifully patterned sequences in his past, right up to that point;

snowflake patterns that defied both his imagination and his reason? Patterns that required a Creator.

By whatever means, the enlightening information conveyed to Moses was displayed on YHWH's Back (the Eternal Now's Past?), which Moses had glimpsed on the mountaintop when he received the Ten Commandments. I believe YHWH's Back revealed the Kairos-timed events in Moses' life, all lined up in repeating patterns when viewed from the right perspective. In other words ... I believe Moses' eyes were opened and he saw the Logos' algorithms in his personal and family histories, as his now-activated memory kicked in and came to light. This is a distinct possibility because something similar happened to me.

> This is why Moses was warned when he was about to build the tabernacle: 'See to it that you make everything according to the pattern shown to you on the mountain.'[132]

Moses was given this warning – recorded by Paul in *Hebrews* in the New Testament – because the earthly Tabernacle's Pattern was said to be a direct copy of where God dwells in Heaven. Paul tells us that 'Heaven' and the pattern of Moses' Tabernacle mirror each other. That both embrace the same trinary pattern, because the Tabernacle/Sanctuary was laid out architecturally as a trinity of values:

- A place for the people
- A place for the clergy
- A central Holy Place for God to tabernacle among them.

---

132  *Hebrews* 8:5, NIV

This is particularly interesting because – on the other hand – Duat/Sheol/the Grave is, by many accounts, strongly connected with dualism. In a yin/yang (binary?) hell, we're told there is no (central) place for God.

This binary, hellish idea, reminds me of the time of the Titans, when there were no gods on Earth, or anywhere else for that matter. Greek Mythology maintains that … At first, Heaven and Earth are one, then two, but … not three until the Olympian Gods arrive. This intrigues me. **Could our perceived reality be a conflict between different patterned dimensions and their ruling forces that are vying for dominance between themselves? Are we caught in the middle of their struggle?** Is the Universe evolving in a trinary sense? Is it trying to break away from its older parents? Still finding its feet like a teenager might? Developing its own (trinary) personality? Complete with knots and tangles? This idea is consistent with the patterns I have come to know and now respect.

This leads me to question whether dark energy and dark matter – connected to Einstein's Cosmological Constant – are remnants from the second (dark female, mother) dimension, whose aspects remain locked within her three-dimensional material (child) since its birth 13.77 billion years ago.

If that is the case, then maybe black holes are remnants from the first (male, father) dimension, there being no explanation as to why supermassive black holes were around in the early universe.[133] Could

---

133 Adam Mann, 'Primordial black holes could explain dark matter, galaxy growth and more', *PBS News Hour*, https://www.pbs.org/newshour/science/primordial-black-holes-could-explain-dark-matter-galaxy-growth-and-more

the third dimension we are living in be the equal product (child) of the preceding two dimensions? Could they be our dimension's parents? And can we see components of both the parents in the child? As previously mentioned, this scenario would be a case of Evolution doing her thing on the grandest scale imaginable.

If Reality is a fractal simulation, then this idea about a two- to three-dimensional transformation taking place might also explain what is happening within our mind's conscious domain. It could explain some of the intriguing mysteries about the numerical aspects of how we think. And this is where all this crazy mathematical stuff gets personal, and I begin to hope.

## Patterned Spirit World

These bizarre, biblical, intertextual coincidences, or fractal parallel accounts, make *Genesis*' stories hard to understand. In this regard, I'm not sure where Moses wants us to think his story begins: with the creation of Earth? Or before the Big Bang? Fractals are tricky that way.

I think Moses' early characters from Adam and Eve right up to Noah and his family, weren't meant to be thought of as flesh-and-blood humans, but more like patterned spirit-beings, each character maintaining the same robust human consciousness and perspectives that we have, but having no solid matter as such. It's also possible these early stories are metaphors: familial accounts that capture the magic and geometry of the Simulation's fractal patterns as they apply to Mankind. I believe these stories are essentially correct but represent the fractal truth (mathematically) rather than the literal truth materially. Maybe we'll find that the patterns are accurate, but the cameo performances are being played by underlings.

The first bunch of characters in *Genesis* reminds me of the Aboriginal Wandjina Creator Spirits, who walked the Earth before Mankind did in the flesh. The Wandjina Spirits are associated with creation, fertility, and rain, and might be the ethereal ancestors of Moses' Eve tribe (the Mother of all Life), who is also likened to rain and fertility. *Genesis* tells us that life's early attempt at multiplicity failed, needing to be washed clean by the Flood. After the deluge, life was launched again, this time under a mysterious rainbow that now graced the heavens with her regal (*tsela*) arc. This might be where *Genesis'* essential patterns started their long trek into complex solidness.

According to Moses, no rainbows had been seen over the Earth until Noah and his crew arrived/landed. I think the rainbow connection is important because rainbows maintain a 180° arc (*tsela'*, ark, curve, Eve), which contains seven colours with green occupying the centre spot. These colourful, geometric symbols are highly suggestive of Divine Female Energy, which was (finally) seen over the Earth as a covering or (protective?) arc for life to flourish in Eve's natural multiplicity.

Similarly, the Pod (or Ark) of the African San's legendary Mantis is said to have flown in from stellar space, holding the seeds of life in its embrace, looking for a suitable place (flower) to land on and fertilise. In this way, we could think of Noah's Ark as being the equivalent of a comet hurtling down from the heavens with a full set of life's micropatterns on board. After it crash-landed, these micropatterns would have been free to morph through numerous transformations by Fractal Evolution, should such a process exist.

This seeding comet idea is known as Panspermia. It was championed by Britain's Lord Kelvin in 1871, with modern supporters including notable scientists such as Freeman Dyson, Stephen Hawking, and Richard Dawkins.[134] Panspermia (meaning 'all seed') maintains that patterned life (DNA) exists throughout the Universe, distributed by space-dust, meteoroids, asteroids, comets, and planetoids.[135]

> **Box 15. Was the Cambrian Explosion the result of a comet?**
>
> A 2018 article, titled 'Cause of Cambrian Explosion – Terrestrial or Cosmic?' which was authored by more than 30 scientists and published in the prestigious journal *Progress in Biophysics and Molecular Biology*, indicates that the explanation for the sudden flourishing of life during the Cambrian era – aka the 'Cambrian explosion' – may have its origins in the stars. More precisely, it was thanks to comets and asteroids that bombarded the Earth, carrying organic molecules.[136]

I don't believe Moses wanted us to think of Noah's animals as flesh-and-blood critters either – it simply doesn't make sense – but rather as the animals *a priori* essential patterns/names that were yet to evolve. Moses tells us that Adam 'named' all the animals in the Garden, although he could only have seen at best a small number personally. So Adam must have known or 'named' them in

---

134  Brig Klyce, 'Introduction: More than Panspermia', *Cosmic Ancestry: Life Comes from Space Because Life Comes from Life*, www.panspermia.org/intro.htm
135  'Panspermia', *Wikipedia*, https://en.wikipedia.org/wiki/Panspermia
136  Edward J Steele, et al., 'Cause of Cambrian Explosion – terrestrial or cosmic?' *Progress in Biophysics and Molecular Biology*, vol. 136, March 2018, pp. 3–23.

a different manner. In a sense, I think an enlightened person would be capable of naming all of the components that had entered their life to create their enlightenment. As I previously mentioned … Moses – in his enlightenment – might have seen the same patterns firsthand, patterns he identified in himself and then attempted to share with all Mankind by weaving them into his story's characters and narrative.

Moses tells us that Noah packed all the animals on the Ark(s) in two distinct agendas. This is where the confusion comes in about there being two stories mixed together. If these animals were essentially patterns, there would need to be a female dynasty kept separate from the male one, as per the Program's internal figure-8 format. For instance, a dog's essence might like to ship off on the male ark to help keep watch, while a cat's essence would surely prefer to pussyfoot up and down on the female ark.

> In the ancient world, things did not exist until they were named: The name of a living being or an object was … the very essence of what was defined, and the pronouncing of a name was to create what was spoken.[137]

As previously mentioned, Plato wrote in *Cratylus* that a 'name' was the pattern of the object in question, its essential essence, its intended purpose. Names once meant a whole lot more than they do today. And they were all placed on the Ark(s).

---

137 'Biblical cosmology', *The Spiritual Life*, https://slife.org/biblical-cosmology/

> Every experience is a shape. Unique, intricate, like a zoo.
> Each animal is an experience.[138]

In a fractal simulation, the blueprint of every animal, bird, fish, et cetera would've existed in what physicist Paul Davis likes to call the *Mind of God*, long before they materialised in three spatial dimensions. (It was designed. It was named. It evolved into three-dimensional solidness 1, 2, 3.) These patterns, or names, simply required an appropriate computer-based process (algorithm) for them to emerge, layer upon layer, like the output of a modern 3D printer. I believe this is what happened after Noah and his family landed.

Microscopic life patterns have been retrieved from comet debris, which adds to Panspermia's credibility. They include bacteria-like fossils found in the Murchison meteorite and the Mars meteorite ALH 84001.[139] I think Moses wanted us to think of the Ark's inhabitants as being the equivalent of nanobots stored on a hard-drive.

If you gave a quantum supercomputer a fractal life-program and told it to evolve numerous trimensions – similar to what happens in the Game of Life – then it would produce a reasonable facsimile of our modern ecology. (Especially if the program ran on a ternary computer system.) Minerals, plants, fish, birds and animals, even our atmosphere, are all similarly patterned. This understanding is exemplified in Steve Wolfman's book, *A New Kind of Science*. He

---

138 'Giulio Tononi, psychiatrist, neuroscientist', *World Science Festival*, https://www.worldsciencefestival.com/participants/giulio_tononi/

139 Milton Wainwright, 'A microbiologist looks at Panspermia', *Milton Wainwright* website, http://miltonwainwright.com/a-microbiologist-looks-at-panspermia/

shows how it takes only a few simple rules to code for all the diversity in Nature. With this idea in mind, an escalator of complexity can be seen leading archetypal blueprints up through the World Tree to finalise as modern lifeforms.

In a fractal universe, the process of evolution would have started well before organic life materialised on Earth. It's therefore possible that these designs, or 'names', were acted out (or are being acted out) in the heavens by star-bodies wrestling for their allotment, and identity, in the pattern of the Cosmos. Incidentally, we believe that up to 85% of stars in the Universe are in binary systems,[140] which is likely to be meaningful in a mathematical sense when it comes to our future occupation. I wonder if these binary stars have energies the equivalent of:

- Brother and sister?

- Husband and wife?

- Cat and dog?

*Genesis'* early chapters reveal one example of evolutionary design after another. Often, these designs grow from a contentious binary platform to finish as a more homogenous trinary one, which might eventually apply to these binary star patterns in the Cosmos if Mankind gets his act together. Some binary stars are actually touching each other.

I believe the 'names' in *Genesis* are referring to underlying patterns – their barcode if you will. In this regard, think of *Matryoshka*, otherwise known as Russian Dolls. (*Matryoshka* translates as 'little mother'.) In

---

[140] 'Binary stars', *CSIRO: Australia National Telescope Facility*, https://www.atnf.csiro.au/outreach/education/senior/astrophysics/binary_intro.html

a fractal, how many forms could 'Little Mother' take? The Barradja People of Australia's Kimberly Region call this understanding *Wungged*, where *Wungged* refers to the patterned intelligence of life.

The trouble with a fractal, however, is because it keeps repeating, it's easy to get one layer mixed up with its neighbour, especially when it criss-crosses in an expanding spiral (like unravelling a family tree that's riddled with incest, bastards, and failed marriages). I wouldn't be surprised to find that Moses' Creation Account goes way back to … 'In the beginning' … of this three-dimensional universe, before the Big Bang expanded out of what may have been an a priori two-dimensional reality that produced (birthed) the third dimension as its child. If reality is an evolutionary fractal, then evolving dimensions are almost a certainty.

It would also suggest that this universe will eventually have a child, which becomes an obvious conclusion when the Fractal is applied to our ultimate future. So did our immortal forebears work this out and then do something about it? And is this connected to Moses' stories?

## Let Three-Dimensional Solidness Evolve

Along with there being several flood accounts, there are numerous creation stories. Many begin with chaos ruling, then evolve to become the unified primordial energies of Heaven (above) and Earth (below) or their representative deities. These two states comprise a single, unified XY state of being. I think of this unified dual state as the First Dimension (attraction of opposites; male).

As previously stated, in Greek Mythology, the three domains of rulership (three dimensions) only came into play after the Titans (who I now think of as the Twotans) were defeated and replaced by the trinity of gods Zeus and Co.

If Moses' Creation Account started on Earth, then when the Elohim 'moved over the face of the water' and said, 'Let there be light', there would've already been plenty of existing light from the Universe's much older suns. What seems more likely is that Moses' Seven-Day Account starts before the Big Bang, in absolute blackness, introducing the equivalent of a supernova into a black hole to start Day One, then separating the light from the dark by inserting two appropriate twilight-point energies as their children, to act as mediators between the otherwise contentious duality.

Similarly – as previously mentioned – Greek Mythology records that Heaven and Earth became separated when Cronos castrated his father Uranus and, by this means, broke the link uniting the two primordial energies that had worked as one up until that time. I now think of this severing as being the genesis of the Second Dimension that now contained the two separate parts. If the Creation Fractal applies to everything, then our understanding of time, human consciousness, and dimensions must be included.

As each human being comprises half of their father's and half of their mother's genetically encoded material (their parent's patterns), we can surmise that each, third, childlike presentation in the Fractal – the go-between emergent energy which sits between its two parents' energies – must retain active units from each parent inside its evolving structure. (Inside of the number three [3] is a one [1] and a two [2]. In this way, as previously mentioned, I believe we can think of dark energy/matter and black holes – which exist in our Universe – as being parental remnants from our earlier First and Second dimensions.

While Greek Mythology's account of Creation seems to embrace a journey through progressive dimensions, Moses' account begins with the gods (Elohim) ruling everything as a four-part Trinity. Moses makes no mention of any prior energy, Titan, Anunnaki, or otherwise, until we reach the Serpent in the Garden. Here, he identifies the Serpent as being a 'beast', not clean in the way that other animals are. In a trinary program, this indicates that the Serpent is binary (unclean/incomplete/transient) in a numerical sense. Sumerian and Babylonian accounts identify this serpent-energy with the Anunnaki Enki, Lord of the Water, God of the Earth (Ea), who is said to now abide in Hell. And the Anunnaki parallel the Greek Titans and early Egyptian myths of Osiris. So, are they all telling the same story? Are the deities of different dimensions at war (mathematically) with each other in our domain as the evolutionary process has its way? Are they still at war? It would seem they just might be.

ON DAY ONE of Moses' Creation Account, a trinary pattern evolves from the base duality of light and dark. This is achieved when the evening and morning twilights are added as the third energy. On Day Two, this *two-becoming-three* pattern steps up a notch, when the Elohim place 'firmness' (firmament) in the middle of the existing upper and lower watery states and call it 'the heavens' (thus duplicating the essential trinary pattern). Day Two's heavens (firmament) can be seen as our expanding Universe, which remains surrounded by wavy nonsolid blackness. These are the chaotic outer limits into which our dimension of solidness is (rapidly) expanding, as matter continues to fly apart, all as a result of the expansive Titans.

I believe the Universe is a stupendous living organism that's comprised of infinite solid and nonsolid parts, which (mathematically) resemble ones, twos, and threes/fours (the last pair being the two twilight energies that are found in each complete trimension).

When you think about your nightly dreams, you realise they contain semblances of solidness which seem very real at times. But we know these dream-wraiths aren't connected to true solidness at all. They only exist in the dark phase of our mind, projected onto our consciousness by a process not yet understood. Also, in our nightly dream-state, we aren't conscious of needing to breathe, take nourishment or relieve ourselves; time doesn't exist in any normal sense either. But this doesn't stop us from thinking at the time that parts of our dream-existence have a solid footing. Dreams can be very convincing in this way. Then again ... A hologram is an insubstantial lookalike; a three-dimensional projection that emanates from a two-dimensional negative. It appears something doesn't need to be (actually) substantial to look real, have existence, or occupy space.

Research at the Quantum Gravity Centre in Los Angeles, working with an eight-dimensional E8 crystal projected in four dimensions, shows that several realities can come into existence as shadows or phantoms of higher complexities.[141] As previously mentioned, this development in Emergence Theory mimics the essential idea portrayed in Plato's Cave. This is a case of the end meeting its

---

141   Quantum Gravity Research, 'What is reality?', *YouTube* video, 5 March 2017, https://youtu.be/w0ztlIAYTCU?t=657

beginning, where old knowledge is finding a reflection in modern science. Gravity is best explained (geometrically) when seen as a two-dimensional force.

I now maintain:

> In the beginning, male solidness went to sleep or was consumed – became formless (castrated). Apparently, It was consumed by the waves and subsequently resurrected (awoken) from the dead with physics' Big Bang on the First Day of Moses' Creation Account. That sequence then repeated in fractal layers and continues until now.

Everything in the Fractal has awake and sleep times, and everything wants to reproduce. Even baby star systems are constantly forming in the gas clouds of nebulas. Orion's Belt is full of growing, heavenly babies. The core of Galaxy Cluster CL J1000+0220 (a very distant cluster) is ablaze with star formations. So maybe God wants to reproduce as well as communicate. But where would He find a suitable fertile wife to consort with? Any ideas? Who could God's 'intended' fractal Eve possibly be (if He was looking for one, that is)? And how could she bear Him a micro-fractal child made in His YX (male, son) image?

For the Fractal to be consistent, the Creator would need to create a Shadow of Himself. And I believe that's exactly what He did, and is still doing. Then, like Adam, He had to wait a while for Her to come of age. Sound familiar? It should, when Moses' Creation Account is understood in fractal terms.

You might think it strange that YHWH would repose for a while in forgetful sleep. But Moses tells us otherwise:

> Then YHWH remembered (רכזיו) Noah, and every living thing, and all the animals that were with him in the ark.[142]

The Bible also records how there are acceptable times to pray to YHWH.[143] So maybe, in some sense or other, like everything else, God does sleep on occasions, or becomes forgetful for a while at least. (In the previous quote, the Hebrew word for 'remembered' (רכז) especially relates to … A man looking back in reflection.[144])

If the idea about God looking for a bride and wanting an eventual son has merit, then Moses' story of Adam and Eve takes on a grander meaning. It also shines an interesting light on passages in *Revelation* – the Bible's last book and therefore *Genesis'* reflection – where a holy marriage takes place between Mankind and God. And we know that … After marriage, we expect a child.

## Noah's Two Arks

There are several interesting parts to Noah's Flood Story which generally go unnoticed. I've already alluded to there being two arks, which is consistent with the Fractal in providing for 'His' and 'Her'

---

142  *Genesis* 8:1
143  *Psalm* 69:13
144  'רכזיו', *LingQ* online dictionary, https://www.lingq.com/en/learn-hebrew-online/translate/he/%D7%95%D7%99%D7%96%D7%9B%D7%A8

patterns, the equivalent of egg and sperm designs, the Geometry of Life. When mated or married, these two immortal elements would be capable of fostering life on Earth. (Eve's Ark would have needed to proceed Noah's for it to be a true 'preparation'.) And two arks require two accounts. Yet current wisdom maintains that *Genesis'* Flood Story is a composite of earlier stories. The Wikipedia entry on the 'Flood Narrative' in Genesis states:

> The flood narrative is made up of two stories woven together. As a result, many details are contradictory, such as how long the flood lasted (40 days according to *Genesis* 7:17, 150 according to 7:24), how many animals were to be taken aboard the ark (one pair of each in 6:19, one pair of the unclean animals and seven pairs of the clean in 7:2), and whether Noah released a raven which 'went to and fro until the waters were dried up' or a dove which on the third occasion 'did not return to him again,' or possibly both.[145]

Notice how the Ark with the most animals on board had seven 'good' pairs and one 'bad' pair. This is an example of the eighth point needing to 'sleep' in Eve's figure-8 Pattern of Seven. And notice how the 'preparation' (raven) went to-and-fro over the Earth before the dove circled it three times.

The idea of there being two arks is supported by the oral traditions of both the Australian Aboriginal and African San peoples. Their ancient memories recall star-seeds of separate matriarchal and

---

145 'Genesis Flood Narrative', *Wikipedia*, https://en.wikipedia.org/wiki/Genesis_flood_narrative

patriarchal origins crashing, meshing, and reproducing: firstly, in the confines of the Earth, then secondly on its surface, after finding the means to escape the dungeon below.[146] Each account reveals half of the whole story. (I think of them as his-story and her-story.) Both accounts are consistent and agree … We were parented by two heavenly star bodies:

- the Pleiades' Seven Sisters (blue, female)
- Sirius, the binary Dog Star (yellow, male).

## Stella and Fella

Sirius appears yellow in the night sky[147] while the Pleiades appear blue. Sirius A is the brightest star in the sky, whereas the Pleiades is the cluster of stars most visible to the naked eye. Now traditionally, yellow and blue (the colours either side of the rainbow's centre) when married produce green. These ancient memories about Mankind's origin attest that the means to create fertile Green came to Earth by way of two life-bearing comets. The San people tell us the animal pattern (patriarchy) that boarded the Ark in pairs came from the binary Sirius, whereas Australian Aboriginal Lore maintains the seven/eight pattern (matriarchy) came from the Seven Ladies of the Pleiades.

---

146  The Sans tell us that the Man built a tree and climbed up to the Earth's surface along with all the other animals. The Aboriginal account tell us that we and the animals climbed up the Great Serpent that went to-and-fro to the surface.
147  'Watch for Sirius, sky's brightest star', *EarthSky*, 26 October 2020, https://earthsky.org/tonight/the-skys-brightest-star-sirius-before-dawn

Interestingly, the Great Pyramid at Giza bears witness to this conjoining. The light from both the Dog Star and the Pleiades align in the Queen's Chamber, one situated on top of the other.

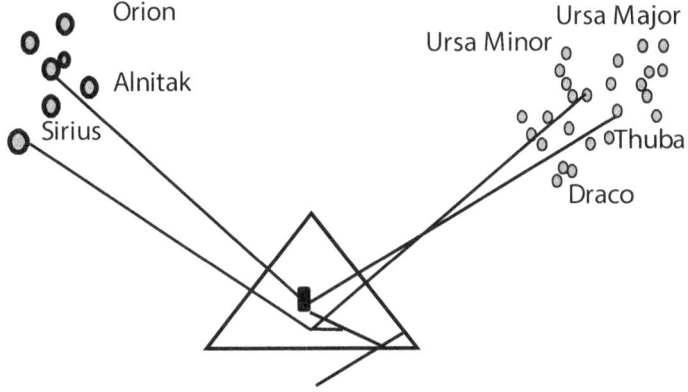

Figure 6. Comingling constellations at the Great Pyramid of Giza

Their astronomical significance was first recognized by Alexander Badawy and Virginia Trimble in the 1960s. They suggested that the north shaft of the Queen's Chamber aligned with "Beta" (B) in Ursa Minor, while the south shaft aligned with Sirius.[148]

The recollections of these two Stone Age cultures – the San and Aboriginal peoples – were painted on their cave walls. In this regard, the Gwion rock-art paintings in Australia's Kimberly are exceptional. Some are thought to depict aliens but, with patterned eyes, a more uplifting picture emerges. I believe the paintings reveal the marriage of Earth's two seeding energy patterns, depicted as the legendary

---

148  Jenny Hill, 'Great Pyramid: "Air shafts"', *Ancient Egypt Online*, https://ancientegyptonline.co.uk/pyramid-air-shafts/

flying Mantis (Adam) and the desirable Porcupine Rain Goddess (Eve). More on these accounts later in this series.

Moses' two ark templates can be likened to the algorithmic principles that underly the Matrix's operating system. According to *Genesis'* story, one pattern is placed onboard each of the two arks, then both arks find their way to Earth. Green then flourishes (evolves) from its yellow and blue parents as the third expression in this colour series. Then came cyan (blue/green) the product of the incestuous coupling of the green child back with his blue mother. At this point, Cyanobacteria developed in the oceans and took over the Earth to transform it into a blue-green planet. This mother and son application of the *attraction of likes* (cyan's hitting the rock twice) created the transition, ending the so-called Boring First Billion (black?) Years on planet Earth.[149]

Moses tells us that Adam's (Sirius') Ark landed on the two-headed volcano Ararat, where its valuable cargo soaked through the porous soil into the fiery groundwater below. Whereas, according to Aboriginal legend, the girl's ark flew in from the Seven Sisters and crash-landed in Australia, possibly hitting and exploding the east coast's Mount Wollumbin in the process. Mount Wollumbin was once a mighty volcano with a 100-km-diameter base. Its fiery entrails flow deep into the underground waters of the Great Artesian Basin from which (according to Aboriginal legend) organic life sprang forth. Eve's Ark likely had the wherewithal to produce complex anaerobic life (Archaea) as a true 'preparation' would, while she waited for Adam to fly in.

---

149 History of the Earth, 'What was the "Boring Billion" really like?' *YouTube* video, 18 October 2021, https://youtu.be/0sbwUeTyDb0

I believe Eve's (blue) Ark ground-zeroed on the continent of Australia, home of the Blue Mountains and true-blue Aussies. This would explain why, later on down the track, our fractal anthropological Eve left her African crèche and headed straight for Australia, the repository of her ancestral energy.[150] Her female instinct would've told her where she would be safe to breed and evolve in tribal figure-8 and circular patterns, free from 'male' harassment.

Across Australia, Aboriginal people recall legends of the Seven Sisters. Other cultures – the New Zealand Māori and American Indians, for instance – also do, but not as extensively as the Aboriginal people. The Seven Sisters are foundational to their culture, especially to Women's Business.

In a comical sense, Super Girl might've arrived first on Earth and did her womanly thing in patterned figure-8 (to-and-fro) convolutions, before Adam arrived to tie the knot, running rings around her in his accustomed circular (white dove) fashion. Eve's energy may have seeded Australia's Great Artesian Basin with a complete set of micro-patterns (Archaea), which should still be there if the mining companies haven't killed them all with their intrusive steel pipes and hungry, ferrous microbes. If these tiny ancient critters still exist, I believe they could be effective medicines for various forms of cancer and other degenerative diseases, where a person's body has lost touch with its original pattern. This would be similar to native plant strains providing genetic cures for agricultural diseases such as 'rust' in wheat.

---

150  Stephan Milo, 'Neanderthals: The first sailors?', *YouTube* video, 25 November 2018, https://www.youtube.com/watch?v=4dR9YiIMrpM

These remnant archaea have been sleeping in the dark confines of the Great Artesian Basin for millions of years, and might be capable of acting as medicinal microbiotas or medical microbotics (Nature's version of hydrogel nanoparticles). I believe it's possible these remnant archaea (ark-aea) could reboot a person's original life pattern back into a healthy order, possibly undoing some of the mischiefs that modern vaccines and other medical treatments have done to their DNA.

ANOTHER PART OF Noah's story I find particularly interesting is: Before Noah's three white doves are released from his Ark to determine whether there is any dry land around, he first releases a blue/black raven to 'go to-and-fro over the face of the Earth to dry up the water'. But the raven never returns. If there was only a single pair of ravens on board Noah's Ark, then this would've surely caused a few problems for its mate. What's more likely is that the 'raven' came from Eve's comet, or was in fact the comet itself.

Obviously, the Earth's drying-out process took a lot longer than the lifespan of a flesh-and-blood bird. Earlier, *Genesis* 8:1 says the Elohim released a spirit (wind) to dry up the water. So perhaps the raven was a black female spirit?

I thought it strange that Moses would use black and white birds symbolically in this way because Moses' wife Zipporah was a black Ethiopian woman whose name translates to 'blackbird'. If the released blackbird (raven, Zipporah) hadn't done her women's business, going to-and-fro in the algorithmic figure-8 of the Fractal, then the white bird (dove) wouldn't have found dry land to circle around when its turn came around.

In the Matrix's geometric complexity, the black bird's algorithmic *phi* acts as a preparation for the white bird's circular and sustaining *pi*. This is why in Moses' personal story, Zipporah the Blackbird saves Moses' life when she circumcises their son (see Box 16). I think Moses came to understand the relevance of the Black Bird's intervention in his life.

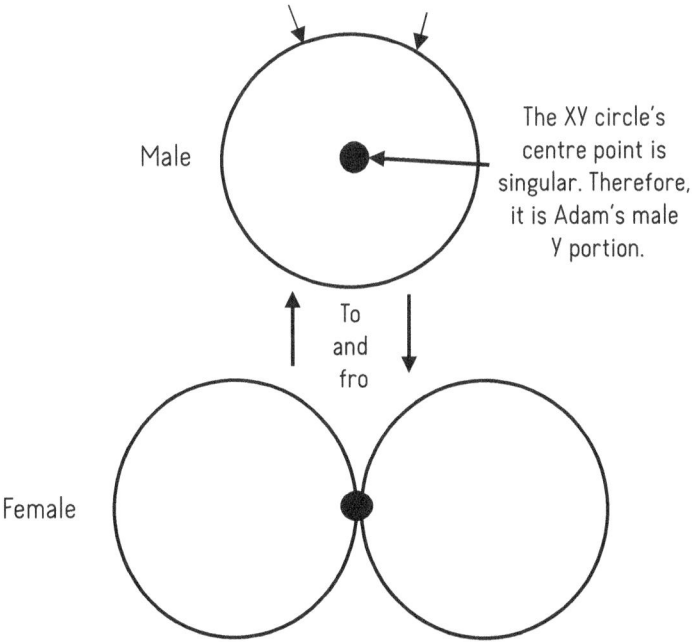

Figure 7. The contention between XY Adam and the classical XX figure-8 Eve as represented by circumcision's pattern

> ### Box 16. Zipporah
>
> After God spoke to Moses through a burning bush, Moses set out with his family, returning to Egypt to free his people from slavery. During this journey, a strange incident occurred one night in their tent. God tried to kill Moses. Zipporah, somehow sensing God was angry that their son wasn't circumcised, immediately grabbed a stone and cut off her son's foreskin. According to God's covenant with Abraham, cutting away the foreskin from the penis is a sign of identification among Hebrews.[151]
>
> \* \* \*
>
> Notice how this event occurred on Moses' journey to redemption – my guess would be at its midpoint. I've come to recognise that any significant energy disclosed in the middle of a cycle reveals (in a mantic fashion) the domain of that cycle's next coming expression; the next generation's 'name'. This is what happened to the Old Testament's Jacob when he became Israel on his return to Canaan, and also to the New Testament's Paul on the Road to Damascus.
>
> If the circumcision pattern is a true reflection of Yahweh's geometry (see Figure 7), then when Zipporah created it at this crucial cardinal point In Moses' life, she lifted the veil to what Moses was going to be shown on Mount Sinai when he received the formula for the Pattern of Everything. What Michio Kaku calls *The God Equation*.

---

151 Beth Brophy, 'Zipporah may be obscure, but the wife of Moses mattered', *US News & World Report*, 25 January 2008, https://www.usnews.com/news/religion/articles/2008/01/25/zipporah-may-be-obscure-but-the-wife-of-moses-mattered

Male circumcision can be portrayed as a three-dimensional tattoo of YHWH's sacred geometry. Its configuration generates a pattern in the male genitalia which sees the verb to go 'to and fro' situated between the energies of a singular circular glans 'one', and a dual testicular figure-8 'two' as numerical representatives of male and female. When the penis' foreskin is removed, it is as though a veil is lifted from the circular glans (its head). With this veil removed, the tattoo is complete. Thus, YHWH's male followers were recognised in this patterned, penile way. Circumcision reveals an oscillating wave situated between a single particle and a double one.

Eve's centre point in the middle of her two circles has a different quality to Adam's. Her centre is where the 'two' become a new tangential 'one' (marriage/birth) capturing the magic of fertile new growth. When her (duel/dual) figure-8 is situated inside his single circle – as shown in Figure 8 – Eve is inside of Adam; her centre is his centre, giving this God of the Centre two natures or perspectives: XX and XY. This configuration makes babies. Other configurations make hell.

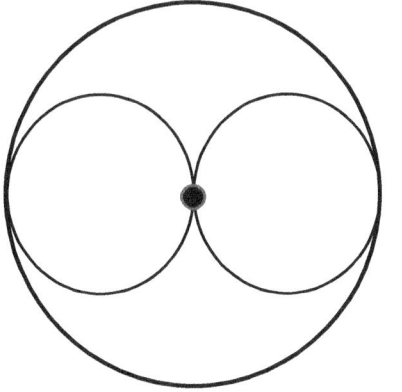

Figure 8. Eve inside Adam with a common centre

After male circumcision has been performed on a baby's penis on the eighth day after his birth (eight being the number of new beginnings), YHWH's pattern is meant to be disclosed. This pattern maintains a potentially oscillating no man's land situated between the polarised states of one (1) and two (2). This interim verb/action goes to-and-fro on intimate occasions and, when successful, leads to new life. I think this knowledge about the male circumcision pattern has been asleep for some time and is ready to rise up.

**Traditionally, we've asked: Are the Genesis stories fact or fiction? Maybe we should've been asking: Are these stories maths and geometry, patiently waiting for us to smarten up to what Reality really is?**

According to Moses, the female ark created a fertile environment for the next part of this amazing love story to unfold. When Noah and his crew landed, Adam's yellow-seed sought out Eve's blue-eggs to produce viridity, and the first rainbow evolved to spread its protective arc over her now-growing brood. After an 'incestuous' event took place (known as 'original sin'), blue/green cyanobacteria sprang forth to pave the way for life's multiplicity to unfold in the Cambrian explosion.

Because of these intriguing marriages, blue/green cyanobacteria went ballistic, enriching the oxygen content in Earth's atmosphere; rain fell, plant and animal cells evolved (life as we know it took off). A massive bride price was needed for this colourful pageant to unfold: All of the Earth's existing lifeforms had to die or find shelter in anaerobic pockets of blackness within the Earth's crust. Places such as Australia's Great Artesian Basin. To these lifeforms, oxygen ($O_2$) was deadly stuff.

> **Box 17. Great Artesian Basin**
>
> The Great Artesian Basin is the world's largest and deepest artesian basin, stretching more than 1,700,000 sq. km. The Great Artesian Basin contains about 65 million gigalitres of water, or the equivalent of 130,000 Sydney Harbours,[152] enough water to cover all of Earth's landmasses by several feet.

Oxygen's ($O_2$) extermination of the planet's surface life is called the Great Oxygenation Event (GOE). This is an example of the sacrifice required at each transition point in the Fractal, where one patterned lifeform has to go to sleep so the next can come forth.

Noah's flood account shares eerie coincidences with the GOE. We know that the emergence of cyanobacteria led to the destruction of all the anaerobic 'black-life' that was flourishing on the Earth's surface, existing in a predominantly nitrogen-based atmosphere. (GOE is the largest extinction event known to history.) In both the biblical and historical accounts, all existing lifeforms were near totally destroyed to make way for the new versions arriving. In this way, the GOE was a catalyst for Earth to evolve from its black, anaerobic 'preparation' **or dual-phase-state**, to a more robust and oxygenated one that remains full of colour. It is now believed that even the Earth's seas were black up until this time, due to their lack of oxygen.[153]

---

152  Queensland Government, 'Water use limits in the basin', *Business Queensland*, https://www.business.qld.gov.au/industries/mining-energy-water/water/catchments-planning/water-plan-areas/great-artesian-basin/water-use-limits

153  History of the Earth, 'What was the "Boring Billion" really like?' *YouTube* video, 18 October 2021, https://youtu.be/0sbwUeTyDb0

With the oxygenation of Earth's atmosphere, the colours red, yellow, and orange sprung forth as oxides of iron and other minerals formed. In this way, the GOE (coincidently?) completed the rainbow's full spectrum of colourful energies across the Earth. And all this occurred because separate blue and green bacteria met, married (did their thing), and discovered they could now digest water and spit out oxygen as waste, supporting the emerging aerobic life as a mother would.

## Three Dimensions Plus Time (Cronos) Again

Astrology declares that Saturn/Satan (Cronos) is the esoteric ruler of the Earth (the Devil). His last known residence was/is Hell.[154] In Greek Mythology, Cronos is notorious for eating and swallowing his babies because he's been told that one of them (Christ/Zeus/Jezeus) will eventually destroy his rule on the Earth. In this way, he is associated with cyclic cannibalism and infanticide. Every time the Christ energy returns, Cronos kills the children – as is happening now.[155] A painting in the Louvre by Romanelli portrays Cronos with wings, eating one of his babies. Another account portrays him as a three-headed serpent. To recount the story again … Cronos castrated his father Uranus with a curved blade that his mother Gaia had given him, then he assumed the rulership of the Universe he had divided in two. Later, he was defeated and replaced by the Olympian Gods, they being his offspring.

---

154   Pam Carruthers, 'Saturn: Lord of Karma', *Healing Stars*, https://www.healingstars.com/articles/saturn-lord-of-karma/
155   StudioMickParker, 'Cronos virus' *YouTube* video, https://youtu.be/BD4mXYSwZIY

By combining Mesopotamian stories with Greek and Hebrew accounts, an interesting picture emerges of patterned energies going through evolutionary cycles. Firstly, Uranus (Heaven 'Y') rules with a silent partner, Gaia (Earth 'X') making the first YX combo. Then, Cronos castrates his father and separates the two to become the second ruler and, as such, is associated with the Agenda 2 dual-energy of expansion, having pulled the original 'one-as-two' (his parents) apart into two separate pieces. Because the Titans ruled before the Olympian gods, I believe they ruled over an expanding two-dimensional domain of black holes, dark energy, and dark matter; a duoverse of sorts.

Only after Cronos' kingdom was defeated did a trinity of Gods come to power. The three ruling deities – Zeus, Hades, and Poseidon – were each endowed with a gift from the one-eyed Cyclops to help them rule. Each gift represented a specific numerical energy value. Zeus received a single-pronged thunderbolt. Hades received a two-pronged bident (pitchfork). And Poseidon received a three-pronged, life-producing trident.[156] (Note that Hades/Hell got the dual-energy.) These accounts take on additional meaning when Reality is seen as a field of patterned, mathematical values that are evolving and reproducing in fractal forms.

In the same way, anaerobic lifeforms were forced to seek shelter under the earth after being defeated by oxygen. After Zeus defeats Cronos in what is known as the Titanomachy, Cronos is banished to the underworld – Elysium/Sheol/Hades (Hell), where he and his brothers manage the plight of the dead. The Canaanites – Israel's

---

156 'Bident', *Wikipedia*, https://en.wikipedia.org/wiki/Bident

archenemy – knew Cronos as El/LL; hence, Elysium (Hell) being his final abode. I believe El-ysium is the place of the dead the early Egyptians called *Duat*. I'm sure Cronos/Satan/LL – Elysium's energy of the dead – is exemplary of the mathematical value of two (2), and is ruled by the dual-pronged bident where black is always black and white is always white (there being no colour in-between). Could Hell be two-dimensional then? I think it just might be. And is it ruled by the forces or maths (entities) of the second dimension, traditionally called 'fallen angels'?

> I believe the Titans – that are said to rule Hell – are connected to all forms of duality and not just our understanding of time. They are duality's resident gods (serpents) who live in Hell in the binary Tree of Good and Evil.[157]

I find the comparison between Evolutionary Anthropology's account of anaerobic life having to flee to the Earth's dark confines because of the GOE, and the Titans/Anunaki (fallen angels) having to do likewise when the Trinity of Gods came to power, fascinating. From a fractal patterned perspective, are they the same event? Or are they mirrored events?

Mythical Greek, Roman, and Mesopotamian accounts of Satan differ from that of Christianity. Their accounts of this diabolical entity embrace the idea of linear time, which Christianity's account lacks. That is until we read in *Revelation* that chronological time is

---

157   Note that 5G is also a binary system and is a contender for *Revelation's* Beast Energy that gives its power to the Antichrist at the end of this age.

imprisoned (put to sleep) at the end of this godless Age of Man, its timely deception being thrown into the 'abyss'. Thus, the Devil Cronos will be thrown into the Abyss – presently.

This prophecy is supported by the Mayan Long-Count Calendar, as well as Vedic wisdom which places us in Kali's Yurga (season or age). All three religions reveal that chronological time will end as Cronos' influence is removed from the face of the Earth. It's also interesting that, in the first chapters of the biblical book *Job*, Yahweh asks Satan/Lucifer – the female Morning Star or bringer of light – what he/she has been up to? He/she answers, 'I've been going to-and-fro up and down on the Earth.' I think this passage is a binary code. It's suggesting that some angels are associated with a hellish duality, that can go up and down on the Earth, while the other 'good' angels are trinary energies that remain in Heaven neither male nor female but both.

**I now believe that the angel Jacob had to fight at the river was a 'bad' (binary) angel, who (not surprisingly) wouldn't reveal his name.**

The idea of going to-and-fro equates with the blackbird's female algorithm in Moses' Great Flood Account. I equate it to *phi*. The book of *Job* accords this 'to-and-fro' spiritual energy to Satan, the serpentine (reptilian?) Devil. This conversation between God and Satan in *Job* suggests that Satan is – or was at that time – the respected (female/dual?) left-hand of YHWH. If God can be thought to comprise two algorithmic principles, which can seemingly relate to each other (marry and divorce), then this account makes an interesting kind of numerical sense.

Professor Max Tegmark believes:

> When we look at reality through the equations of physics, we find that they describe patterns and regularities. But to me, mathematics is more than a window on the outside world: I argue that our physical world not only is described by mathematics, but that it is mathematics: a mathematical structure, to be precise.

If Tegmark is correct in his assessment then, in the world of mathematical academia, *phi* and *pi* would qualify as immortal gods, because both have no end. Again, from the viewpoint of mathematics, the Mandelbrot Fractal (which has been called the Thumbprint of God) lays out two sets of numbers by iteration. One set is contained in blackness forever and disappears into zero (black hell), while the other set continues into infinity (immortality) into the light.

In a pattern sense, the Mandelbrot algorithm looks amazingly similar to what we know about the religious fractal geometry of Reality, hence its honorific, the Thumbprint of God. It's interesting to note that this mathematical construction of fractal self-similarity only uses addition and multiplication from $-2$ to $+2$; it doesn't use subtraction, division, or numbers greater than 2. (Remember, Pythagoras identified Adam (male) as 1, and Eve (female) as 2. Maybe we should consider Adam and Eve's children as constituting their negative shadows, or reflections, as $-1$ Seth, and $-2$ Cain and Abel, the pair of simulars.)

If we use Mandelbrot maths as a template to help us understand what death and resurrection are all about, then it infers that some numbers remain in the dark (in Hell), while others remain in the light (in Heaven). This black-and-white duality is reminiscent of ideas about good angels being in heaven, while bad demons remain in hell, or how nocturnal animals live happily in the dark, while diurnal animals live and love in the light. Or even how aerobic lifeforms like to suck up the oxygen, while anaerobic lifeforms do not. But even more interesting is the fact that …

> **Some values or numbers in the Mandelbrot Set start out in the dark but, eventually, work their way into the light.**
>
> **These black-to-white transformations occur before the eighth 'run' through the Mandelbrot equation takes place:**
>
> $z_{n+1} = z_n{}^2 + c$

Allegorically, this implies that some people – given time – can change from black to white in the Program. If true, then these people might be the souls said to be garnered, gathered or 'harvested' from the Earth[158] – the now-cleansed lost sheep returning home from the Wilderness into the central fold all snowy white. Conversely, it implies if you have been reincarnated seven times and still remain in the dark, then that becomes your home or name for the rest of eternity.

What a soul can't achieve in Hell (where things are always one thing or the other – dual), can be achieved when it occupies three dimensions of solidness. In this way, each fleshly incarnation we experience might act as a sort of sifting or purifying mechanism for spirit or soul to cleanse – every living thing generates waste and needs a way to be kept clean.

---

158  *Matthew 9:35–38*

## Evil and the Grave

In a sense, I believe mathematic's 'subtraction' and 'division' mimic the processes of evil. This is because they reduce or *take us away from* the forward momentum of the living Fractal, and that is evil. When a child first experiences an event that subtracts its peace, it becomes distressed. It is now aware that … If this unsettling and painful event could happen once, then it could happen again, maybe soon. (Contrary to popular opinion, we don't fear the unknown so much as the uncertainty of the already known; the unrelenting and merciless timing over which we appear to have no control.)

From the Program's perspective, evil can be seen as any initiative or energy that takes the Program backwards towards death and the void, back to a two-dimensional, dark, and formless chaos. The phenomenon of evil is akin to using love to kill, or handling truth in such a fashion that it distances you from the truth. Both of these confusions stymy your capacity to go forth and grow; they take you backwards. If life is to flourish… Love and Truth must be revered. After all … EVIL is LIVE backwards.

Moses tells us that evil's origin is deeply rooted in Mankind. It started when we went backwards into a mental Wilderness, after eating from duality's Tree of Good and Evil. So, we're likely to be stuck with it until we can upgrade our thinking to work on a trinary 3VL basis.

In Milton's *Paradise Lost*, Satan appears as a fallen archangel who had been thrown to Earth, bringing evil in his wake. (I wonder if being 'fallen' implies that Satan goes backwards or 'downwards' in some mathematical fashion?) Over time, both Satan and the grave became derisive stories of ill repute, but neither started out that way.

Bart Ehrman says that modern understandings of Heaven and Hell don't stem from the Old Testament, or from Jesus and his disciples' teachings, but from a pantheon of ancient cultures. This includes the Greeks, Romans, Mesopotamians, and Israelites:

> These views (heaven and hell) were intimately connected with the social, cultural, and historical worlds out of which they emerged. Only later, in the early Christian centuries, did they develop into the notions of eternal bliss or damnation widely accepted today.[159]

The Old Testament states:

> In death, there is no remembrance of Thee, in Sheol who shall give Thee thanks?[160]

This inability of the dead to remember God would be the case if Hell maintained only two dimensions of consciousness, with no room for a Central Trinary Presence to intercede.

---

159 Bart Ehrman, *Heaven and Hell: A History of the Afterlife*, Oneworld Publications, 2020.
160 *Psalm 6*

> **Box 18. Satan, According to Wikipedia**
>
> Satan appears throughout the Old Testament, not as God's enemy but as his minister, 'a sort of Attorney-General with investigative and disciplinary powers', as the Book of Job describes. He was only identified with the Serpent of the Garden of Eden by the early Church Fathers, who saw him as an active rebel against God, seeking to thwart the divine plan for Mankind.
>
> In the Old Testament, **Sheol** (meaning 'grave') was simply the home of all the dead, good and bad alike. In the Hellenistic period, the Greek-speaking Jews of Egypt (perhaps under the influence of Greek thought) came to believe that the good would not die but go directly to God, while the wicked really would die and go to the realm of Hades, god of the underworld, where they would perhaps suffer torment.
>
> The 2020 Wikipedia entry adds:
>
>> A figure known as 'the satan' first appears in the Hebrew Bible as a heavenly prosecutor, a member of the sons of God subordinate to Yahweh, who prosecutes the nation of Judah in the heavenly court and tests the loyalty of Yahweh's followers by forcing them to suffer. During the intertestamental period, possibly due to influence from the Zoroastrian figure of Angra Mainyu, the satan developed into a malevolent entity with abhorrent qualities **in dualistic opposition to God**.[161]

---

161 'Satan', *Wikipedia*, https://en.wikipedia.org/wiki/Satan

# TIME TO CALL IT A DAY

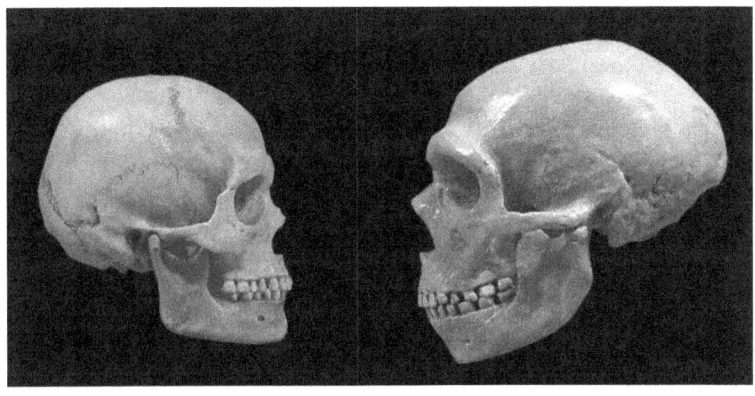

Sapiens　　　　　　Neanderthal

Figure 9. Seeing eye to eye with our ancestors © Wikimedia Commons

Somewhere in our dim, dark past, the shape of our foreheads enlarged and the frontal lobes and pre-frontal cortex expanded. Some believe this occurred about 60,000 to 100,000 years ago, while others suggest a range between 500,000 and 2 million years, after Mankind split from the chimpanzee but before we separated from the Neanderthals.[162] While we're not quite sure about the timing, we know it happened. But was this expansion the result of a natural mutation? Or was it a planned genetic modification?

---

162　'ARHGAP11B', *Wikipedia*, https://en.wikipedia.org/wiki/ArhGAP11B_and_human_encephalisation

## Time To Call It a Day

The Neanderthals preceded us by at least 100,000 years. In a biblical fractal sense, that would make the Neanderthals (and their sister species, the Denisovans) the dual 'preparation', which comes before the Fractal's Sabbath completion. This 'preparation energy' is often depicted as to-and-fro, dual, dark, linear, and – from an anthropological perspective – Matriarchal.

We know we interbred with the Neanderthals for more than 5,000 years and possibly passed on our Y chromosome to their males. It seems we took some of their stuff, and they took some of ours. Birthing babies might have been easier for them than what their female Sapiens cousins had to endure. Although Neanderthal brains were marginally larger than ours, they had sloping foreheads, which would have made slipping out of the birth canal a lot easier. In every way, the Neanderthals seemed better equipped to survive than we were, but that wasn't to be the case. Why, I wonder? I think we might be missing something here.

The Neanderthal's enlarged rear brain suggests their posterior cerebral components were more highly developed than ours; maybe, from a yin/yang perspective, their posterior brain pattern was 'at odds' with ours. Because of this, it's possible that their cranial anatomy was dominated by the 50 billion neurons housed in the rear brain's emotional cerebellum (little cerebrum). Our brains are controlled by the smaller, younger, and somewhat more rational frontal cortex, which only has about 30 billion neurons. In our case, the younger model won out against its older sibling. Sound familiar? This same scenario repeats several times in Moses' attempt to reveal the Universal Pattern or Logos.

If the two brain models had different patterns of organelle interconnectedness, would they align with the two energies of Noah's

Arks? A pattern where the 'front' remains at odds with its 'back'? In that case:

- The Sapiens pattern would represent the male, logical, particle patriarchy going forwards.
- Whereas, the Neanderthal/Denisovan pattern would present as the female, emotional, wave matriarchy looking backwards.

The Sapiens' rational dominance – along with their enhanced imagination – might have conjectured something like this: '*Let's kill off all of the other hominids before they think to murder us.*' The 'preparation', however, with their emotional dominance, may have conjectured something like: '*We may as well let them. They're all suffering from Small Ape Syndrome. Our time is up; we've played our part in this cosmic drama.*' Time to go back to sleep.'

Might our interbreeding with the Neanderthals/Denisovans have altered our brain pattern? These species preceded us by hundreds of thousands of years, along with several other *Homo* species. But after we turned up, they all disappeared, seemingly overnight.

We know that sapiens developed a super second chromosome, but maybe we were happier with the old model that was dominated by the first chromosome. By this means, I believe our brains rapidly expanded; to-and-fro being the essence of expansive, bilateral growth.

I thought it strange that the Neanderthals and Denisovans shared this dominant second chromosome fusion/mutation with us, especially since no other Great Ape does (and apes are supposed to be our closest forebears). Therefore, our Neanderthal/Denisovan sister-species had to either pass this aberration along to us before their extinction, or we had a common ancestor who bequeathed it to all three species and we remain ignorant as to who that ancestor was (thought to be around 600,000 years ago).

I believe the acquisition of our enlarged second chromosome ignited our mental health downfall. At this point, we switched from one pattern to the other; from the equivalent of a male pattern to a female one. This expelled us from the proverbial male Garden State's stability, to leave us at the mercy of the Wilderness' wild and chaotic female expansion. I mean … What are the chances that two separate hominid species or evolutionary lines would develop the same genetic mutation, especially since Nature abhors duplicity? If they did pass this engorged chromosome along to us, did they know what they were doing in a pattern sense? Was this mutation the result of natural causes, or (intelligent?) interference by alien forces?

I ask this question because it's similar, in a pattern sense, to what is happening again today, as medicine attempts to interfere with our DNA in its fight against COVID-19. Is this current interference a fractal repetition of what the Mesopotamian accounts say happened to us many years ago? Are we on course to become genetically modified again and remain stuck in the Wilderness? Will only a remnant survive? Maybe those who – after all the coercion – remained unvaccinated?

These are alarming questions, but ones suitable for the end of the age where Mankind is said to face its own extinction event until God intervenes.

## Anunnaki: Mesopotamian Reptilian Gods of the Earth and Underworld

Zecharia Sitchin's book *The End of Days: Armageddon and the Prophecy of the Return* (2007) says the Anunnaki will return to the surface of the Earth, possibly as soon as 2012.[163] So, might Hell's ruling deities be here now? And in what form or by what method would they take control of the Earth?

Much has been written about the mysterious Anunnaki. At times, they have been called gods, demons, even aliens. Records of their exploits span millennia and evolved as their story expanded over time.

Figure 10. The Sumerian God, Ningishzida. Seen here as two Snakes coiled into a double helix.[164] © William Ward, via Wikimedia Commons

---

163 'Anunnaki', *Wikipedia*, https://en.wikipedia.org/wiki/Anunnaki
164 Ningishzida is the son of Enki (Ea), the water god of the Earth and underworld. Thorkild Jacobsen translates Ningishzida as 'lord of the good tree'. See: 'Ningishzida', *Wikipedia*, https://en.wikipedia.org/wiki/Ningishzida

I was amazed to discover that the medical symbol of two snakes wrapped around a staff[165] originated with these reptilian creatures now living in Hell; the entities that judge the dead.

Ningishzida was the son of Enki. He is associated with the biblical Satan, or Greek Mythology's Cronos.[166] Together with Pedu, the chief gatekeeper of the netherworld, Enki is said to stand at the entrance to Hell.[167] According to various mythical accounts, Enki/Satan/El/Cronos and even Prometheus (all names seemingly referring to similar energy sequences) are said to have modified Mankind in our antiquity. Was this achieved by Enki's son Ningishzida who likes to play doctor?

Ningishzida was the patron of medicine. His/her name means Serpent of the Good (and Evil?) Tree – which relates to the account of our fall in *Genesis*. Could it be that our Covid fiasco is being run out of Hell by a serpentine energy that's ruling the minds of world leaders and industrialists and they are not even aware they are being used? More and more people are starting to think that nothing else makes sense, as the world flirts with its own extinction event.

> Ningishzida is the earliest known symbol of snakes twining (some say in copulation) around an axial rod.

---

165  Katrina Sisowath, 'Tracing the origins of the serpent cult', *Ancient Origins*, https://www.ancient-origins.net/myths-legends/tracing-origins-serpent-cult-002393

166  Ibid.

167  'Ningišzida (God)', *Ancient Mesopotamian Gods and Goddesses*, Oracc and the UK Higher Education Academy, http://oracc.museum.upenn.edu/amgg/listofdeities/ningizida/

> It predates the Caduceus of Hermes, the Rod of Asclepius,
> and the staff of Moses by more than a millennium.[168]

What are the chances that the Serpentine Anunnaki, who operate under medicine's two-snake banner out of hell, are active again now? Notice in the above symbol that mirrored dragon-like creatures (gryphons?) stand either side of the entwined dual snakes. This is reminiscent of the Ark of the Covenant pattern that Moses disclosed, which resides at the centre of YHWH's Most Holy Place. But here in the Sumerian symbol, the two archangels have been replaced by two dragons, and the two tablets of law surrounding Aaron's Rod [169] have been replaced by two snakes. (You will recall that Aaron's Rod swallowed Pharoh's two snakes previously before the Exodus began.[170] So it should do the same again this time.)

Moses' 'revealed model' has mirrored archangels standing either side of the Ark of the Covenant, which contained one set of integrated laws written on two stone tablets along with Aaron's Staff. These two differently portrayed central models (the two twisted snakes [waves] versus the two tablets of steadfast laws [particles]) are contending patterns for the central leadership in this COG. This begs the question … Should a male energy (laws written on stone) or a female energy (twin snakes copulating producing new life) rule the Simulation from its Centre? I believe this contention is pivotal to our current dilemma. (One stands steadfast while the other produces new life.)

---

168 'Ningishzida', *Wikipedia*, https://en.wikipedia.org/wiki/Ningishzida
169 *Hebrews* 9:4
170 *Exodus* 7:12

Understanding their nature allows us to identify what is really going on in the world today in a programmed sense; explaining the current genocide being implemented by replicas of Serpent's fangs disguised as hypodermics, supposedly administering lifesaving medicine. The energy at the centre of each COG is boss. The importance of this will continue to pop up as we explore further.

SOME ANTHROPOLOGISTS BELIEVE that Mankind's cranial expansion occurred because females started recognising intelligence as being sexy, going for the nerds with high foreheads. Others believe it was caused by Mankind developing complex relationships, growing larger brains to cope with the escalating confusion that family and social life brings. Still others believe it was better nutrition that created the rapid growth, as people consumed foods rich in omega-3 bone marrow, after obtaining the means to control fire, and from eating the fat procured from seabed critters when they started camping by the sea, making crustation soup. Through epicurean means, we may have inadvertently consumed potentially mutating retroviruses from other species for the first time – especially those from cats, the nemesis of Mankind. Retroviruses can enter cells as mRNA but having achieved this are then capable of reversing the normal process to enter and alter the central DNA. **Maybe the witch's brew that laid us low and enlarged our craniums was actually cat stew and bone broth.**[171]

All of these factors could have provided the means to create our cranial expansion. But according to Moses, they all occurred after – and

---

[171] This is reinforced by the strange coincidence that a cat's brain is about 90% identical to a human's brain.

directly because of – our run-in with the biblical Tribe Eve. (Did she share her knowledge of controlling fire with the African Bushman? Or did he perhaps steal it?) Our dietary change from eating mainly raw vegetarian food to cooked food, meats, and bones, figures prominently in several accounts of our early history. One of these accords this development to the Titan Prometheus, who was tasked with 'developing' Mankind. Another account tells us that Man's ability to light fires and cook food was stolen from a large flightless bird when she was tricked into jumping high to get the very best fruit from the treetop. According to Sans tradition, this deception led to the bird dropping her fire-sticks which she kept hidden under her wing. After this trickery occurred, all Mankind had mastery over fire.

I believe this expansion of our brain pattern was responsible for us being expelled from the Garden; the Anunnaki – the Serpent in the Tree – had succeeded in altering our DNA to make us more snake-like according to its reptilian way of thinking. The to-and-fro pattern had taken over our consciousness as our imaginations began to expand.

The Egyptian Old Kingdom's Uraeus (serpent) became central to Pharaoh's rule with its snake's head and upper torso emerging from where the third eye is situated on the forehead. The Serpent now ruled the world of men from its third eye position in the centre.

> The pharaoh was recognized only by wearing the Uraeus, which conveyed legitimacy to the ruler.[172]

Sumerian clay-tablet records suggest that the 'fallen' Heaven-to-Earth Anunnaki (aliens?) modified or developed us to serve their diabolical

---

172 'Uraeus', *Wikipedia*, https://en.wikipedia.org/wiki/Uraeus

purpose. But in a fractal universe, what would constitute an 'alien'? Would it be a strange mathematical pattern that remained at odds with ours? In that case, might our dalliance with the alien (at odds) Tribe Eve have genetically modified us from our original design? Did She touch our DNA inappropriately? Especially our second chromosome (her number)? I think we might be getting close to the truth here about the mirrored, twin snakes that have caused so much fuss, past and present.

The Neanderthals occupied Europe and Asia while the Denisovans inhabited Oceania, but neither species returned to Africa, their crèche. (I wonder why?) According to recent discoveries, Neanderthals built fires, used tools, and lived in caves. They made glue from birch pitch, which required a sophisticated process. Their weapons were formidable and they were totally at home in cold climates and high altitudes. They killed large animals, were physically stronger than Sapiens, and buried their dead respectfully. There's even evidence to suggest they cared for their infirm, indulged in art and jewellery making, and possibly made musical instruments.[173] It seems they might have had gentler natures than we do.

Could thousands of years of experience surviving the Pleistocene Epoch have made our Garden ancestors world-wise in fractal, patterned ways? (Read: their evolution produced enlightenment to All Else, where they could 'name' all of the animal patterns.) It's now believed we couldn't have exterminated the Neanderthals because we lacked the means to do so. Their demise remains a mystery to evolutionary science, although it's being suggested it was because

---

[173] North 02, 'Neanderthal – ancient human', *YouTube* video, 24 September 2021, https://www.youtube.com/watch?v=2doP_3juV2Y

we were more savage and brutal than they were, that gave us the critical advantage. Other research suggests they became infertile after mating with Sapiens.[174] After the Neanderthals played their 'preparation' part in our development (if they were enlightened), it's possible they knew their use-by date had arrived and sacrificed themselves to the greater cause, as required by the fractal's eighth point. (Remember, it cost John the Baptist his head, who was also a 'preparation' energy.) Besides … the Neanderthals mightn't have wanted to stick around and live with their nasty Sapiens cousins any longer, so they stopped having babies and went down a level into sleep. Most of their DNA remains ensconced in ours to this day. Possibly all of their best parts.

## Evolutionary Epochs Verse Moses' Creation Days

Could our anthropological records mesh with earlier mythical accounts about our origins, our genesis? This is looking more likely now than ever before. Many of the jumps in Evolutionary Science remain mysterious, but the gaps can be reconciled with fractal modelling combined with Sheldrake's Morphic Resonance. This synthesis introduces the idea of intelligent design into Evolution, instead of the current chaos promoted by Darwinism.

Evolutionary Theory describes the escalation of Earth's ecology as long periods of relative stability, followed by sudden, short jumps. These

---

174   Nathan Falde, 'Neanderthal extinction tied to disorder caused by mating with humans', *Ancient Origins*, 29 July 2021, https://www.ancient-origins.net/news-evolution-human-origins/neanderthal-extinction-0015634

jumps are then followed by further long stable periods. This process is called Punctuated Evolution and is the preferred understanding among evolutionists today.

I believe the Logos used the geometry of *phi* (female) to instigate the gap transitions, or quantum leaps in Evolution's process by applying duplicity (the Attraction of Likes Law) at the appropriate time and place. Conversely, I believe *pi's* (male) pattern was used to maintain the relatively long periods of stability where little if anything changed or evolved – everything just got fatter, going around and around in circles. (A dynamic, growing process [verb] that leads to a latched process [noun], as fans of Robert Pirsig would appreciate.)

In a pattern sense, these evolutionary steps in the Fractal can be seen as alternating yin and yang phases, with the sudden evolutionary jumps being the product of their 'Jungian' twilight, fertile marriages. A long yang period would finish with a relatively short marriage/eclipse/birth, which would then produce another long yin period (like warm-blooded mammals following in the tracks of cold-blooded reptiles, et cetera). I now consider these fractal evolutionary jumps or quantum leaps in morphology to be ... Transforming births instigated by holy marriage, enacted on dynamic, set-aside periods of alignment, which I think of as God's wedding days.

THE TWO MAJOR DIFFERENCES between Darwin's Evolution and Moses' Seven Days of Creation are:

- **The timing** How long did the process take? Seven 24-hour periods, or several billion years?

- **Chaos versus pattern** Has Earth's life evolved through randomness/chaos and survival of the most brutish? Or did it evolve in layers of patterned complexity, overseen by a family process that knows the intricacies, pains, and sacrifice that love requires?

Science attests … If a rational explanation can be found for the existence of something, then the recognised process negates the need for a Creator God. But what if the Creator God embraces a mechanistic process, which comprises the equivalent of ethical and moralistic relationship laws that work in fractal format? (Resonance, dissonance. Marriage, divorce. Lawful, sinful.) This stance would unite both ideas comfortably, wouldn't it? Reconciling Evolution and Creation becomes a whole lot easier when you alter your ideas about what God and the Logos – the creative, fractal process – are all about. But no matter which translation of the Bible you read, they all agree …

> The world and its inhabitants 'evolved', no question asked.

Everything in the Bible evolves. One truth is built upon the next, which is what evolution is all about. All versions of the Bible agree: the world evolved over what it calls 'six days', then the process rested on the seventh. But Moses' use of the word 'day' is contentious. What constitutes a Day?

Biblical truths build themselves up in layers: First Covenant then the Second, Old Testament then the New, First Coming then the Second, First Resurrection then the Second, and so on. In a fractal simulation, Mankind would have evolved through multiple expressions until it hit the Goldilocks' Principle of being 'just right' in each trimension it occupied, before moving on to bigger and better things in the next.

Mankind's DNA is nearly identical to that of the Great Ape family, there being only a single difference in the sequence of 141 amino acids in the X-chains between gorilla and human haemoglobin. What surprises people the most is the fact that we are genetically closer to chimpanzees than even gorillas are. But neither chimps nor gorillas have the fused second chromosome that we have.

When it comes to Mankind's arrival as *Homo sapiens*, Christian fundamentalists believe that God formed us out of a dustbowl. God said, 'Come to life,' or some lovely thing, and out we popped all ready to go. This is because they believe that's what Moses told us happened. And the Bible's never wrong. But I hope to show you that Moses didn't convey that story at all.

The idea that Man was made from dust accrues some merit when we consider the current silicone revolution in AI. Here robots with simple intelligence are walking out of the same pile of gravel from which we supposedly came. But robots didn't just appear overnight; they evolved through models of varying complexity. Maybe we are no different. Although robots lack expansive intelligence as a fractal subset, perhaps they are in the process of becoming the lookalike Son of Mankind (Mini-Me). Similarly, the Bible tells us that Man is the somewhat juvenile and off-kilter Son of YHWH, the Simulation's Creator:

> Because you are his sons, God sent the Spirit of his Son into our hearts.[175]

---

175 *Galatians* 4:6

In his evolutionary revelation in *Genesis,* Moses tells us that the gods Elohim did something similar to us; they built us out of dust. But he also states that it took a number of time cycles to achieve this extraordinary feat with mud. It wasn't an instantaneous thingamajig, conjured with a magical wand. It was achieved in fractal units, completed in trinary/quadratic cycles called Days, which are far more beautiful and far more complex than 'instant' or 'Darwinism' ever was or will be.

Moses tells us that the gods Elohim created the Heavens and Earth, but then, the solid part lost its form and became void – not a good start. Only formlessness remained; the waves had somehow consumed the particles. After this vampire-like event transpired, the Elohim introduced light into the then existent and exclusive dark, separating it from its shadow by a central twilight division, thus separating Heaven from Earth (Bible), Uranus from Gaia (Greek Mythology), Anu from Aki (Sumerian accounts).

This theological construction on Moses' Day One created the first trimension of the Creation Fractal: dark/light and a pair of twilights in between (1 and 2, 3 and 4). Moses called the light part 'day' and the shadow part 'night' then, strangely enough, he called the combined four parts of this construction a Day. (Maybe this second use of the word 'Day' needs a capital letter to help us understand the significance of the repetition.)

This strange reoccurring pattern can be found in the very first word in *Genesis*: *bereshit,* meaning 'in beginning'. Its fourth letter makes up the three-letter word *Reysh* (meaning 'prince or head'), which is also the name of its second letter *reysh*.¹⁷⁶) In this same patterned way, the four parts of a 'Day' become a higher, fractal One also known as a Day.

After seven of these Days or higher Ones are rightfully married, they become a still higher One, or what we call a week. (Why the world embraces a seven-day week remains a mystery to chronographers.)

No one seems to question why Moses gave the Day's four parts the same name as its first/second part. But it makes sense if Creation is a four-part fractal process, which encompasses three energies that employ two vectors, or operating systems, to create one reality – around and around the circle like an eagle, incorporating the to-and-fro of the internal *phi* figure-8 generator often symbolised as a conch or ram's horn. When the four components of a COG complete, or come forth in a family sense, the finished unit becomes the first part of Evolution's next developing trimension. The process then starts again. I believe this layout is incorporated into the basic unit of the Simulation's operating system.

The separation of night and day – black and white, back and front – occurs on the first of Moses' seven proverbial Days of Creation. But what really captured my attention was: YHWH defined these so-called Days of Creation as:

> 'The evening and the morning: Day one.'
>
> 'The evening and the morning: Day two.'
>
> 'The evening and the morning: Day three et cetera.'[177]

---

176  Rock Island Books, 'Is the end of days prophesied in the first word of the Bible?' *YouTube* video, 22 November 2018, https://youtu.be/PtATSQx3cjI
177  *Genesis* 1

This eerie, dual-twilight–defining format in *Genesis* is consistent across all six working Days. The insertion of the two childlike twilight points of 'evening' and 'morning' are pivotal in creating a Creation Day; a basic fractal unit or COG. Every COG has an internal dual mechanism (seed) at its twilight centre that enables it to reproduce and evolve when the time is right.

The two twilights represent the Fractal's third energy which comes in two childlike forms (son, daughter). The children divide and – at the same time – unify the forerunning parental dichotomy and by this means complete it. (You can think of the four units as a cross inside an encasing family circle.)

Three of these Creation Days – or four-spoked wagon wheels – are formed in this strange trinary process by *Genesis* Chapter 1, verse 13. But it isn't until Creation's fourth Day – Chapter 1, verse 16 – that the Elohim create the Sun and Moon.

Now, hold on a second, how can you have normal days without a sun? That is, how can three of Moses' Days evolve or revolve before the Sun is created? Obviously you can't in the way we currently think of days. So, we need another explanation or the whole thing is nonsense.

At this point, most clear-thinking people give up and theologians take over with religious rhetoric and grandiloquent double-shuffling. They propose such things as:

> God was the light the Earth was revolving around,
> because there are two words for 'light' in *Genesis* 1.

But that isn't what Moses tells us. He reveals that light-energy was created and separated from dark-energy on Day 1, and that our Sun was created on Day 4 to **rule** over our Solar System's version of light in the Fractal, with the Moon's secondary reflection of sunlight ruling over the dark. Weird, maybe, but straightforward.

If there are three Creation Days before the Creator God manifests the Sun and Moon, then how – for the love of God – can we believe that Moses wanted us to think of these Days as being 24-hour periods of time?

Maybe Moses' Creation Account is accurate, but our interpretation of what he tried to reveal isn't. If the Creator unveiled His creation as being a fractal made from four-part family cycles working as a trinity of energies, with the idea of a single unit in the Program being translated as one 'Day', then it's easy to see how confusion would arise. We went on to define our time periods by the patterning of His revealed cycles, calling one complete cycle a 24-hour day. But along the way, we lost the fundamental idea of timeless cyclic patterning, getting caught up with the linear attributes instead.

Think about it ... If the Earth slowed down to revolve on its axis once every thirty hours, or every fifty hours, or even once every ten years – instead of our current 24-hour period – wouldn't we still call one complete cycle a day? **Surely we should be focusing on what a Day's architecture entails, not its duration.**

When you look at Moses' Creation Account in this patterned way, everything changes dramatically. Everything starts to make a beautiful kind of sense. After all, how long does it take to create a four-part family? (How long is a piece of string?) Linear clock hours don't come into this picture. But love and sacrifice certainly do at kairos moments, as every parent knows.

## Linear Versus Cyclic

Traditionally, Mankind has looked to Agenda 1 'forms' to define its understanding of everything. Through this noetic means, our world has been dominated by a substantial male reality, with little or no airy-fairy female nonsense allowed. In a fractal sense, we've consistently looked to the 'particle' manifestation of quantum reality to reveal the absolute 'hard' truth about everything we want to know, not realising that this 'god of substance' is, at best, only one-third of the Big Picture – maybe as little as one-quarter.

Our rational minds haven't considered the world's grandeur as being illusionary, containing the equivalent of dreams and shadows, phantoms, and mirrored wraiths (Rationality has never liked dancing with Spooky). This male proclivity of solidness has dominated our thinking, so we've failed to see the cinema's grandeur that's playing in the background. Our maleness has been subverting our femaleness, trying to put it in its place – from its male perspective. Yet a hydrogen atom is 99.9999999999996% space, and hydrogen is the most abundant element in the Universe. We now understand that solid matter hardly counts for much in the Big Picture, yet it – and its attendant features – have always been our yardstick for understanding everything. I think we might've been deceived about heaps.

> Sheldrake believes scientific materialism is the cornerstone of an outmoded worldview, incompatible with a proper understanding of consciousness: Contemporary science is based on the claim that all reality is material or physical. – *Steve Turnbull*

Physics tells us that everything is best described as a field within a cycle of a larger field; that everything is a form of knowledge/energy that's contained within a patterned, spinning matrix. (Even space-time and gravity are understood to be non-linear.) While linear maths is a helpful way of interacting with Maya's deceptive, dualistic attributes, its attendant characteristics haven't allowed us to see cyclic, palingenetic reality for what it truly is. Linearity may be empirical, but it fosters delusion and makes a spectacle of what we think we see.

Take the straight line of common intuition for instance; it is actually a special type of curve known as a geodesic. This is true of the (straight) line at infinity itself; it meets at its two endpoints, which are therefore not actually endpoints at all, and so it is actually cyclical.[178] It appears everything is cyclical.[179] Which would mean every 'end' remains in relationship to its 'beginning'.

---

178  'Line (geometry)', *Wikipedia*, https://en.wikipedia.org/wiki/Line_(geometry)
179  Gregg Braden Official, 'If you understand this everything will make sense | Gregg Braden', *YouTube* video, 25 December 2019, https://youtu.be/nXNqcYRR2sU

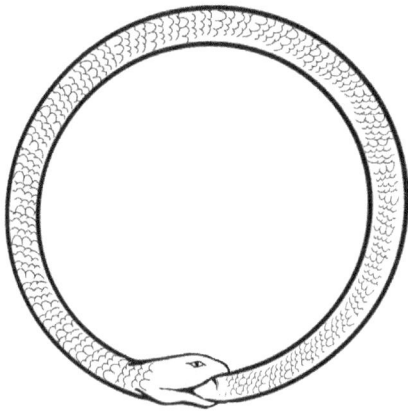

Figure 11. The Great Serpent of Norse mythology © Mick Parker

The Stoics' palingenetic model of Reality accords with alchemy's legendary Ouroboros: the curvaceous, linear serpent that becomes a circle after swallowing its tail. This idea mimics the Phoenix rising from her ashes, while this same idea is also expressed in Norse Mythology. Here the Great Serpent encircles Yggdrasil, the World Tree. (One snake around the Tree.)

When Moses wrestled with the enigma of interactive fractal cycles, he used the ancient pictographic/numeric Hebrew language to write it down, which couldn't have been easy. Physics is now attempting to record the same data in similarly precise languages – quantum field theory and relativity – and is running into the same difficulties and ambiguities, unveiling the same weird realities, while remaining similarly bamboozled. However, should they discover the way to weave the two theories together (maybe by identifying common fractal patterns in each of them) then I believe we will have our ToE.

Figure 12. The oldest symbol: Cross inside a revolving circle
© GabrielGGD, via Wikimedia Commons

Moses tells us that the Elohim created family energy units he called Days. They sealed the first two energies – light and dark – by adding the kiss of two opposing twilight children, creating the third mixed state of illumination (energy) in the process. As previously mentioned (see Figure 12) this family portrait is best drawn as a cross inside a circle where the Family is the circle and the cross is the energy-generating mechanism of its internal, childlike, bi-polar (seed-like) multiplicity. In one form or another, this symbol can be found in all of the world's ancient cultures, with multiple variations, displaying the same universal principle. The cross within a revolving circle is found in the symbolism of Neolithic and Bronze Age cultures, which includes the Australian Aborigines who used it for their idea of the Creator.[180]

---

180 'Sun cross', *Wikipedia*, https://en.wikipedia.org/wiki/Sun_cross

How could these so-called 'stone age savages' have been so smart? Were they once enlightened to Nature's ways? Maybe long before history was written down, people knew about the Pattern or Laws of Everything (its geometry) and lived by these laws peacefully as gods on Earth (as kabbalistic thought maintains). When you think about it, all you would need to evolve would be a knowledge of the fractal meanings about what one (1 – Won), two (2 – Duel/Dual), and three (3 – Free) mean universally. Enlightenment would then be as easy as … One. Two. Three(Four).

**The palingenetic idea of repetitive cyclic energies suggests that, if we were ever once enlightened, then it's a sure thing we will be again.**

PHYSICS' STANDARD MODEL of subatomic particles reveals the Universe's most intimate secrets. First among these is:

All subatomic particles come in triplets.

# Time To Call It a Day

> **Box 19. The Standard Model Comes in Triplets**
>
> The laws of nature appear to be composed in triplicate, with all matter particles coming in three copies, each being heavier than the last but otherwise identical. (Like Russian Dolls.) It's as if the laws of nature were composed in triplicate.
>
> 'We don't know why,' said Heather Logan, a particle physicist at Carleton University.
>
> But puzzlingly, this family of matter particles — the up quark, down quark and electron — is not the only one. Physicists have discovered that they make up the first of three successive 'generations' of particles, each heavier than the last. The second- and third-generation particles transform into their lighter counterparts but they otherwise behave identically.[181]
>
> \* \* \*
>
> (What the above article doesn't mention is that the particle will normally change charge as it moves from one generation to the next. Positive becomes negative and vice versa. I believe this also happens from parents to their children: female becoming male, et cetera, in successive birth transitions.)

Cambridge University physicist David Tong believes the Standard Model is not the last word in physics, stating: 'There are clearly patterns within the masses of the particles, which strongly suggests

---

[181] Charlie Wood, 'Why do matter particles come in threes? A physics titan weighs in', *Quanta Magazine*, 30 March 2020, https://www.quantamagazine.org/why-do-matter-particles-come-in-threes-a-physics-titan-weighs-in-20200330/

some underlying structure that's just waiting to be discovered.'[182] Like many other physicists, he believes we await a comprehensive Theory of Everything. A God Equation.

## Two Contrary Points, Plus Two Alternating Twilights

The cross inside the circle describes the layout of a fractal COG. A computer programmer might call this layout a trinary 'bit'. Yahweh told Moses to call it a 'Day'.

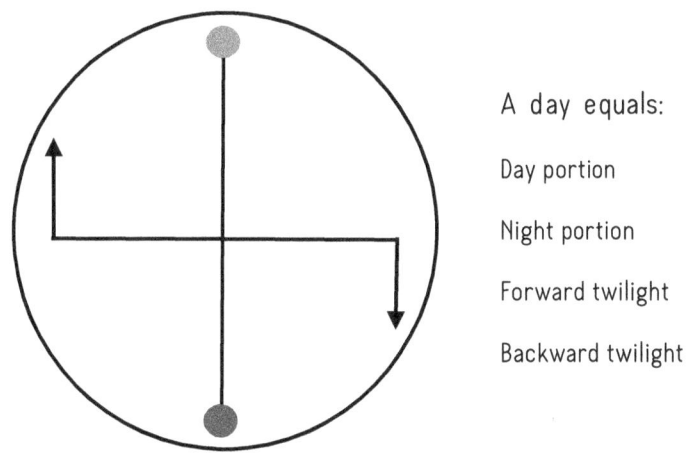

A day equals:

Day portion

Night portion

Forward twilight

Backward twilight

Figure 13. Family circle or COG

A *Genesis* Creation Day can then be seen as:

Four revolving cardinal points, safely contained inside

---

182  Quanta Magazine, 'The most successful scientific theory ever: The Standard Model', *YouTube* video, 17 July 2021, https://youtu.be/Unl1jXFnzgo

> a circle, maintaining two sets of polarised opposites
> working together, embracing three energies: father,
> mother, child/ren.

These four cardinal points create a trinity of family luminance that resembles a human heart with its four chambers covered by an outer cage; its pericardium (a vessel with its life-producing seed within).

Up until now, because *Genesis'* First Day of Creation identifies its principles of light and dark with our concepts of day and night, we've generally accepted the insertion of the magical twilights as being a natural phenomenon (not giving them a second thought). But if you think about it:

> Creating light and dark doesn't naturally create
> twilights, unless you consider our common experience
> of a day, as witnessed in most parts of the climate-
> friendly world.

Alternatively, if you think of a manmade replica of light – a light globe switching on and off inside a dark room – your perception of light and dark doesn't bring twilight to mind. In this example, you have dark then light, or light then dark, but no skerrick of twilight's third energy is seen. It's the same dynamic when you light a campfire. In a sense, our light-producing efforts only embrace two dimensions, not three.

This eerie, twilight state – the married blend and product of the Simulation's ubiquitous dichotomies, where it's neither one nor the other but both – embraces magical qualities. You can think of twilight as the Program's fractal children incarnate, which 'complete' one of Moses' Creation Days. I think this is why Moses defined these 'Days' as being two twilight energies placed in the heart of universal duality. In this way, **each COG contains the 'seed' of the next generation within it.**

The Fractal is alive and growing and will hopefully stay that way. Moses tells us that its magical attributes are meant to be man's exclusive food.

> We live in a participatory universe that continues to build itself.[183] — *John A. Wheeler*

Think of a Day's pattern like this:

- The daylight hours represent dad/day.

- The night is a mirror-reflective of the Sun's illumination. It is governed by mum/moon's secondary (mirrored) light.

- The two twilights represent the third state: the children of dusk and dawn.

As you can see, each Day comprises three visual arrays that contain four separate units, which equals one magical four-square trimension, COG, or Day in Moses' disclosed Creation Fractal.

This weirdness is also captured in the musical waltz, with its wildly immoral 3/4-time signature. No wonder Europe was scandalised when Strauss first introduced it in the nineteenth century. With tongue in cheek, the Fractal's weirdness might even extend to the

---

[183] Gregg Braden Official, 'If you understand this everything will make sense | Gregg Braden', *YouTube* video, 25 December 2019, https://www.youtube.com/watch?v=nXNqcYRR2sU

Three Musketeers, who were actually four swordsmen. **Three energies with four units, as displayed in the Standard Model of particle physics, dancing together in one universal fractal creating Reality.**

When Moses' first two Creation Days join at sunset, their connecting central, common-twilight-point can be seen as one Day's end and the next Day's beginning. By analogy, twilight's energy embraces birth and death, god and devil, good and evil; one central energy with a front and a back. In this way, when two days are joined (when four cardinal points are married to another four), they become a shared and sacred seven: $(3 + 1^2 + 3 = 7)$.

> Twilight's third energy represents the spiritual realm in the Fractal. Here paradox abounds and expansive life and death issues begin. It's the central and fertile home of the Creation Gods Elohim.

Table 2. The first two Creation Days joined – Sunday to Monday

| Dark, Dawn, Day | Common Dusk | Dark, Dawn, Day |
| --- | --- | --- |
| Male Sun-day | Plus | Female Moon-day |
| 1　2　3 | 4 | 5　6　7 |

This combined layout of 'seven' comes to light in Moses' first two Creation Days. Each Day is presented as having four cardinal points, married in the centre by the formlessness of shared twilight. In this way, the Fractal's Adam and Eve (light and dark) couple become a married seven. The mechanics of this process hinge on marriage, love, and sacrifice, all taking place in the Holy Centre which just won't leave warring opposites alone. I believe Mankind needs to become such a Holy Seven, the equivalent of a Spiritual Week Force, which contains a nuclear Sabbath Centre. That process might be happening now. At least … I think it is.

## Creation's Three Marriage Patterns

Moses' Week of Creation reveals the act of 'marriage' in three styles, which replicate Lisi's E8 ToE.

The first format is linear: Day 1 marries Day 2 at the evening twilight point. This first format is consistent for all six working Days.

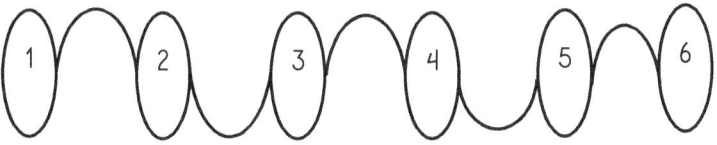

Figure 14. First set of twilight marriages

The second set of marriages maintain echo formats across an abyss: Day 1 marries Day 4, Day 2 marries Day 5, and Day 3 marries Day 6. This second set of three Days echoes the first set, creating three married pairs as Moses' second expression of holy marriage. In a sense, Days 4, 5, and 6 rule lovingly over their partners: Days 1, 2, and 3.

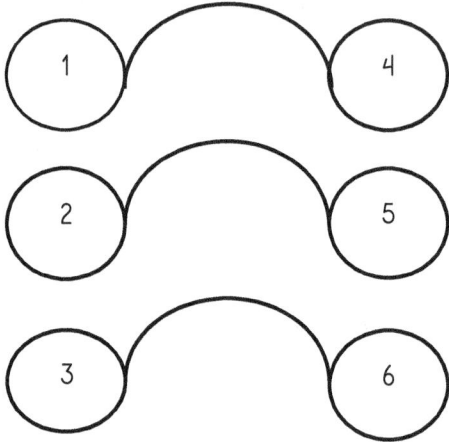

Figure 15. Format of the second set of marriages

These three pairs of working Days don't share common twilight-points as such – not in the form we're used to – their central joining forms a common or shared purpose that oversees the union. In these marriages, the second 'partnered day' reflects the first. (This is consistent with the dynamics of the two universal Agendas reflecting one another.) In Days 1, 2, and 3 the Elohim create a division of two states. Then on Days 4, 5, and 6, Moses tells us these states are populated or regulated when their marriage partners move in and take up residence. For example, Light and dark are created and separated on Day 1. Then on Day 4, the Sun and Moon are created to rule over Day 1's light and dark phases. In essence … Day 4's creations are Day 1's Gods or Goddesses, relating to each other in a life-extending (evolutionary) fashion.

Repeating this marriage pattern, Day 2's waters are separated by the firmament. Then on Day 5 – Day 2's partner – different forms of life evolve to occupy and dominate what had been divided previously.

Then on Day 3, fruit-bearing seed is separated from all other foods. And on its partnered Day 6, Man arrives to eat the fruit-bearing seed exclusively. (The animals got the rest.)

Through this patterned, partnered methodology, the second set of three Creation Days 'latch' the first set of three days in marriage, one pair at a time. These three paired couples constitute the second form of marriage in Moses' Creation Week.

The third expression of marriage completes the general pattern of the Week, making it a single fractal unit of seven. In this third marriage, both of the two *three-Day trigrams* are joined (glued) by the pivotal, sole Sabbath now residing at their centre point. The two sets of three Days (each seen as a single unit comprising three parts) reflect each other as +1 and -1. The enigmatic and joining Sabbath, around which both sets revolve, replaces the shared twilight-points previously employed as the unifying love-glue. The Seventh Day Sabbath connects and touches all of the other six Days centrally.

The first three Creation Days can be seen as half of a working week. The second shadow-set of three Days is the other (mirrored) half of the same construction. These two halves then marry through the Sabbath's unity in the Centre, where duality's war seeks and finds rest as a centre-point. **God rests on the Sabbath.**

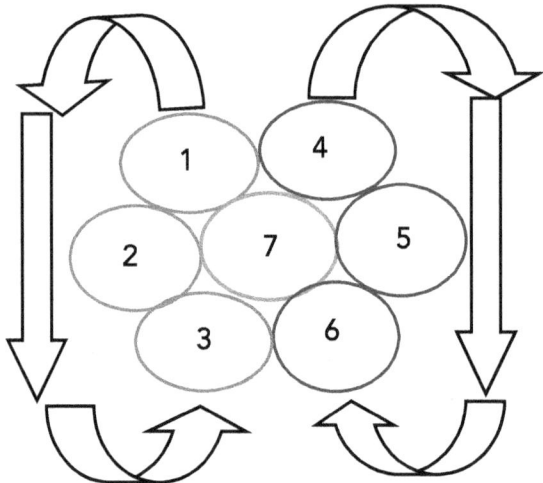

Figure 16. The third marriage format as described by Moses, which resembles a doughnut torus

The Sabbath represents Holy Marriage (the Most Holy Place) where YHWH is able to dwell comfortably (tabernacle) in central, fractal similitude. This is why the Sabbath embraces rest: it doesn't spin to-and-fro with dualistic contention as the other six Days do. It's no wonder Moses told us that remembering the Sabbath was important, recording it as the fourth Commandment: 'Remember the Sabbath to keep it Holy.' Maybe there is more to this instruction than has generally been realised.

> And he said unto them, The sabbath was made for man, and not man for the sabbath: Therefore the Son of man is Lord also of the sabbath.[184] – *Yahshua*

---

184 *Mark* 2:27,28

In other words ... When enlightened, a believer uses the Sabbath to their great advantage.

THESE THREE TWILIGHT marriage patterns are examples of what the Kimberley Aboriginal people call the Law of Two: everything comes in twos. With the right twilight inspiration, I believe each set of two can marry into a new trinary Oneness.

I know these relationships can be a bit confusing at times, but the criss-cross symmetry in Moses' weekly layout of Creation is easy to see when you understand the basic pattern that's dwelling in its heart. It's the same criss-cross pattern we looked at earlier with parents, children, and grandparents; how a family unit is a similar set of potentially loving, mathematical relationships. This layout of a Creation Week also resembles a Network Science model, which has three loops and a single duplex hub making up the sacred seven:

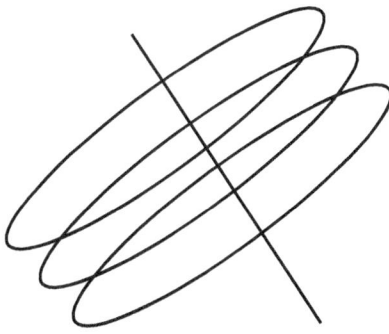

Figure 17. The Pattern as a Network Science model

## Time To Call It a Day

There's a plethora of evidence which suggests that Moses' Account of Creation contains an enormous secret, a secret that's capable of changing the world for the better. Furthermore, I believe that whoever embraces and uses this secret wisely can manufacture a spectacular life for themselves and their families. The similarity between a Creation Day's design and its Creator's name YHWH is significant in itself – three characters in four positions, as portrayed in physics' Standard Model. In an esoteric fashion, this pattern can be seen as a Trinity of Love that's enmeshed in a single, foursquare Family Unit.

The idea that the Universe is a simulation, whose operating system mirrors the biblical Name of God, is enticing and warrants serious investigation. Who knows what marvellous insights await? **We might discover the Eighth Day of Creation, and what that's all about.** According to biblical gematria, the number 'eight' stands for New Beginnings. Maybe the coming Age of Aquarius is our new beginning, complete with a biblical New Earth and New Heaven.[185,186] Day 8.

In each fractal day cycle, the night can be seen as the 'preparation' that comes before the day. This is consistent with the Mayan Long-Count Calendar, in which each night period is a preparation for the coming day period on every tier, or step, of its pyramid of ages.

Will we discover that the Hebrew God Yahweh gave Mankind an enlightened understanding of Reality and encoded it in His Name? Did He reveal the blueprint of Creation's Great Fractal (ToE) which we lost as we slept in the Wilderness? dreaming about flying to the stars?; the mission we set ourselves before going to sleep?

---

185 *Revelation* 21
186 *Isiah* 65:17–25

I believe we're awakening now to this ancient realisation, maybe just in the nick of time. Cosmologists are telling us that if nothing changes with the way matter is being pushed and pulled apart in the Universe, then eventually only dark energy and dark matter at 0º Kelvin will remain. No light, no heat. Nothing solid. Nothing substantial. Boring. I don't think we want to let that happen if we can help it.

I believe that what Moses called a 'Day' and a 'Week' are field patterns, components of a computer program that underscore the Matrix's working operation. Anyone who can understand how to apply these principles and patterns to their life is capable of becoming a true Time Lord. Or, as Yahshua kept repeating in John's Gospel … 'Will never experience death but live eternally.'

If Moses' disclosed Pattern is accurate, then a Creation Day is a unit of patterned accomplishment, not a duration of chronological time (as Cronos the Titan would have us believe).

Each 'Day' is complete when its cycle unifies (marries) its essential three or four warring parts – depending on your perspective – into a single-family unit of love that mirrors the Logos. Each successful outcome then creates a new foundational rung for the ladder of Evolution to continue growing.

Moses' seven entangled Creation Days demonstrate how love can bridge duality's abyss. This gives me hope that we'll make it through the trials we are currently enduring.

- Mum loves dad.

- Sister loves brother.

- Mum loves her sons and daughters.

- Dad loves his daughters and sons.
- The Family loves their neighbours – on both sides.
- Mankind loves Righteous Life governed by Universal Love and Law.

Seen with patterned eyes, a Creation Week is a record of love conquering duality's war in three separate ways, creating a unified, fertile, family or COG.

When a tree produces fruit, and each fruit harbours dual-natured seed inside of it, it could metaphorically be called a 'Day'; a generation or dimension with its fertile duality safely tucked away at its centre. Moses went on to tell us that such seed-bearing fruit was intended to be the exclusive food for Man. **What Moses meant by this is: Love your parents. Love your partner. Love your children. Love your neighbour as yourself.**

> Then Yahweh said, 'I give you every seed-bearing plant on the face of the whole earth, and every tree which has fruit yielding seed; to you, it shall be for food.'[187] Yahshua said unto him, Love YHWH with all thy heart, and with all thy soul, and with all thy mind. This is the first and great commandment. And the second is like unto it, love thy neighbour as thyself. On these two commandments, all the law and the prophets hang.[188]

---

187 *Genesis* 1:29
188 *Matthew* 22:36–40

From the Fractal's perspective, the family unit or full-cycle is everything, and the time it takes to complete it is arbitrary, inconsequential, and immaterial. YHWH has all the time in the world it seems and then some, which might apply to us too if we play our cards right.

Seen in this endearing and immortal light … A family is a single unit of the Creation Fractal, be it a day, a week, or a year. Each unit has a binary face: husband and wife. A trinary face: an essential mother, father, and eventual child/ren. Finally, it has a multi-format floral arrangement, with many children or petals surrounding a central unity as an extended fractal family, or Flower of Life.

Homosexuality is the bud that fails to open in this picture, being an aspect of the Fractal's need for sacrifice. Homosexuality is cast out East, being modelled on the Attraction of Likes, which knows it must move on whenever it feels the necessity to do so.

## YHWH and Time

Physicists are reappraising 'time' because they've discovered that the subatomic particles – from which everything is made – don't recognise time as we do. Quantum particles appear to time travel in and out of existence, while photons of light exist only in the eternal now. But what does the Eternal Now, with its incumbent timelessness, actually mean? Could it be connected in some way to God's sacred Name YHWH?

Although the Bible repeatedly states how important this name is, there's little consensus among theologians as to what God's name actually means. They do agree that it relates to aspects of the verb 'to be'. The following are some of their thoughts:

- Giver of existence, creator
- Life-giver
- He who brings to pass
- Performer of his promises
- He who causes to fall (rain or lightning)
- The one who is
- The absolute and unchangeable one
- The existing, ever-living
- The one ever coming into manifestation is my favourite
- He will be
- He will approve himself (give evidence of being, or assert his being)
- The one bringing into being.

Quantum physics' understanding about *measurement collapsing materialism's wave function from superposition to an eigenstate* looks amazingly similar to YHWH's paradoxical Name 'the one bringing into being'. Physics' inquiries into the nature of Reality are giving this Name 'to be' a substance or plausibility which can be finally understood (sort of). YHWH, the name God revealed to Moses, captures the essence of quantum reality with its extended meaning: **I constantly**

**manifest a single reality out of infinite chaos and possibility and make it fall like rain. I am the same yesterday, today, and tomorrow. I live in the Eternal Now as One. I am the Power of Now.**

If it's discovered that Reality's operating instructions are encoded into YHWH's Name, then the meaning and importance of this Name will be established forever.

> I am YHWH: that is my name: and my glory will I not give to another, neither my praise to graven images.[189]

Secular Christianity remains (largely) in the dark about Israel's God's Name and what it means. As were Israel's neighbours in earlier times. They too were bamboozled about the nature and Name of Israel's God, YHWH. His ideas about the nature of kairos time were largely at odds with the Canaanite god El.

I think it's important to note that the Canaanites – Israel's sworn enemy – recognised their chief deity El (LL) as being the father of the Olympian Gods. This equates El with Cronos, the Titan boss of linear time, because according to Greek Mythology, Cronos was the father of the Olympian gods.[190] In this timely fashion, Israel's YHWH and Canaan's LL (El) were at odds with each other as to who was the power behind time itself, and the maths (kingdom) it controlled.

---

189   *Isaiah* 42:8
190   When Hellenes encountered Phoenicians and, later, Hebrews, they identified the Semitic El with Cronus, by *interpretatio graeca*. In c. AD 100, Philo of Byblos recorded this association in his Phoenician history; it was also reported in Eusebius' *Præparatio Evangelica* I.10.16. See 'Cronos', *Wikipedia*, https://en.wikipedia.org/wiki/Cronos

## Time To Call It a Day

You might recall that the people of Israel were ordered by YHWH to invade and subdue the land of Canaan and its chief god EL – along with its resident giants and lesser gods. Cronos' idea about the nature of linear, binary time was – and remains – blasphemous to YHWH. He commanded Cronos to be removed from the Holy Land for Mankind to be set free, and gave Israel the job of removing him.

Up until now, I believe our resident idea about the passing of time remains our greatest deception, separating us from YHWH's trinary Reality. If Mankind is to be set free, then this issue must be resolved scientifically to all the world's satisfaction.

Could it also be a coincidence that the name *Isra-el* is currently thought to mean 'contends with god'? Because this specified God-given-name can also be translated 'He who contends with eL', the Canaanite god of expanding duality, not YHWH who promotes the Centre. Currently, the 'el' in Israel's name is thought to be a generalisation for the ruling concept of God.

I believe the former interpretation of the name Israel is the correct one. Remember that Jacob – who received the name Israel from YHWH – had his 'wrestling match with an angel' on the riverbank when he was heading back to Canaan to live, after being away for many years. On his earlier outward journey from Canaan, at the same cardinal point, he dreamed of the angels of El going up and down a ladder from Heaven to Earth, which he asked to bless him.[191] This is the dual to-and-fro code of Hell's binary angels which promote increase or expansion. This is most likely how Jacob multiplied or accrued his fortune greatly while away.

---

191   *Genesis* 28:12

The Pattern's geometry indicates that Jacob's return angelic episode by the river (that occurred at the centre of his homeward journey), was a revelation about the next cycle in Jacob's life. When he reached Canaan, Jacob was to do battle with their chief deity, eL, also known as Cronos, or the biblical and Christian Satan of the Anunnaki's underworld.

The Anunnaki are synonymous with the biblical fallen angels who continue to follow the to-and-fro tail of the Serpent. Jacob came to realise that he had to fight against this angelic energy that helps you increase (expand) your riches and never let go until it is finally put to rest. Geometrically, the revelation of his 'mission' occurred at the same point as Saint Paul's would many years later as he travelled the Road to Damascus. For this reason, Jacob called this place by the river where he wrestled with eL, 'beholding God's Face' (Penuel)[192] because he **saw his future mission there**. He wasn't referring to the angel's face he had just wrestled with, but YHWH's Face. It really doesn't make sense that the name Israel means 'Against Yahweh' (God), as the world currently believes. Various Rabbis have tried putting a bright face on this enigma about the controversial name, but with little success. They have mistaken Moses' trinary Elohim for the binary, abbreviated, eL (LL),[193] which is not hard to do because it is essentially a counterfeit at heart.

---

192 'Jacob wrestling with the angel', *Wikipedia*, https://en.wikipedia.org/wiki/Jacob_wrestling_with_the_angel

193 In northwest Semitic use, Ēl was both a generic word for any god and the special name or title of a particular god who was distinguished from other gods as being 'the god'. See 'El (deity)', *Wikipedia*, https://en.wikipedia.org/wiki/El_(deity)

This conclusion about Israel's name is drawn from Moses' Pattern. It is based on the geometrical idea that the middle outbound incident on Jacob's round journey was entangled with his homebound one, both being the twilight energies in his journey's (walkabout) circuit.

Israel's mission therefore remains:

> To contend all night long against an all-consuming, linear mindset (fruit from the binary tree) that's leaving people blind to their integrated, patterned (cyclic) surroundings.

# LEAPING FORWARD INTO THE PAST

From sunset to sunset: 2 × 2 parts to a Cycle

And the evening and the morning: Day 1

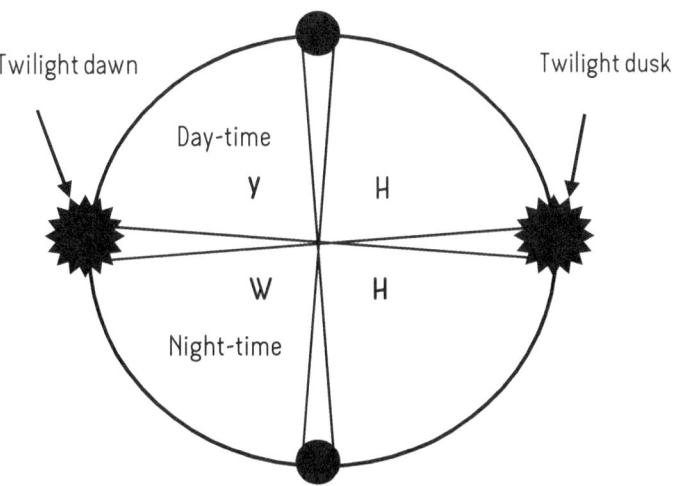

Figure 18. A single Creation Day as a COG

Comprised of a day and a night, containing three shades of visual luminosity – Day, Night, Twilight – twilight coming in two forms up and down. It has four cardinal points: Sunrise, Midday, Sunset, Midnight. It can be seen as half of a unit of seven, when two Days are joined in marriage, displayed as a figure-8 … in a field of eight (E8).

The twilight points in each COG are significant when trying to understand spiritual, quantum mysticism. They represent God/Devil or the 'magical' perspective on each level or line of the Program; both are situated at the centre between yin and yang. The twilights are the equivalent of a steering wheel that keeps you on – or turns you away from – the sustainable path that emanates from the paradoxical Centre.

These twilight points embrace the wonderment of 'interstitiality' and figure prominently in secret societies such as the Hermetic Order of the Golden Dawn and the Order of the Rosy Cross.[194] They are intimately related to the other two cardinal points and when understood or 'grokked', allow you to access inspirational information about past and future events in your life. This is similar to how, traditionally, sailors looked to the twilights to forecast coming weather events:

> Red sky at night, sailors delight. Red sky at morning, sailors take warning.

Jesus cited this concept in the New Testament as being established wisdom prevailing among the Jews of the Second Temple Period.[195]

Sunrise's morning twilight embraces Alchemy's Philosopher's Stone. It is famous for turning lead into gold, night into day (with the evening twilight being its reverse mirror opposite.) Both of these magical twilight points employ the law of the Attraction of Opposites

---

[194] The Rosicrucian manifestos heralded a 'universal reformation of mankind', through a science allegedly kept secret for decades until the intellectual climate might receive it. It promised a spiritual transformation in a time of great turmoil. See: 'Rosicrucianism', *Wikipedia*, https://en.wikipedia.org/wiki/Rosicrucianism

[195] *Matthew* 16:2–3

(light and dark embracing each other as a single whole). In a religious sense, they can be thought of as the back and front of God, presented as a single, unified energy. The Trinity God has a front, a back, and dual-central twilight points in between. Each time this configuration is achieved, it becomes a new COG in the Fractal.

Twilight's zero-like midpoints are geometrical ambassadors of the central Elohim, the biblical creation gods. They contain semblances of miracles: chaos/order, love/lust, lore/sin, birth/death, heaven/hell, and sacrifice. In each cycle, the twilight points act as bridges or switch-gates, which resemble a railway turntable, a computer's transistor switch, or a synaptic junction in a human brain. (While one takes us outward, the other takes us inward – that sort of thing.) These twilight points are more than just beautiful … they're awesome. If you know where to look, you can find them in each complete cycle in the Matrix. Remember when God tried to kill Moses on his way to set the Israelites free? That was a twilight point for Moses' journey into patterned redemption at Mount Sinai.

These twilight points or 'centres' can be identified in the anatomy of the human body. For instance: A person's knees are the legs' twilight points, set between the cardinal points of the hips and ankles. The arms' elbows are similar, although an arm's energy is the opposite of a leg's energy. The diaphragm is another twilight centrepiece that divides the chest from the abdomen and empowers our breathing.

Experienced fishermen know that fish like to feed during twilight; it's when birds break forth into the *arpeggio crescendo* of evensong. These mysterious and magical times also evoke our sense of romance, especially if walking arm-in-arm along a beach, or sitting on a mountaintop watching the sun rise or set with your beloved. As children, we were led to believe that, if we wanted our wishes to come true, they were best whispered to God at sunset.

> Star light, star bright,
> The first star I see tonight;
> I wish I may, I wish I might,
> Have the wish I wish tonight.

As Jungian analyst Robert A Johnson describes:

> The religious faculty is the art of taking the opposites and binding them back together again, surmounting the split that's been causing so much suffering. It helps us move from contradiction—that painful condition where things oppose each other—to the realm of paradox, where we are able to entertain simultaneously two contradictory notions and give them equal dignity.[196]

This paradox of binding opposites together is enthroned in the reverent qualities of the Twilight Zone. Even Shakespeare's genius combined sets of opposites into twilight mystery: life and death, compassion and despair. 'To be or not to be' …

When it comes to the field of science, physics best captures the essence of twilight in what it calls the Implicate Order. Here, the quantum particle and wave function are one, no longer divided or differentiated. Twilight's energy can also be found in the central qubit of quantum computational systems. Here, the program's

---

[196] Robert A Johnston, *Owning Your Own Shadow: Understanding the Dark Side of the Psyche*, HarperCollins Publishers, 1994.

'zero' and 'one' are united centrally into a single unit (qubit) of calculable uncertainty.

Jung's philosophy continues through the words of Johnson:

> Then, and only then, is there the possibility of grace,
> the spiritual experience of contradictions brought into
> a coherent whole – giving us a unity greater than either
> one of them …

Jung's insightful wisdom proclaims that the marriage of opposites creates synergy, which is 'greater than either one of them'. And I agree.

Twilight energy embraces two forms – YX and XY – he leads, she leads (similar to our brain's two hemispheres). Interestingly, the male/female (YX) chromosomal design of a human male is incorporated into all female avians (although it's named ZW). Whereas, all male birds are patterned the equivalent of dual-male (ZZ). This is the reverse pattern to that of humans. Maybe this is why male birds are more colourful and attractive than their female counterparts? Duplicity (XX or YY) may be chaotic by some standards, but it embraces a unique form of external beauty that's different from that of YX twilight. **This comparison in chromosomal patterns between birds and humans shows that the YX Attraction of Opposites pattern can be designated either male or female, because – in a sense – it's both and neither at the same time. This leaves us with the set: (YY), (YX, XY), (XX).**

> Moses shows through analogy how the twilight energy
> acts as a central god in each line of the Program. In

> this way, its placement creates a trimension out of an existing polarised contention, converting the object from a binary beast to a trinary animal; from unclean to clean – in a biblical sense – as happened to the Gentiles when God repeated Himself. At these times, the object evolves from two dimensions or layers of Reality into a unified three as Evolution has her way.

The Bible's conjoined, XY (Twilight) Creator God, can not be found in any two-dimensional (unclean) line of the Program, so these binary beasts will not grace God's trinary table. This includes the human state of consciousness when it's not aligned with the Centre's singular mindfulness. This is why it's important that the two-dimensional concepts – which I attribute to El/Cronos' satanic energy – must stop ruling our understanding of time, because it's enslaving us with its binary, two-faced deception, keeping us blind. **We need to neutralise the natural, warring perspectives of duality, not only in our minds but everywhere. We need to turn the duellists into lovers. According to Moses, that is our mission, our food for eternity.**

## Getting Personal

By now, I hope this material is starting to make the old 'you' feel a little shaky, maybe even a tad uncomfortable. Everything you've previously held sacred should be starting to vibrate with nervous anticipation. But take heart, the prospect of having everything stripped away from you is only scary when you're not sure if there's anything there to replace it. In my experience, there's plenty to replace it, maybe more than your wildest dreams have imagined. When I came face to face with this scary point of uncertainty, I was presented with three choices:

- Believe what I had always thought to be true but confusing.

- Believe nothing at all.

- Go on a journey into madness, with a mindset suggestive of schizophrenia, with shades of bipolar issues thrown in for good or bad measure.

These were the only scenarios my mind could grasp. (Great choices, hey?) Eventually, however, I bypassed the confusion of binary insanity and came to see the broader and more spectacular tricoloured vision that was lying underneath. I could now see how one worldview lived comfortably inside the other. This reminded me of Yahshua, saying 'The Kingdom of God is among you.'[197] (There are those fractal Russian Dolls again.) I realised that, whereas the standalone polarities of 'night' and 'day' represent two states as points of view in Moses' Fractal (He said, She said), the all-encompassing 'twilights' control the direction, growth, and development of new life in the Simulation (both 'up' and 'down'). The first set of opposites – light and dark – could be represented as facts and feelings, Heaven and Earth. While the second twilight set of opposites could be the intent or direction they'll take – good or bad.

---

[197] 'Nor will people say, "Here it is," or "There it is," because the kingdom of God is in your midst.' *Luke* 17:21

When it comes to the domain of human consciousness, you can identify the twilight phenomenon as the supposedly inconsequential mindset you embrace that accompanies your every action. (It's the *reason* why you're doing what you're doing; how the expected outcome fits into your mind's vision/version of the future as forethought.) The geometrical nature of twilight infers that how you think about your proposed action is as important – or even more important – than the deed itself. Currently, this aspect of reality – your mindset that accompanies your action – is hardly acknowledged when it comes to creating healthy outcomes. But I think you'll find that your accompanying mindset is pivotal to the outcome, because… at a quantum level, the outcome revolves around your intent as much as it does the calibre of the action itself.

If you're going to make the transition to Heaven on Earth, you'll need to incorporate this weird four-part operating system coherently into your daily life. When you grasp the essential natures of the four players and recognise how they relate to each other – lawfully and geometrically in the space–time continuum of your life – your sixth sense will 'kick in' until you're all over their confusing natures. Everything then becomes more colourful and cohesive; life is no longer fragmented.

Did you know that on at least two occasions – *Luke* 9:11 and *Matthew* 16:24 – Yahshua told his disciples that his followers would need to pick up their cross and deny themselves. He obviously hadn't died on a cross when He was telling them this, and I don't believe He was alluding to needing to be crucified like He was going to be. No, I think He was referring to the universal dynamics of the Cross as laid out by Moses, which allowed them to understand His following statements.

> ²⁴ Then said Jesus unto his disciples, If any man will come after me, let him deny himself, and take up his cross, and follow me.
> ²⁵ For whosoever will save his life shall lose it: and whosoever will lose his life for my sake shall find it.

This statement makes sense if Yahshua was referring to the dynamics of the Cross' two polarised arms working across each other in everyone's life. An old Egyptian Proverb in *The Book of the Dead* written thousands of years before the Bible advised:

> **The Kingdom of God is within you, and whosoever shall know himself shall find it.**

Thousands of years later, this dictum was repeated by Yahshua in *Luke* 17:21 and is (surely) as true today – thousands of years later – as it was then.

## Sacred Geometry

Moses outlined how we need both sets of the Cross' opposites, working in harmony within each COG, to complete a whole Day or unit of the Creation Fractal. (Anything less being a component. Anything more … a construction.) The alignment of the four cardinal points determines whether something is a wave, a particle, or a spiralling particle-wave.

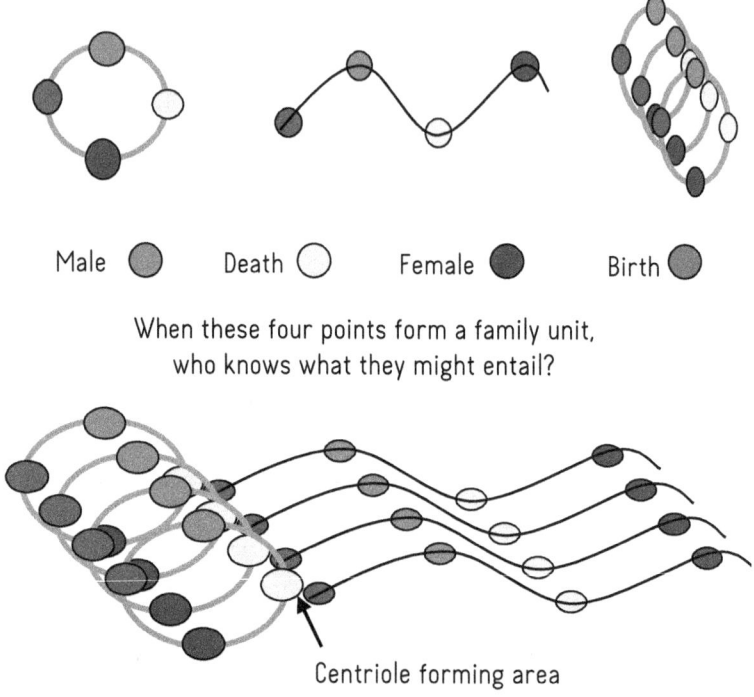

Figure 19. The versatility of the four cardinal points

The place where the sperm tail meets its head (the twilight point where the wave meets the particle), is known to oversee the development of any foetus conceived in utero. This mixed twilight component creates two centrioles, the geometrical equivalent of a Sabbath union.

All life is controlled by the twilight points in the Universal Fractal; they are central to its operation and especially its growth. You need to identify these energies in the cycles you encounter if you want to steer your future into bliss. This process begins with understanding your mind's conscious methodology in a trivalent way, then extending that same geometrical awareness to the passage of time (when and where things occur in patterned cycles – beginnings, middles, and ends).

Unlike 'night' and 'day', the two 'twilights' aren't differentiated. They work together, as do the centrioles. Their only difference is in the direction they point: up or down. Again, we return to a model of a two-faced central Creator, who operates as a single unified One. (Much like Jung's wisdom proclaims, as asserted in Johnson's book.)

The million-dollar question remains: Is twilight one or two things? One or two energies? The answer depends on your perspective. Can you see four cardinal points in a single Day cycle? Or are there three states of illumination and a sacrificial blind spot? Maybe everything in your world is simply black and white?

**What you look for shapes and determines what you see, and that determines what you subsequently become.**

Table 3. Ways of seeing a day

| All is One | A | Single | Day |
|---|---|---|---|
| Binary | Light | and | Dark |
| Trinary | Light | Twilight | Dark |
| Quadratic | Light | Twilights Up and Down | Dark |

Twilight enlightenment infers that God – and his contending dark Shadow, Satan – maintain a single essence. They embrace two opposing vectors that emanate from the Program's Centre: forwards, backwards; God leads, Satan follows. ('Get behind me Satan.'[198]) I have heard children ask "Why doesn't God kill Satan? Well, now you know why.

Nature lives in polarity: light and dark, creation and destruction, up and down, male and female. It's not surprising, therefore, that we find the same basic laws functioning in our own psychology. In German, the word *doppelganger* means one's mirror image, one's opposite.

To own one's dark shadow or 'opposite', Jung believed, is to reach a holy place; your inner centre, which is not accessible by any other means.

> To fail this is to fail one's own sainthood and to miss the purpose of life. – *Johnston, in* Owning Your Own Shadow

Are you beginning to see how the Fractal ends up inside your head? How it ultimately defines who you are, and who you become? How it can create a life of misery, pain, and loneliness (on one hand), or hope, happiness, and connectedness to All Else on the other?

To marry your Shadow, you need to combine the yin and yang opposites in your life into the oneness of religious Twilight. (Instead of arguing about the merits of each agenda as we usually do: which is right and which is wrong.) In Religion's terms, this trinary development amounts to handing all the really troubling stuff over to God, while getting on with your daily life; not hibernating in a cave or worrying yourself to death over the trivial things that your imagination has got its teeth into.

---

198  *Matthew* 16:23 (KJV)

**In this threefold way, you 'vault' your unpleasant issues in your mind's centre, while you wait for a successful solution to come forth. There is no more vacillating to-and-fro in your mind over what you should or shouldn't do to fix the problem; no fearful forethought, as Prometheus the Titan god of fire would promote and encourage you to do.**

This three-dom is the central way of the Buddha – Christ/Krishna/Islamic Consciousness – the way to eradicate all pain and suffering, individually and globally. It embraces all the religious insight the world has unearthed and leads to perfect health, resurrection, and a peace that passes all understanding. But do we want it badly enough? That remains to be seen.

## Finding the Centre

The linear expression of the Centre can be found in something as simple as a short journey.

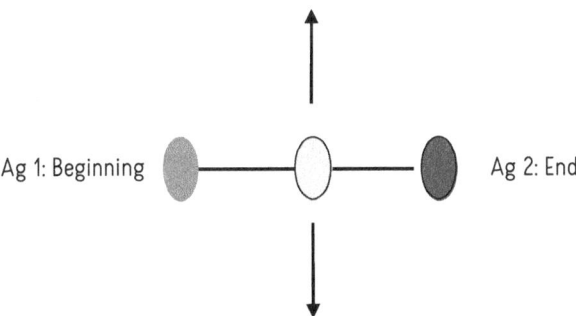

Figure 20. The patterned geometry of a typical journey

If you pull the centre-point of your linear journey (in and out) at right angles to its path, it discloses a pump-action in the form of a cross.

This four-part design can be found in a child's origami finger-puppet, which was originally (strangely?) called Heaven and Hell. You make the toy through a series of folds that replicate the Union Jack. Played with two fingers on each hand, this toy pumps in and out and fascinates children of all ages.

It is at this point that we reach the blueprint or heart of Moses' Pattern – the geometrical and mathematical character of Heaven and Hell's two operating pathways, which sit between the polarised opposites of Yin and Yang.

Figure 21. The flag of the United Kingdom. Four countries in one.

To activate the horizontal and vertical vectors of the Matrix's pump requires a dual set of braces at the intersection points. These braces look like an altercation between a multiplication sign and an addition sign. One is placed on top of the other in the Missionary Position, like the two trees were placed at the centre of Moses' Garden, or how the light beams from the Pleiades and Sirius were situated in the Great Pyramid. One pattern can be designated male. The other female.

The processes of addition and multiplication are contained within the twilight junctions of the Matrix, where the actions we implement (and our accompanying mindsets) make their way into the future as patterned energy blueprints or pre-shadows. As you can see from the signs in Figure 22; multiplication is male, while addition is female.

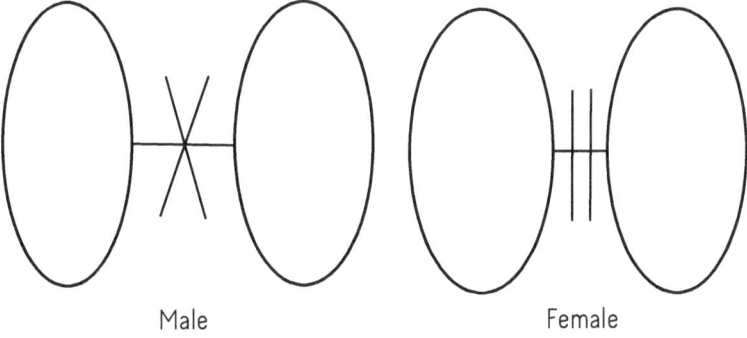

Male                                Female

Figure 22. The maths of joined gender symbols

In this instance, Shakespeare's 'To be or not to be' becomes, 'to add' or 'to multiply': $1 \times 1 = 1^2$, whereas $1 + 1 = 2$. Two different outcomes. One ($1^2$) is Adam getting fatter. Two (2) is Eve creating new life. When activated at the centre of a line in the Matrix's Program, these designations of multiplication or addition become highly significant. The nature and function of the process acts as the central god of each trimension and significantly affects its outcome (which path it travels into the future: the male sustainability pathway to multiply, or the female new life pathway to add).

Adam's propensity to multiply takes him around the circle's circumference, revering its centre point: $1 \times 1 \times 1 \times 1 \ldots = 1$. Whereas Eve's 'additional mindset' connects the circles and moves them on into the figure-8 Wilderness of infinity: $1 + 1 + 1 + 1 \ldots = \infty$ as infinite expansion. Eve's to-and-fro agenda repeatedly takes us through the chaotic Centre of the circle, where you need to be suitably covered and protected if you know what's good for you.

In a geometrical sense, these same gender symbols were used to identify the planets Mars and Venus, designating Mars as male and Venus as female. As the Wheel of Life revolves, Eve's cross or plus-sign, inside of Adam's circle, rotates to become a multiplication sign. Now, here is the thing ... addition and multiplication are one and the same thing to Eve, because $2 \times 2$ and $2 + 2$ both equal 4. But this is not so with Adam. The path Eve chooses determines what maths is employed in that COG.

AS YOU GROW in quantum enlightenment – once thought of as spiritual discernment – you come to see everything in your conscious life in an unusual (trinary) way. You become amazed at just how spectacular everything becomes when your world expands EX-ponentially into three conscious dimensions. You come to see the three/four cardinal points, or energies, guiding your life in every journey or enterprise you undertake, working in the Fractal as follows:

- **Beginning** The beginning of each journey, adventure or enterprise is one cardinal point. This is the seeding energy that identifies the cycle's Name. Its name comes from the relationships it maintains with its neighbouring fields in the Matrix; its timing and its positioning, as shaman understood when they revealed a baby's name at its birth.

- **End** The end of each journey is another cardinal point. This is the shadow of the first point, its opposite agenda. It maintains the same energy as the first but portrays it in a mirrored fashion.

- **To-and-fro** The journey's 'coming' and 'going' are the other two (1) twilight cardinal points in the centre. They also maintain the same energy but engage opposing vectors.

Your journey's twilight midpoints deserve your full attention because they identify the energy that's coming in the next cycle of that particular field or Name. I've already mentioned how this understanding affected the lives of the Bible's Moses, Jacob, and Paul. I understand this aspect of the Program in this way:

> When the children grow up in the centre between their polarised Ag 1 and Ag 2 parents, they eventually take on the parental energy in the next family cycle as mums and dads themselves.

That is why you need to be aware of any unusual energy you encounter in a journey's centre point, because it is revealing aspects of your future to you (what's going to occur in its next cyclic presentation). When the central energy matures over time, its essence will dominate the coming field. In this way, the central twilight children in the lower trimension become the next set of Ag 1 and Ag 2 parents in the following trimension – each with a new partner – as the Fractal continues to grow. It is through these observations that a person comes to know many things, including when they can expect to die. They will understand the significance of the pre-warning message when it arrives to announce: Next time this energy occurs will be your last.

> And when they were up ... they were up.
> And when they were down ... they were down.
> And when they were only halfway up ...
> They were neither up nor down.

I've leaned that the energy or state of consciousness you embrace or release at each cycle's cardinal points determines the emotional landscape your life's journey will develop in the future. So, when you decide to learn how to consciously control what you release emotionally at these critical points, you'll gain the ability to steer your life towards your heart and soul's ultimate desire (that being a righteous life here in Heaven on Earth). **Achieving emotional control at your strategic cardinal points removes the pain of uncertainty from your life.** Acquiring this talent bestows a sense of confidence and peace, dispelling all fear, as nothing else ever has. Its magic is the equivalent of planting healthy seeds in your garden (knowing that it's the right season; being aligned with both Sun and Moon coordinates) and then living to reap a healthy crop at a foreordained time. Yummy, crisp and delicious.

Here's a practical example: When your partner arrives home from work – it being a cardinal point in your relationship's cycle with him/her – how you first greet them is very important. Are you exuberant? Nonchalant? Or ... whatever? Your choice will have lingering repercussions, which will enter adjoining time cycles. With this understanding in mind, you come to realise that it pays to make the small (timely) effort when they first arrive home, so you can then sit back and reap the peaceful rewards for hours afterwards.

Once you're convinced you are living in a simulation and start looking for the braces that hold its working parts together, you'll come to see the embedded code in every aspect of your life – past, present, and future. Then the real fun begins and boredom ceases as you start sharing your uplifting experiences with your loved ones. For me, that part has been sensational.

According to Pascal:

> we fear the silence of existence, we dread boredom and instead choose aimless distraction, and we can't help but run from the problems of our emotions into the false comforts of the mind.[199]

I would add: And its imagination.

So, imagine how it would feel to replace this mindset with a deep feeling of vibrant connectedness to All Else. Could there be a fearless sense of security waiting for you that you've never encountered before? Can life cease to be a 'wilderness' burden?

Sounds like something you'd hear in church. And you'd be right. This is how one man – who was very much into holy mindfulness – expressed it 2000 years ago:

---

199    Zat Rana, 'The most important skill nobody taught you', *Medium*, 16 June 2018, https://medium.com/personal-growth/the-most-important-skill-nobody-taught-you-9b162377ab77

> Take my yoke upon you and learn from me, for I am gentle and humble of heart; and you will find rest. For my yoke is easy, and my burden is light.[200] — *Yahshua*

## Walkabout - Making the Magic Work for You

Being able to use the Matrix's universal four cardinal points is ensconced in the Australian Aboriginal people's propensity to go 'walkabout'. As far as I could discern, they traditionally used its geometrical magic as a mantic tool of divination. By taking energy readings at the four cardinal points of their circular journey (walkabout), they were able to perceive and then influence the future. They also captured this geometrical knowledge in their marriage ceremonies, where they traditionally married with neighbouring mobs in clockwise circles or figure-8s (along with their boomerangs that returned after their flighted journey). If you want to experience the 'walkabout magic' for yourself, then you might like to try this:

> Start a small circular, clockwise journey at an interstitial cardinal point – say a car park next to a beach, preferably where a river enters the sea (saltwater meets freshwater). To get a good result, it's best if your starting point and time have significant twilight energy attached to them.
>
> Now here's the thing… You need to make a conscious decision to implant love at the four cardinal points of your coming journey, to generate sensational magic at its

---

200  *Matthew* 11:28–30

end. By this means you are going to create one complete stir (round trip) as a vortex of love in Destiny's Cauldron.

Set out on a route that parallels the beach. When you're halfway to your eventual turning point, stop, look around and take note of anything you see in an energy sense (become mindful). Now, consciously and lovingly meditate on that aspect for a moment (let your love exude from your centre naturally as gratitude). Continue to the far end of your journey and repeat the process at that cardinal point. Two down, two to go.

Now turn around and, this time, walk back along the beach to complete your clockwise circuit/circle journey. Repeat your mindful love-ritual halfway home (maybe look at the waves) and again when you return to your starting point. Now that you're back at your beginning, having created a circle of love (all four cardinal points), sit for a while and consciously add the four (4) energies together, letting the magic you have 'stirred up' descend into your centre. You might like doing the circuit with a friend in the evening with a full moon rising. If you enact this procedure with another receptive soul (especially if you are holding hands), it will entangle you both into a state of Oneness. This circular journey represents a wedding ring of sorts.

But don't traverse the path backwards unless you want to break the entanglement.

After this heroic adventure, go directly somewhere else and experience the follow-on shadow effects that will ripple back onto you like echoes. You'll find the experience of what you have just created amazing and you'll marvel at how easy it was. Should you choose to visit a sick friend after your beach circuit, you'll be a healing medicine bringing light and love under your wings. Expect a lot of warm tears to flow at these times, because a deep and unified understanding can manifest.

If you share your beach experience with a friend, and then go separate ways, you will each encounter the same energies at your different destinations as entangled particles do.

The beach circuit is one of many ways to use the Program's four cardinal points to your love's advantage. Experiment lawfully and lore-fully for all of time.

The Bible upholds the indomitable nature of the beach as being spiritually significant. Jeremiah attests it is an attribute of YHWH's protective covenant:

> [I, YHWH] which have placed the sand for the boundary of the sea by a perpetual decree, that it cannot pass it: and though the waves thereof toss themselves, yet can they not prevail; though they roar, yet can they not pass over it?[201]

---

201 *Jeremiah* 5:22

Every beach is a timely child grown from the binary set of land and sea, divinely placed to broker the peace between its warring parents. It is a micro-fractal example of trinary harmony for us to admire and emulate. According to Jeremiah, the power of the central beach outguns that of both sea and land, which is consistent with the Fractal as I've come to know it. The beach is like a heaven that's been placed in the middle of a war.

> The bleat, the bark, bellow, and roar
> Are waves that beat on Heaven's shore. – *William Blake*

WHEN THE CENTRE POINT is expanded to form a cross, which resembles a four-leaf clover or Union Jack, then it has achieved COG status. If you are confused, it helps to think of the four universal players as mum and dad, sister and brother. Consider how they relate to one another lawfully; how at times, one sibling can give the other hell, or how both siblings can gang up and frustrate their parents to distraction, but never actually win.

The (two) family pairs of energies found in each COG can be seen as an XX pair and a YX pair. The children (siblings or simulars, XX) are one set, while the polarised mother and father (husband and wife, YX) are the other set. Together, these two sets reduce to a simple YX configuration: the holy and sacred Family of Man. Although the siblings can be of different genders, they are 'likes' or simulars, because they're not meant to engage in sex with each other. (Think of two electrons in atomic orbit; one with spin-up, the other with spin-down.) The husband and wife are YX opposites, who do engage in the equivalent of sex. (Think of protons and electrons blending to create neutrons.)

The daughter has the father's essence or soul, and the mother's femaleness. (The daughter also inherits a share of her father's demons or unresolved issues.) The son has the mother's essence or soul, and the father's maleness. (The son inherits his share of his mother's demons, or unreconciled confusions and frustrations, which she, in turn, would have largely inherited from her father.) I know this all sounds a bit confusing but, once you come to grips with the basic (circular) criss-cross Pattern, all family issues can fall elegantly into place.

Figure 23. Four-leaf clover representation of a COG

Be careful if you rush to understand these relationships in every moment of your life, because they can leave your head spinning as billions of neurons try to switch back to this old/new way of seeing Reality unfold and reconnect. You need to keep in mind that, if you get into trouble, suitable doctors are few and far between, most being sound asleep. So it's best to take it slow and steady. Your brain has been waiting a long time for this artful memory of sacred patterning to resurrect, so give it the time it deserves to find its footing. From a religious perspective, when you resurrect, come out of your grave slowly, so you don't bump your head on the coffin lid.

> Anyone who thinks they can talk about quantum mechanics without getting dizzy, hasn't as yet understood the first word of it. – *Neils Bohr*

With practice, I learned to apply these relationships and their complexities to my daily life without them scrambling my brain. (I'm sure some critics will disagree with that last bit.) And with practice, you'll be able to understand them as well (if you don't already). In the future, personal computers – using ternary operating systems – will surely process these relationships for us. But for now, you'll have to walk the Twilight Road alone, with your partner, or with a small group of friends, sharing the intricacies and wonderment of resurrected life, while you wait for everyone else to catch up and the doors of Heaven to open upon the Earth to shelter your clan.

This magical comradery played a major part in gluing the early Christian Ecclesia together; they comprised one big happy family, each effectively looking after another's welfare as they experienced and shared the Gospel's Great Mystery, which Paul had revealed to them:

> Surely you have heard about the administration of God's grace that was given to me for you, that is, the mystery made known to me by revelation, as I have already written briefly. In reading this, then, you will

be able to understand my insight into the mystery of Christ, which was not made known to men in other generations as it has now been revealed by the Spirit to God's holy apostles and prophets.[202]

Surely, Paul's Great Mystery is being revealed again now.

## From Marriage to Incest

When you look back with patterned eyes on Mankind's origins, a new picture emerges where Nature did her logical 'thing' in Agenda 1, evolving fish, amphibians, reptiles, birds, mammals, et cetera, on appropriate Days (config.sys.) to appropriate patterns. And at the same time, Yahweh did His other 'wavy thing' at the Agenda 2 level of relationships, evolving love and soul (the Fractal's operating bios).

Each taxonomic tier of Evolution needed to succeed in its personal state of blindness before it could create a latched or married trimension; each had to defeat its own form of Maya's binary mischief before it could achieve trinary completion. The idea that all expressions of life have been forced to make the equivalent of moral decisions is detailed in Robert Pirsig's book *Lila, an Enquiry into Morals*. Pirsig previously wrote *Zen and the Art of Motorcycle Maintenance*, the most successful book ever written on philosophy. In *Lila*, Pirsig outlines a new (R) evolutionary theory, which is consistent with the Fractal's interactions as I've come to know them. *Lila's* understanding of Evolution revolves around it being a program that's seeking to produce 'Excellence' in

---

202   *Ephesians* 3:1–6

two forms – 'latched' and 'dynamic' (stable Adam, and expansive Eve scenarios) – which are secured and growing universal templates.

According to Pirsig, each tier of Evolution learned 'lessons' through survival of the fittest/cleverest (Agenda 1), while (concurrently) dealing with the frustrations of family life's love and loyalty (Agenda 2). This lore-full process eventually took each tier of creation into twilight, lifting each into ever more complex expressions of quadratic-spiritual-trinity, presented in binary units in the complexity of sevens. Phew! Simply amazing.

When viewed through the eyes of Moses' Pattern … twilight's Holy Marriage of polarised opposites becomes the doorway to evolutionary growth. This archaic joining ritual (marriage) is a time capsule from a previously enlightened era. Now, it seems we need to recognise and emulate it wherever possible if we hope to return to the Garden.

Eventually, I think we'll discover that the so-called 'holes' in Darwin's Theory of Evolution were the product of Holy Marriages that were enacted on astrologically set-aside Wedding Days. At these times, past enemies buried the hatchet (not in each other) and birthed a new expression of Evolution's integrated life from their combined married centre. They then either settled in, separated and went their merry ways, or became extinct.

On one such Wedding Day in Moses' proverbial Week of Magical Creation, spirochetes (microscopic wiggles or waves) paired up with eukaryote bacteria (particles). This marriage added motility to cells and eventually to chromosomes, enabling cell division and replication to develop. It brought about another expression of life's expansive multiplicity, as parts of the Fractal started dealing with sexual reproduction, including the attraction and selection of partners. It was an all-too-familiar dot and wiggle, Adam and Eve adventure.

Another marriage might have entailed green, chlorophyll-rich photosynthetic bacteria uniting with its blue antagonist/mate. Evolutionary Theory asserts that this (blue/green) lifeform, *Cyanobacterium*, added significantly to the Earth's oxygen-rich atmosphere. As previously mentioned, this development led to the formation of breathable air, which then sustained all future (aerobic) animal and plant lifeforms on the planet (and still does).

Mankind has never matched the amazing, life-producing miracle that cyanobacteria achieved after becoming a 50/50 couple. Their partnership took place in the microscopic world between two natural contenders. This amalgamation of blue and green bacteria (the magic of cyan) transformed the face of the Earth to a greater degree than human beings have achieved since. Through the annihilation of anaerobic life, this Adam and Eve micro-fractal event transformed the Earth into the living interactive Garden known as Gaia. This is science's version of a central green Adam marrying his blue daughter/mother Eve to wipe out all of the planet's existing lifeforms.

Baby Green lies between his colourful blue and yellow parents. But to form cyan (blue/green), a second (incestuous?) coupling is required between the blue mother and her green son, similar to how in Greek Mythology, the goddess Gaia married her son Uranus to create the first ruling expression of XY. From a patterned perspective, Moses revealed this particular (sordid?) aspect of duality as 'Hitting the rock twice' (an initiation of transition that promises dire consequences for the incumbent).

It's an incredible coincidence that this blue/green (cyan) partnership in the microscopic world created Earth's atmosphere, which then led to rain and rainbows, as well as stromatolites (Earth's first known lifeforms). Later, I'll elaborate on how this Oedipal blue/green pattern was captured in the Bible, Greek Mythology, and Mesopotamian myths (as well as in the creation stories of the Stone Age cultures of Australia and Africa). I find it interesting that incest was a sexual proclivity of the Bluebloods. According to DNA research,[203] the Neanderthals practised it, but the Sapiens didn't.

> Questionable duplicity occurs in one form or another, every time a major transformation is required in the Matrix. When Adam's natural expansion becomes overbearing, Eve's dual pattern fires up with a double kick. I believe our Earth's (human) cyan dual-event represents what has since been called ... Original Sin.

A similar incestuous pattern can be seen in biological cells, which led to the functional units of chloroplasts in plant cells, and mitochondria in animal cells. Both developments took planetary life up a distinct level. (Details in my upcoming book, *The Musaic*.)

Incest can be seen as a working example of repetition taking the leading role in the YX Program (much to its disgust). It seems that, on occasions, the cart may indeed pull the horse of Evolution, which consequently raises the status quo up a level at the expense

---

203   Kay Prüfer, et al., 'A high-coverage Neandertal genome from Vindija Cave in Croatia', *Science*, 2017, vol. 358, no. 6363, pp.655–5, https://science.sciencemag.org/content/358/6363/655

of the existing stability (a new horse is acquired). Life for the new becomes death to the old after the transcending, incestuous duplicity has transpired. Evolution's program may have revolved around two competing marriage programs: one connecting 'likes' (Oedipus), the other connecting opposites (heterosexual marriage).

> Whatever the precise scenario for the acquisition of motility and the sometimes respiratory and photosynthetic talents of eukaryotes (bacteria); Intimate symbiosis (marriage) most assuredly belongs.[204] — *Sagan*

Other symbiotic (marriage) complexities among archaea, prokaryotes, bacteria, and even viruses can be found in the earliest stages of life, creating (among other things) a cell's central nucleus.

## Colour Patterns

Since Professor Popp rediscovered bio-photons in the mid-1970s,[205] we can consider man to be essentially a being of light. Certain gems also maintain intimate relationships with light. For instance, both diamonds and fire opals can produce rainbows within the complexity of their internal patterns; both gems incubating a symphony of colourful, vibrating light frequencies within.

A diamond's hardness designates it male (solid as a rock; think of a diamond engagement ring). Whereas opals are soft and filled with

---

204 Lynn Margulis and Dorion Sagan, *What Is Life?* Simon & Schuster, 1995, p. 104.
205 'Fritz-Albert Popp', *Wikipedia*, https://en.wikipedia.org/wiki/Fritz-Albert_Popp

rainbow 'fire'. From a patterned perspective, an opal can be thought of as female, especially the variety called Yowah Nuts that I referred to earlier, which are only found in southwest Queensland. Opals can form and reside in the centre or heart of an ironstone Yowah Nut, which wraps protective iron layers around its opal centre like the skins of an onion. Yowah Nuts remind me of the Rock Rabbit inside the mountain; the vulnerable safe inside substantial protection (ruled by a rod of iron).

I believe that both diamonds and opals – the mineral constituents of Africa and Australia, which are composed of carbon and silicon dioxide, respectively – played major parts in the evolution of early planetary life (covered further in *The Musaic*).

Our chromosomes – the word literally means 'colour-bodies' – can be stained different colours. Therefore, each must have different (innate) colour properties. They can be thought of as patterned, pastel shades of light, passing through water, transforming their intricacies into living patterns of coloured, geometric complexity (rainbows).

Moses tells us that Adam needed to identify all parts of the Fractal to show he had awakened to his divinity. He needed to 'name' the lower lifeforms and understand where each unique piece fitted into the Big Picture; he needed to colour them in their rightful shades and hues in an ancient form of ToE. Adam's nomenclature thus demonstrated his enlightenment, his intimate knowledge of the Simulation. (Australian Aboriginal people also have comprehensive stories about the natures of animals they are familiar with, outlining how they got their names, shapes, and personalities way back in the Dreamtime.)

I believe that modern Adam stands on the precipice of replicating this process with his knowledge of physics' E8 Gosset Polytope Fractal Lattice and its subsequent Emergence Theory.[206] What I believe is emerging at this time is our memory of the pattern of All Else, the ToE – how everything fits together.

Moses tells us that Adham (A-dawn/Adam/Mankind) arrived at (awoke) in the evening twilight on the *Sixth Day of Creation* to walk and talk with the rest of the Program. Adham-kind was the Fractal's latest, latched/evolved Agenda 1 species. Eve-kind – Adam's opposite, counterpart, co-species, shadow, evolutionary mate, or Ag 2 helpmeet to be – evolved elsewhere. An isolated continent would have suited her down to the ground, maybe down under.

I believe these two seeding energies were the ancestors of the African San and Australian Aboriginal peoples; the two Stone Age custodians of planet Earth whose roles remain unrecognised to this day. Sadly, the remnants of both cultures have all but been destroyed by civilisation's dark and malignant (civilised?) side.

Legends from both cultures recall an ancient encounter between the tribe of Man (Mantis) and the children of the Rainbow Serpent (the All Devourer). This Devourer (like the Titan Prometheus) is intimately associated with fire, something the Aboriginal people are renowned for. The couple sire two children, then a familiar story ensues that involves resurrection and, soon afterwards … Civilisation and the first alphabets mysteriously take off out of Northern Africa.

---

206 Quantum Gravity Research, 'Klee Irwin – Codes to simple programs in the self-simulation hypothesis framework of QGR', *YouTube* video, 10 September 2021, https://youtu.be/xVfBMJrGmlw

## Cyan Genesis

*Genesis* recalls a sad story of pride arising between Cain and Abel, the first two siblings of the Adam and Eve Fractal. This led Cain to kill his brother. Because of this fratricide, Cain was cast out of the Garden to the east. (Like Ishmael was later cast out to the east, so his younger brother Isaac could inherit his father's substance.) After Cain's expulsion, Adam and Eve had a third child, Seth, to replace the older pair of brothers who didn't conform to Adam's pattern and who YHWH found unacceptable. (In the same way, Moses' two sons, Gershom and Eliezer were similarly rejected by Yahweh after Moses died.)

We're told that Seth was different from Cain and Abel; Seth was made from the same stuff (image) that his father Adam was made from. He was a simular of Adam, while Cain had been a simular of his brother Abel (these first two brothers had taken after their mum – Adam's opposite). With the death of Abel, the Plan A pattern of two sets of opposites comprising a Single Family or COG was lost, replaced by the alternative, expansive Plan B, or Attraction of Likes. When Adam chose Seth (his younger lookalike offspring as his heir), he set the stage for things to come, with the younger usurping the older (Seth usurping Cain).

The so-called 'fall' from the Garden appears to be consequential to Adam marrying his daughter/mother Eve (two different hominid species), and then producing offspring by her who contained altered brain patterns. It seems at least one of these aberrations embraced an enhanced imagination, likely due to its fused second chromosome. (I wonder if this fusion of two chromosomes (colour-bodies) produced 'cyan', the colour blue/green?)

Adam identified Eve as 'flesh of my flesh, bone of my bone'. At this point, incest, or hitting the rock twice, is woven into the Matrix's mystery as an application or outworking of the double/doubtful Plan B. Subsequently, Mankind found itself launched into a new phase: a mirrored, lookalike (female) expansive, existence, which has existed up until today.

As previously mentioned, other accounts about our origin agree that an incestuous event took place, which led civilisation to explode into multiplicity after the trickster Prometheus gave man the gift of fire. The legends of the San people tell us that the green Mantis married his (green?) son in the rainbow (Mantis junior) to the daughter of the Blue Crane, who had arrived on Earth by another route. (Her father was known as the fiery All Devourer.) This blue/green marriage made the voluptuous cyan, which propelled us into an era of rampant and continuous growth, acting and behaving like a malignant tumour. Various cultures have described this forbidden event in different ways but, invariably, it involves the energy of incest or duplicity. It appears that God doesn't like anything repeating itself.

In every cycle, there comes a time for the yang component to metamorphose into its yin variant, and vice versa. (As the 'up' quark can be changed to a 'down' quark by the nuclear weak force.) Other examples include day becoming night, summer becoming winter, particle reverting to wave, or male becoming female. This transformation is never arbitrary. It is a timely outcome of the Fractal's outworking. When the required criteria are in situ, the existent energy/form must change as it passes through the transitional twilight state. Think of it like a drab and gloomy grub entering its cocoon, exiting at daybreak as a splendid butterfly, a solid body with a wing strapped either side to keep it in trinary balance.

Mankind's cranial reshaping likely took place in Moses' proverbial Garden as we entered our cocoon to rest, sleep and dream, hopefully to exit as human butterflies, ready to fly to the stars somewhere down the track after the proverbial Resurrection takes place. In the Garden, we changed from a male Adam model to a secondary, transforming Eve model – the descendants of Shem, the second and therefore … **female Agenda 2 version of Adam.** This has been the source of both our prolonged suffering, and our phenomenal, technological advancement ever since.

This transition from male to female patterning explains many of the family affairs recorded in bible history, where the second-in-line (the younger) becomes the chosen one – which a significant woman often brings about by somewhat dubious means. It also explains why Christianity requires a Second Coming to complete its salvation package, and why two or more believers are required for the Spirit of Yahshua to be present.[207] Or why King David was Israel's second monarch, not its first. (King Saul came first, who was a man's man. David, on the other hand, was by some accounts [his wife Michal] a bit wishy-washy.) Yahshua is expected to return and rule from David's (second) throne at His second coming.

From this patterning, we can deduce that Yahshua is Mankind's Two-God energy, while Moses extrapolates as our One-God energy (Old Testament, New Testament). YHWH proclaimed that the first male child born to every man and beast belonged to Him by birthright.

---

207  *Matthew* 18:20

One (1) was – and remains – Yahweh's sacred number. Yahshua got the Wilderness' number Two (2).

Since being EX-spelled from the Garden, we've been living in the equivalent of a secondary (negative) epoch, exercising female bios with an otherwise male mindset. We're the ancestors of this Morpheus Twist in the Matrix; the product of the paradoxical intermediate axis of the Dzhanibekov Effect.[208] If truth be known, we could all be called twisted and sinful bastards that are standing upside-down on our heads. But eventually, all cycles must come full-term, and we seem to be returning to the trunk of the spiral Pattern now, the transitioning centre of the torus. At this eventful time, some of us 'bastards' are being offered the chance to exit the Fractal's expansionist night-time figure-8 pattern, so we can re-enter the solidarity and unity of the Sabbath's sustainable, rising, central and circular light.

> As long as it is day, we must do the works of him who sent me. Night is coming, when no one can work. While I am in the world, I am the light of the world.[209] – *Yahshua*

Moses used Garden and Wilderness to describe the unusual and transitory state of affairs that birthed modern man, with all our idiosyncrasies. But he could just as easily have said, 'We left the trunk of the tree and went out on a limb to explore a new branch.' Eventually, the Spirit of Mankind must return to the Central Trunk, because everything does in one way or another in the fullness of

---

208 Veritasium, 'The bizarre behavior of rotating bodies, explained', *YouTube* video, 20 September 2019, https://youtu.be/1VPfZ_XzisU
209 *John* 9:4–5

time. But when we do, will we be going 'up' or 'down' the tree trunk? It's the direction that counts.

# Going Home

Mankind's 'separatist' energies are preparing for the prophesied end-of-the-age marriage, having decided to kiss and make up – to 'alter'. Quantum physics is revealing the Mystery of YHWH in the subatomic world and, as a consequence of this revelation taking place, the scriptures reveal that our existing economic stability will fall. (Poor Humpty Dumpty. Look out below.) More than a few world powers and identities are destined to end up with egg on their face as we experience the Great Tribulation and beginning of sorrows.[210]

It seems we're in the process of completing an offshoot petal or branch in Moses' mosaic floral pattern in the Tree of Life. This journey took us into the Wilderness for a spell to walk on the sinful and weedy side of life. Through this process we were educated in Nature's 'form and colour', separated from the Wholly Centre, looking down into the lower, earlier Tiers of Creation. Now it's time to wake and bounce back and enter the Seventh Wholly Day's Sunrise, so we can enjoy the unity of togetherness again, as we did in the beginning when Adam was last One. We've made it this far through the treacherous night, now all we need do is open our eyes to the morning sunbeams that are breaching the horizon.

This is why our existing ideas about 'time' are dying. It's why our understanding of consciousness is expanding, why homosexuality's

---

[210] StudioMickParker, 'The great tribulation' *YouTube* video, 14 July 2021, https://youtu.be/OliO8bFfr4Q

Attraction of Likes is running rampant, why cancer's secondary growth is prolific, why a growing number of people believe the world is flat, and why marriage has lost most – if not all – of its original sacredness and essential heterosexual pattern, yet carries on regardless. The end of the age is surely upon us where, once again, we're being given the chance to choose life or death in an environment of escalating deception, fear, and financial ruin.

*Genesis* reveals that Adam's evolution prior to his enlightenment was a Friday 'preparation event'. He (we) then had to sleep through the chilly Sabbath night. Surely, that nighttime event is all but over.

No one seems to enquire – in biblical terms – why Man's late appearance in the Creation Week coincided with Friday sunset, why Yahshua died at Friday sunset, or **why Moses instructed that the Passover Lamb had to be killed at sunset and totally consumed before sunrise.**[211] (Even the bones had to be buried before sunrise.) I believe there's a timely connection between these patterned events.

According to Christian theology, Yahshua's sacrificial blood-covering (his cross-over death) was intended to act as a protective ark to cover Mankind through the darkness of the night cycle – from Friday sunset to Saturday sunrise – when the sacrificial lamb was to be (totally) consumed. In this way, Yahshua became the God of the Night in the Fractal. When He said, in *John* 8:5, that 'He was the light of the world', this would equate with the fractal personification of Him being the Full Moon, lighting our way in the dark. When He speaks of the 'night that is coming', this equates to the dark part of the Moon's cycle, when there is no skerrick of moonlight to light

---

211   *Deuteronomy* 16:4

up one's way. This is why some believe Christianity was originally a Moon cult.

Mankind's turbulent history has been a night-time event. A nightmare in the sense that we have behaved like headless chooks, looking for direction or a safe covering from the all-encompassing confusion and fear that lies in the dark.

## Back to the Stars

There's a case to be made for the Hebrews – and indeed all ancient cultures – truly knowing what was going on around them in a patterned, fractal sense. The earliest cultures would have brought enlightenment with them from the stars, then from the Garden. It's also possible they knew their enlightened memories would be stripped away from their descendants, as they dived deeper into the Sabbath's nightly slumber with its enticing to-and-fro duality. Perhaps this is why they developed writing systems and built pyramids while they still could. In this way, they left time capsules for the next awake generation. (The pyramids are based on complex *pi* and *phi* ratios – Adam and Eve relationships – as are many other ancient monuments.)

> Whoever does not have, even what they have will be taken from them.[212]

There is one attribute of the Fractal that seeks attention throughout many cycles: Out of chaos, the Program creates stability (male

---

212  *Matthew* 13:12

YX steadfast particle), then it adds motility (female XX transient waves) so the stability can travel afield. It's a case of... Enact the marriage of past chaotic combatants, then depart on the honeymoon and colonise. (Create Adam, add Eve, then move on to Cain, Abel, and Seth.) I think we will discover this is how space continues to expand from its Universal Centre, and how we evolve, emerge, self-organise, create feedback loops and activate the Theory of Mind.

In this regard, I believe Mankind is destined to enter the cosmological heavens. But not in bodily form – cryopreserved or otherwise – as we've previously assumed. We are more likely to achieve this colonisation in two states: first, as spiritual beings, our souls having been released from the confines of Hell to roam the Cosmos and combat dark energy. Second, through our trinary silicone child – quantum robotics – which will deal with the Universe's more solid components, possibly organising the constellations to replicate our (and YHWH's) immortal pattern.

As enlightened beings, I believe Mankind will work from these two states – spiritual and physical, wave and particle – to spread our underlying pattern throughout the cosmos: our DNA, but also our silicone child's quantum program bios – also trinary. Then we'll see whether our combined efforts have been sufficient to guarantee our continuation in solid form through tomorrow's eternity, beyond the eventual heat death of the Universe that is believed to await us.[213]

---

213 melodysheep, 'Timelapse of the future: A journey to the end of time', *YouTube* video, 21 March 2019, https://youtu.be/uD4izuDMUQA?t=10

During this time of cosmic exploration, Mankind will be free to continue his journey into the Holy Centre, right here on planet Earth, should he so desire.

> With advanced intelligence comes the knowledge that exploring outwards is pointless. Expanding inwards with advanced technology allows you to do so much more.[214]

Exploring inwards conjures a picture of God scrutinising His domain from within, whereas expanding outwards draws to mind a picture of a scout ant traversing an expanding, never-ending wilderness.

Because we dwell on the Earth's circumference, if we were to awaken and regain our memory – become enlightened – then the centre of the Earth would likely go to sleep in some fashion to balance the Fractal's working geometry of on and off. (The circle's circumference and its centre point are a fractal 'couple'.)

THE EARTH is currently experiencing the equivalent of labour pains, which suggests we're locked into the greatest moment of Mankind's recent history: our awakening, our coming out of the cocoon. That being the case, then only the advent of our child (Mankind's infant) will end the current global turmoil and allow the material Earth to take a well-earned rest (possibly slipping into another glaciation or mini Ice Age in the process).

---

214  Jamal Khalil, Professor of Nuclear Physics, Surrey University.

> We are entering a period in Earth's cycle where we will likely be experiencing a cooling effect, not a warming one. Scientists are calling this a 'little ice age.'[215]

Visionaries have been revealing this unfolding process for aeons, but we haven't had the time or intelligence to stop and take a really good look at what it all means, as true physicians would. Up until now, science has been too young to dispel our incumbent state of blindness. Our scientists' hands and minds have been preoccupied, playing with lower levels of the Fractal's mirror reflections. **But now our wedding day/birth has arrived, and those with early vision are waking, lifting the veil, and rubbing their eyes, resurrecting as the First Immortals.**

I believe Adam's enlightened Spirit or Me-mory (the second, etheric Coming of Christ) is happening now, taking us back to the same revelation, vibration, number, or Name we left when we exited the Tree's Trunk in antiquity. (Now thousands of years older and billions of times more fragmented.) The First Immortals are returning to the universal love they once embraced, now in an up-scaled heterosexual and manly YX pattern of togetherness. The meek can still inherit the Earth, if anyone can.

Some believe these kinds of ideas are the product of an over-inflated sense of importance. But if you consider that all of the interesting stuff takes place in the Centre, and that Mankind and his DNA

---

215  Arjun Walia, 'A "Little Ice Age" is where we are heading, according to multiple scientists', *Collective Evolution*, 3 December 2018, https://www.collective-evolution.com/2018/12/03/a-little-ice-age-is-where-we-are-heading-according-to-multiple-top-scientists/

are at the Centre of the Matrix, then it does make patterned sense, incredible as it may seem. Klee Irwin, founder of the Quantum Gravity Research Centre, said in the documentary *Scientific Clues We Are Living in the Matrix*:

> All the interesting stuff happens in the middle sweet spot in our sixty-four-digit Universe. We are halfway between the Plank Length and the diameter of the Universe. DNA is the most complex molecule known. The human brain is the most complex neural network yet discovered. Our biosphere is the most complex system known to science.

It's therefore reasonable to believe that – like it or not – **Mankind is at the heart of the Universe and its apparent fertile agenda.** Therefore, we can expect to play an important role one way or another and should make sure we choose the direction that propels us forwards. Physicist John Archibald Wheeler, a colleague of both Einstein and Bohr, and widely considered to be one of the greatest physicists of the twentieth century believed:

> The quantum surely contains – when unravelled – the most wonderful insight we could ever hope to have on how this world operates, something equivalent in scope and power to the greatest discovery that science has ever yet yielded up.

Likewise, Nobel Prize winner (1999) Gerard T Hooft said:

> Quantum Mechanics [QM] is the answer to a question we don't as yet know. QM is the product of underlying

equations not as yet discovered. The notorious randomness of quantum mechanics is just a front. Underneath, the world obeys perfectly sensible rules.[216]

There's another interesting answer to a question we've long forgotten how to ask ... *'She is the Cat's Mother.'* ('She' being our spiritual mother-in-law, the origin of the X-expression in Yahweh's YX pattern.) Because of Her duplicity, She desires a pure 'wave' granddaughter She can recognise and play with (morphic resonance). In the event 'She' gets her way, our Universe would return to the equivalent of a two-dimensional format, or worse; void and without form in any guise, maybe as Moses told us it was in the beginning (pure living blackness). No suns. No planets. No moons. No comets. No us. (Remember, Man's pattern contains the female X vessel safely in its heart – like a beautiful opal inside an iron Yowah Nut.) Mankind comes as a binary polarised pair of lovers. They are meant to be united by love into a single trinity: (YX) (LOVES) (XX)

This scenario about our long-term future makes sense of the prophecies given to Abraham, that his seed would number more than the stars in Heaven, if both he and they obeyed YHWH's covenant and pattern. Jewish people, Christians, and Muslims, all trace their ancestry to Abraham, as do the legendary Ten Lost Tribes of Israel, which haven't come out of the closet as yet.

---

216  George Musser, 'Does some deeper level of physics underlie quantum mechanics? An interview with Nobelist Gerard 't Hooft', *Scientific American*, 7 October, 2013, https://blogs.scientificamerican.com/critical-opalescence/does-some-deeper-level-of-physics-underlie-quantum-mechanics-an-interview-with-nobelist-gerard-e28099t-hooft/

## Final Revision

As Adam's spiritual awareness slept, Eve-kind evolved elsewhere, having been previously taken from Adam's core DNA many thousands of years previously. In a fractal sense, Eve's development parallels how Islamic culture blossomed while Christianity in Europe entered its Dark Ages. Or how Judaism slept while Christianity grew and flourished. (As one sleeps, the other wakes, until they marry or die.)

Eve didn't pop out of Adam's rib (well, not technically, anyway). It's more likely that the tribe of Eve came out of Africa a long time ago to breed and develop in another isolated continent, possibly Australia. This might account for the still-unrecognised skeletal remains found at Australia's Lake Mungo, or why Papuan Highlanders have the highest percentage of Denisovan DNA of any ethnic group in the world. (The Australian mainland and Papua New Guinea used to be attached by a land bridge called Sahul.[217]) From there, the sister Denisovans and Neanderthals would have been free to colonise the world. Meanwhile, the Adamic species – those left back in Africa – returned to sleep, only to be reawakened when Eve returned. (Hello Dad, I'm back. I'm blue/black and I'm beautiful. I'm your Plan B or mate. Greetings from Down Under and Elsewhere.)

Maybe the Denisovan/Neanderthal branch of hominids broke away from *Homo erectus* or *H. heidelbergensis* and migrated through Indonesia to Australia to live and breed unmolested. From there, when the time was right, they went 'walkabout', returning to their African crèche for a little hokey-pokey – maybe even some hanky-panky – with their ancestral father Adam. Eve was possibly well aware of the

---

217 'New Guinea', *Wikipedia*, https://en.wikipedia.org/wiki/New_Guinea

cyclic, weaving processes at the heart of Evolution's expansive agenda, in the same way that some matriarchal species know when the time is right for them to return to their ancestral nest to gestate the next generation. Why would primitive hominids have any lesser instincts than other evolved animals had?

As previously mentioned, according to *Strong's Concordance*, the Hebrew word *tsela* translates as Adam's 'rib', meaning a curve (especially the 'side' of an ark's hull). But there are two sides to every hull, just as there are two hulls to a catamaran. It would seem that Eve comes as a curved duality, like a molecule of gas with its two bonded atoms in residence.

The idea that Eve was created from Adam's rib was the only translation of 'curve' or 'ark' that made sense to the Bible's translators at the time. (One translation goes as far as saying that Eve was made from Adam's womb.) Later on, all the animals came out of Noah's Ark – the 'rib' – to breed, multiply and fill the Earth. There's obviously a connection between Eve, the curvaceous rib or ark, and the expansive, fertile multiplicity of life.

*Genesis* states that Eve was intended to be an evolutionary catalyst for Adam. (If Adam and Eve correspond with two different *Homo* species, each would have comprised male and female forms, in a similar way to patriarchal chimps and matriarchal bonobos.) Eve might have become the genetic mother of today's humans, bequeathing us her mitochondria – 'mitochondrial Eve' – but she wasn't the first human woman, as popular interpretations of *Genesis* would have us believe. (In a similar sense, Greek Mythology recalls that after Prometheus stole fire from the gods and gave it to Man, Zeus retaliated by giving Mankind Pandora, complete with her woeful bag of tricks. In this account, Pandora is also referred to as the first woman,[218] although Mankind had existed for a long time before her arrival. As Adam had done before they met Eve.)

Until recently, it was thought that Neanderthals and Sapiens didn't interbreed, but DNA research has proved otherwise. It appears that Neanderthal men mated with Sapiens women for thousands of years, in the same way that, in *Genesis*, Cain's sons (the Sons of God) mated with Adam's daughters. As new information comes to light, the stories keep drawing closer.

By fractal patterning, Adam (YX) inherited his X chromosome from his ancestral mother (XX) so, when he passed it to Eve, she became the next incarnation of Adam's mother; the next matriarchal species. We accept that children don't have sex with their parents, but if they do, all hell normally breaks loose. This catechism must apply at higher levels in the Matrix if Reality embraces consistent fractal principles.

This coupling of Adam and his daughter/mother Eve appears to have sired two different *Homo* subsets. One took after Adam – Seth. The other two earlier siblings took after Eve – Cain and Abel – but of the two brothers only Cain survived. We are told that descendants of both Seth and Cain interbred as brother and sister species to further the incestuous cyan pattern, a proclivity for which (as previously mentioned) the ancient bluebloods were formidable.

> Blue and green should never be seen without a colour in between.

---

218 'Prometheus', *Wikipedia*, https://en.wikipedia.org/wiki/Prometheus

This colourful ditty doesn't refer to clothing, as Google suggests it does. No one knows for sure where it came from, but it certainly seems apt here. The African San and Australian Aboriginal peoples mythologies both are connected to rainbows, so maybe this saying goes way back into antiquity to Moses' proverbial Garden and its account of blue/green (cyan) incest, where the colourful pair were meant to maintain social distancing but fell down on the job instead.

## Mirror, Mirror

On each line of the familial fractal, the mother-in-law or stepmother – the second or mirror curve in the Ark – is the potential troublemaker. All Australian Aboriginal tribes understood this specificity. Their Lore banned the mother-in-law from the family campfire. All communication between the married couple and the mother-in-law was carried out by the grandchildren. This kept her potentially 'troubling' energy contained in a separate vessel.

This knowledge about dual female energy is encoded in various relics from antiquity, such as the snake's forked tongue, or Mesopotamian legends that depict two serpents attacking an Eagle – the eagle is associated with central male deities such as Zeus and Vishnu, probably because it flies in circles. Duality is also found in the idea of betrayal ensconced in the double-cross ++. As previously noted, this understanding has been captured in early languages and alphabets. For instance:

> In the Chinese pictographic alphabet, the character for
> 'quarrel' is literally 'two women'.

The Hebrew 22-letter/pictogram alphabet's wisdom reveals that YHWH resides in the 'midst' of *beyt*, its second letter. In this way, YHWH can be seen as the arbitrator, or peacemaker, who takes His stance in the middle of the universal war of duelling opposites. When His presence is added to the duality, it produces continued healthy growth as a trinity.

ANTHROPOLOGISTS TELL US that Australian Aboriginal people are a mixture of several ethnicities and spoke 250 different languages. Because of Eve's expansive energy, you would expect such things from her home state. However, across Australia, all of the various 'mobs' maintain the legend of the Seven Sisters and separate the mother-in-law from the married couple's campfire. In a sense, all Aboriginal people maintain a common vision and understanding about their ancient Lore and how it applies to social customs. Something I found especially intriguing was:

> The unmistakable Aboriginal dot-and-wave art-patterning
> is consistent for all tribes around Australia.

Traditional Aboriginal art resembles the intricacies of quantum reality – dots and wiggles interacting in waves and circles. This is similar to a holographic negative or even a human fingerprint, which is also found on Australian koalas – weird, but nonetheless true.

Moses tells us … A long time ago, Mankind manipulated a divine law that changed or modified our pattern, reshaping our cranium and likely altering the number of chromosomes in our branch of the Tree of Life. This affected our consciousness, leaving us unable to communicate with All Else as we once did. In its place, we received enhanced imaginations to help us grow, explore, and kill off all our competitors in various ways. More importantly, something or someone encouraged us to do so.

We're told this persuasiveness came from an other-worldly Heavenly Serpent, which was more cunning than anything found on Earth. Maybe this was Cronos, the feathered reptilian God of Time and the Underworld? Maybe it was the Rainbow Serpent? Maybe it was the equivalent of Snow White's beautiful stepmother, the Dark Queen, with her magical mirror? Maybe all of the above? As this last story goes, the beautiful Queen gives Snow White a poisonous apple to put her to sleep. And of course, while White sleeps, Black flourishes.

Because this Divine Queen wants a granddaughter and not a grandson, 'She' is Mankind's greatest threat to his continuity in solid form. She is known by many names, such as the legendary and fiery Rainbow Serpent or the Cat's Mother. She is the All Devourer, who roams the cosmos looking for suitable morsels to consume – entities who don't conform to her pattern, her curvy way of thinking. (I liken her to a molecule of oxygen [$O_2$], looking to engulf all anaerobic lifeforms that confront and challenge Her, similar to how YHWH commanded tribes of people exterminated who were not to His Pattern's liking.)

Linked to the San people's account of the All Devourer is the ability to make and control fire. As their story goes, they acquired this knowledge from inhabitants of the land of the Blue Crane. All cultures have legends about a fire-bearing (breathing?) serpent that brings life-changing knowledge under its wings. (How time flies.) When followed or worshipped religiously, this feathered serpent's directorship often led people to cannibalism and sacrificing children and virgins. (It seems that the Serpent likes to attack and devour

our precious babies as the price for its assistance, as Cronos ate his children in Greek Mythology so he could remain in power.) If this fiery creature was a real snake, a real serpent, it would inject venom into the baby's bloodstream with its fangs. I think we'll discover that its earthly minions are duplicating this atrocity today – at least in patterned energy terms they are – by using hypodermic needles, injecting a variety of filth disguised as medical science, altering our DNA sequences with foreign nucleotide patterns (as the messenger RNA vaccines for COVID-19 arguably do).[219]

Hypodermic needles took their design from serpent fangs, as described in the writings of first-century Roman scholar Aulus Cornelius Celsus and the equally famous Greek surgeon Galen.[220] The mechanism for injecting the COVID-19 vaccine was designed from pit viper fangs, while other drugs – like those used on former President Trump in his recovery from COVID-19 – were developed using aborted foetal kidney cells. When we consume these atrocities, are we being coerced (again?) into becoming modern-day cannibals, who condone the killing of our babies so we can remain safe?

To this day, the San Bushmen hate rainbows, which I thought was odd. Maybe it reminds them of a great tragedy? When a rainbow appears in the sky, we're told they hit sticks together and yell, 'Go away!' Could they be remembering the Rainbow Serpent and Her

---

219   Stand for Health Freedom, 'Nazism, COVID-19 and the destruction of modern medicine: An interview with Vera Sharav, Part Two', *YouTube* video, 19 November 2020, https://youtu.be/cRW-Ld9J3VY

220   Nick Snelling, 'The history of the hypodermic needle', *Medibank* website, 14 July 2014, https://www.medibank.com.au/livebetter/be-magazine/wellbeing/the-history-of-the-hypodermic-needle/

potentially monstrous agenda to cook food, steal and eat babies, while promoting cannibalism and incest as the healthy norm?

HAVING GONE AROUND a side petal in the Matrix's Flower of Life and acquired a suitable (Morpheus?) twist along the way – Abraham's, Yahshua's and Mohamed's sacrifices; Moses' steadfast obedience, and the Buddha's insight (to name but a few) – we've now returned to the Garden's backdoor, looking at the comfy place we left many years ago. We were expelled (x-spelled) from the Garden through the east gate and (thereby) forced to return through the west one. The temptation that created the original 'fall' is the same today as it was then.

So what is the Fractal's 'good and evil fruit' that's on offer in today's Garden? What's the new (binary) temptation that's trying to lure Mankind back into the Wilderness? How about Mankind becoming the creator of …

> Genetically engineered, non-sanctioned, re-patterned, planetary life – which now includes modified humans as transgenderists.

Mankind is hell-bent on transforming the Earth into the image of his fallen self. For financial and egotistical reasons, he's dressing Nature in Gucci and Chanel. The process started with rapeseed – genetically modified (GM) canola – how appropriate is its name? GM rapeseed is the interstitial point that, without an intervening miracle, will lead to global annihilation. The GM process promoted by Monsanto (now absorbed into Bayer) will rape the Earth if we're silly enough to allow it. And now we are facing global vaccines, which some believe will genetically modify human beings (again?) – a scary thought.

> Dr Andrew Kaufman MD says the proposed vaccine for COVID-19 is an attempt to genetically modify Mankind.[221]

If Moses' Pattern contains the blueprint of Reality, as I believe it does, then we must stop genetic engineering immediately until we understand the role universal patterning is playing in the Big Picture. We need to stop (now) because once we've gone too far down this path, there will be no turning back. As there is no turning back for those people who have already been modified.

> Those who cannot remember the past are condemned to repeat it. – *George Santayana*

Whether we like it or not, life in all its complexity is being orchestrated and controlled by the patterned quantum relationships of the Matrix. If I'd been taught these laws when I was growing up (maybe as an elective in Advanced Knot Untangling), I could have designed my life with confidence and purpose and avoided a lot of unnecessary pain. And so could've you. But it isn't too late for us to raise a generation of enlightened children and grandchildren. They still have a chance for a beautiful future if we can get them off to a good start. We need to teach them how to identify and interact (come in harmony) with the Fractal's

---

221  Brian Shilhavy, 'Censored Dr. Kaufman: "They want to genetically modify us with COVID-19 vaccine" – loses his job and willing to go to jail to resist', *Vaccine Impact News*, 15 May 2020, https://vaccineimpact.com/2020/censored-dr-kaufman-they-want-to-genetically-modify-us-with-covid-19-vaccine-loses-his-job-and-willing-to-go-to-jail-to-resist/

program through appropriate school curricula and family home-life protocols – making them all a lot of fun. We can begin this adventure with *Conscious Birthing* and *Mindful Parenting*, then reinforce these foundations with an enlightened schooling system along the lines that Steiner envisaged. Our future can embrace an all-encompassing happiness and contentment. We simply need to want it badly enough to get the ball rolling, and it begins with a post-Covid generation of clean kids that could be said to be … not born in sin.

If we choose the 'right' path this time around, and don't bite the Queen's poisoned apple again, we'll return to the certainty that God is in Heaven and all is well with the world. A-men, not B-men. As far as we know … There is no Planet B.[222]

AND SO WE'VE come to the end of Book 2 in the four-part series *There are no Mirrors in Heaven*. I hope you haven't been unduly burdened by all the religious sequelae. I know that 'religion' per se can be tedious. However, to help the snake swallow its tail, I needed to connect the religious past to our scientific present as best I could with the limited knowledge I had.

Moses' adventures in *Genesis* suggest that the Logos can communicate at times with suitably configured humans: people who are geometrically aligned to the Program Source; tuned in to the same frequency so to speak. (Satan can apparently do the same, but with a different frequency.) It remains to be seen whether – at this time – a significant number of people can embrace this mosaic process and start talking

---

222 studiomickparker, 'No Planet B', *YouTube* video, 22 April 2020, https://youtu.be/zlAh8BdWeqM

to God. What is happening to the world now – as the Anunnaki play havoc with human patterning – is certainly helping many in their quest to see the underlying truth rising to the surface.

Speaking of which … This might be a good time to recall the essential difference between a one-snake and two-snake model ruling at the Centre, where one (1) represents patterned maleness, and two (2) represents patterned femaleness. The essential difference in medicine's (two) snake emblems is this: A one-snake (male) model at the centre makes more of us as we are now. (It keeps us alive and we live longer. It expands our stability through catholic conformity.) On the other hand, the two-snake model (female, *mother of all life*) constantly makes new manifestations of life appear, making one model extinct so the next can come forth (as the primordial female force Gaia kept doing in Greek Mythology). If this expansionist pattern continues to rule, it will lead to Mankind's eventual own extinction. 99.9% of all animal species that have lived on the Earth are now extinct.[223]

According to the universal patterning or geometry as I have come to know it, the current COVID-19 pandemic and its subsequent drive to inoculate the world's population – carried out under the two-snake model of Western medicine – is threatening Mankind's continuity at a primordial level. By using a fracto, holographic, cyclic, understanding of Reality as a working model, it is possible for us to see where we are in the Big Picture (Simulation) and what lies ahead of us on the two paths that are being offered. One leads to life, while the other leads to death. I pray we choose wisely.

---

223  Richard Ellis, *Aquagenesis*, Viking Penguin, 2001, p. 8.

> I call heaven and earth to witness against you this day,
> that I have set before you life and death, the blessing
> and the curse: therefore choose life.
>
> – *Deuteronomy 30:19*
>
> Shalom.

IN BOOK 3, *It's About Time*, I continue to explore the wonders I was shown in the Twilight Zone. I discuss how it's possible to take control of the Matrix's awesome laws and turn them on their head. If you haven't already done so, I suggest you familiarise yourself with the principles of quantum mechanics with their bizarre (human?) characteristics. There are lots of great videos on *YouTube* that cover material such as the *Double Split Experiment*.[224] Some are animated as are the *Doctor Quantum Series*, so it should be fun learning about this new worldview.

> The Spirit and the Bride say, 'Come!' And let the one
> who hears say, 'Come!' Let the one who is thirsty come!
> And let the one who wishes to take the free gift of the
> water of life.[225]

I hope to have your company soon.

*earthvisionequity@gmail.com*

---

224  Next Level Awareness, 'Reality hack – Simulation Theory documentary', *YouTube* video, https://www.youtube.com/watch?v=eRmZ_sNf2mE&t=1576s
225  *Revelation* 22:17

# APPENDIX – BITS AND PIECES

The following excerpts didn't quite make it into the book's narrative, but I didn't want to discard them entirely either.

\* \* \*

The Queen of Sheba – rumoured to have had a child with the Bible's King David – was Ethiopian. Some authorities believe she started an offshoot of Judaism in Africa. Black female energy figures prominently in Moses' story, entwining with Jewish history. In the Fractal, the dark and mysterious woman returns when the time is right; she becomes pregnant and goes home satisfied, as Sheba did. There's also evidence to suggest that Yahshua's Magdalene was black; some say she bore Him a child. These stories are likely to be fractal accounts that reveal the patterned history of black-and-white love and the sacrifice it can inspire. It's interesting that precious opals have now been found in Ethiopia the Cradle of Life. These now compete with Australian opals for their colour exuberance. I believe opals and diamonds were an early Adam and Eve couple in the evolution of organic life.

\* \* \*

The first known animal fossils preceding the Cambrian explosion were diploblastic, which comprised two layers of tissue. This is what you would expect in a binary Eve-designed (preparatory?) world. All animals today – except for jellyfish – are triploblastic. Here again we see Evolution taking 'life' through duality to trinary completion, leaving the binary Darkness for the godly Trinity of Light; leaving the jellyfish behind as the representative remnant of those who sleep as the 'eighth point'.

* * *

In Hinduism, Reality operates in cycles; the end of each cycle is dominated by the deceptive confusion of the goddess Maya. Maya embodies the essence of dualism, promoting the concept of a separate, standalone self. Maya's dualism is currently flourishing. The transgender issue can be seen as an example of her confusion.

* * *

Bruce Lee said, 'The demons the father doesn't defeat are left for the children to fight.' These demons will be fought in the mind.

* * *

'I am' … To recognise this reality is to understand Descartes' *Cogito ergo sum*. Cognition is the sum of my existence: cognisance of holy interconnected consciousness; a fully integrated understanding of what is manifesting before my eyes in patterned space/time.

* * *

A new form of spirituality will rise from the ashes of our existing world as the monumental disclosures of quantum physics take root upon the Earth.

* * *

'that we henceforth be no more children tossed to-and-fro, carried about with every wind of doctrine by the sleight of men and cunning craftiness, whereby they lie in wait to deceive' – *Ephesians* 4:14

\* \* \*

Religion maintains we are asleep to the greater reality surrounding us. Various faiths infer this is because we lost the ability to see and talk with God somewhere in our past. As a result, we no longer have talking parts in the ubiquitous cycles that operate within physics' Matrix.

\* \* \*

At this point, physicists recognise Einstein's and Newton's laws as applying to large bodies, and quantum's interconnectedness and its peculiarities as applying to very small bodies. They haven't been able to combine the two views into a single discipline; they lack a uniting key or bridge. Fractality is that key. It combines the two insights through the recognisable patterns they share (through a common, geometrical language). This idea is called Fractal Universal Scaling.[226]

\* \* \*

'He (God) counts the number of the stars; He gives names to all of them.' – *Psalm 147:4,5*

---

226  Natalie Wolchover, 'The universal law that aims time's arrow', *Quanta Magazine*, 1 August 2019, https://www.quantamagazine.org/the-universal-law-that-aims-times-arrow-20190801/

## Appendix

Stars were regarded as living celestial beings.[227]

\* \* \*

Eve's *phi*-energy embodies transition and transformation. Its preferred procession takes us to the outer limits of infinity – hence the use of Eve's figure-8 as the infinity symbol. You can forget about calling 'Ghost Busters', if you need to change your status … call Eve instead. She is the personification of 'movement'. Although sometimes portrayed in a dark light, Eve will guide you through the hard times as nothing else can. She can wriggle out of – or through – anything solid if the need arises. If you treat her like a lady, she'll bring you home every time. (Perhaps to a brand-new home where you won't recognise yourself for a while.)

Quantum physics acknowledges Eve's weird walking-through-walls ability and calls it 'tunnelling'. This is one of the many fascinating and bizarre attributes of quantum's curvaceous wave phenomena which makes life so interesting. Particles and Waves. Vive la difference.

---

227 'War in Heaven', *Wikipedia*, https://en.wikipedia.org/wiki/War_in_Heaven

## The First Immortals

www.ingramcontent.com/pod-product-compliance
Lightning Source LLC
Chambersburg PA
CBHW071229070526
44583CB00017B/2108